For Duncan McDowall

an admired (and, I
trust, admiring!) colleague

with warmest wishes

[signature]

Carleton University
8 January 1992

NEGOTIATING FREER TRADE

THE UNITED
KINGDOM,
THE UNITED
STATES,
CANADA,
AND THE
TRADE
AGREEMENTS
OF 1938

IAN M. DRUMMOND
NORMAN HILLMER

Wilfrid Laurier University Press

Canadian Cataloguing in Publication Data

Drummond, Ian M., 1933-
    Negotiating freer trade

Bibliography: p.
Includes index.
ISBN 0-88920-970-7

1. Great Britain — Commercial policy.   2. United
States — Commercial policy.   3. Canada — Commercial
policy.   4. Great Britain — Commercial treaties.
5. United States — Commercial treaties.   6. Canada —
Commercial treaties.   7. Free trade and protection.
I. Hillmer, Norman.   II. Title.

HF1721.D78 1989   382.9'11'713   C88-094172-3

Copyright © 1989

WILFRID LAURIER UNIVERSITY PRESS
Waterloo, Ontario, Canada   N2L 3C5

89 90 91 92 4 3 2 1

Cover design by Rachelle Longtin

Printed on acid-free paper

Printed in Canada

Negotiating Freer Trade has been typeset using an electronic file supplied by
the authors.

For Philip Wigley
1941 − 1982

Contents

Illustrations

(The following illustrations appear
between pages 102 and 103.)

Plate 1
John W. Dafoe's *Winnipeg Free Press* and its famous cartoonist, Arch Dale,
were among the campaigners for lower tariffs

Plate 2
Seated left to right, Cordell Hull, Mackenzie King and Franklin D. Roosevelt
sign the 1935 Canada-United States Trade Agreement in Washington

Plate 3
"My old friend." Prime Minister King (left) and President Roosevelt at
Quebec City, 1936

Plate 4
Preparing to ward off the imperialist dragon, a dapper Mackenzie King
arrives at St. James's Palace, London, England, 1937

Plate 5
The prime ministers of the Commonwealth at the Imperial Conference of
1937. From left to right, Savage of New Zealand, Lyons of Australia, Baldwin
of Great Britain, King George VI, Mackenzie King of Canada, Hertzog of South
Africa

Plate 6
The dominion high commissioners and other high-spirited well-wishers see
the British prime minister, Neville Chamberlain (hat raised) off to his conference with Adolph Hitler in Munich, September 1938. First to the right in the
first row, the Australian representative in London, Stanley Bruce; fourth to
the right is the Canadian high commissioner, Vincent Massey; Lord Halifax,
British foreign secretary, is fifth to the right

Plate 7

The dignitaries arrive for the signing of the Canada-United States trade agreement, Washington, 1938. From left to right: Mackenzie King, Cordell Hull, O.D. Skelton

Plate 8

The American president and Canadian prime minister in President Roosevelt's office, just after the signing of the 1938 Canada-United States trade agreement. Dr. Skelton is standing third from the left

Preface

Our collaboration grew out of a mutual interest in the North Atlantic Triangle of the 1930s. One of us had written about British Empire economic policies, the other about British-Canadian political and diplomatic relationships. Quite independently, we became aware that a comprehensive study of the 1938 trade agreements had yet to be written. This book's origins lie in that realization.

We collected documents in four countries, and incurred large debts to the staff members of a great many institutions: in Great Britain, the Public Record Office, Kew, and the Cambridge, Birmingham and Leeds University Libraries; in the United States, the National Archives and Library of Congress, Washington, the Franklin D. Roosevelt Library, Hyde Park, New York, and the Harvard University Library, Cambridge, Massachusetts; in Canada, the National Archives of Canada, the Directorate of History of the Department of National Defence and the Historical Section of the Department of External Affairs, all in Ottawa, and the Queen's University Library, Kingston, Ontario; in Australia, the National Library in Canberra. We also travelled to the National Archives of New Zealand, but found nothing relevant to our enquiry.

Part of the research was carried out with grants from the Social Sciences and Humanities Research Council of Canada and Leeds University. This book has been published with the help of a grant from the Social Science Federation of Canada, using funds provided by the Social Sciences and Humanities Research Council of Canada.

We spoke about the trade negotiations at the Centre for International Studies, Trinity College, University of Toronto, and the Annual Meeting of the Canadian Historical Association. We are grateful to Robert Spencer and Ian Macpherson for those opportunities to make early attempts at sorting out our thoughts on Anglo-American-Canadian trade questions in the late 1930s.

Professor J.L. Granatstein, who examined the trade negotiations while writing his distinguished biography of Norman Robertson, generously shared his research and gave encouragement. Robert Bothwell, David Dilks, John English, the late Donald Forster, and Philip Taylor taught us a great deal about economic diplomacy and much else in the course of many discussions over the years. Anne Hillmer, Paul Kennedy, Angelika Sauer, Gustav Schmidt, C.P. Stacey, and three anonymous Social Science Federation readers reviewed the manuscript, giving us a better understanding of the subject. Rod Cherkas, Linda Lewis, Gloria McKeigan, Vincent Rigby, Christine Rowe, and Loretta Wickens helped with research, typing, proofreading and many of the technical details as we brought the text to completion. Olive Koyama was an effective editor. Sandra Woolfrey of Wilfrid Laurier University Press richly deserves her considerable reputation in Canadian publishing.

Readers will encounter frequent references to *ad valorem* and most favoured nation (mfn). The former is a duty based on the value of the product, not on its size or weight; the latter is a status conferred in trade agreements giving signatories the right to trade advantages and tariff reductions which the parties may negotiate with any other independent country. The symbol / refers to the old British shilling. Two shillings and sixpence (2/6) corresponds to twelve and one-half of the "new pence" now used in the United Kingdom.

Finally, we would like to remember Philip Wigley, a valued friend, ally, and colleague who died in a hill-climbing accident six years ago. Even now, it is difficult to believe that he is gone.

Toronto and Ottawa   I.M.D.
September 1988   N.H.

Introduction

On 17 November 1938 Great Britain, the United States and Canada, after four years of discussion and manoeuvre, signed two wide-ranging and interlocking trade agreements. By the standards of our own recent history, when multilateral trade negotiations have often dragged on interminably, progress was speedy. Compared with the admittedly limited experience of the 1930s, it was anything but. As the economist Allan Fisher wrote in 1937, there was "no indecent haste to dismantle the complicated machinery of trade restrictions that had been built up during the depression, and the story of negotiation and discussion was rather like a slow-moving motion picture the final stages of which had not yet been released for public exhibition."[1] Nevertheless, with the demands, commitments and reservations of the three participants so nearly irreconcilable, and the complexities of the American political-bureaucratic system so nearly unbearable, perhaps it is a wonder agreement was reached at all.

Our study treats the trilateral trade negotiations in which Canada, the United Kingdom, and the United States were embroiled during the year 1938, as well as the foreplay that led up to these negotiations during the years 1934-37. This introduction presents a justification for our study, and places the negotiations in context by sketching the state of scholarly opinion respecting them. The next chapter treats the economic and political environment of the 1930s. Later chapters present a narrative account of the proceedings in order to discover what the actual issues were, how these issues were viewed by the several participants in the three countries, what difficulties and obstacles impeded the progress of the negotiations, and how these obstacles were evaded or overcome.

This book is the first effort, based on the archives of all the participating countries, to reconstruct the painful and protracted

Reference notes for the Introduction begin on p. 169.

process of triangular trade discussion and negotiation from 1934 to 1938. It considers the negotiations from the standpoint of all three countries, an approach that casts the entire process in a very unattractive light. Washington seems to have been all too concerned to make its trade surplus bigger and to widen electoral support for Roosevelt's New Deal government. Both Americans and Canadians were quite prepared to talk of the evil trade-distorting effects of preferential tariffs, while at the same time attempting to direct trade concessions so as to gore the oxen of third countries, such as Mexico and the Scandinavian states. Britain and its Empire-Commonwealth would not turn their backs on preferences; the Americans certainly had not given up protectionism. Precisely when the international skies were dark and growing darker, precisely when war was ever more likely, we find the three allies-to-be greasing the path to oblivion with lard, cocooning themselves with Nottingham lace, and impaling themselves on a shaft of Baltic pine.

We have built up our story from archival materials in four (Australia included) countries, thereby, we hope, avoiding the distortions that can readily occur when a scholar depends on one national body of documentation. In addition, without trying to reproduce every twist and turn in the complex negotiations, we have included enough detail to give a realistic picture of the trials and tribulations that trade negotiators face. Finally, in our concluding chapter we reflect upon the longer-run significance of the negotiations—their political meaning, and their relation to the changes in the international economic regime that would come with the end of World War Two.

The 1938 accords were regarded by contemporaries as a significant international event. Commentators took them as testimony to transatlantic solidarity in a dangerous world; English-speaking politicians and officials expressed both satisfaction and relief, the more so because the dictatorships were thought to be watching the confusions and difficulties with some relish. Academics, too, took immediate note, and drew lessons about the evils of protectionism and the movement towards a freer-trading sanity.[2] As historians looked back in the aftermath of war, however, the focus was on Europe, and on the political aspects of appeasement. The historiographical balance has not been completely redressed by several recent studies of Anglo-American relations, of international economic diplomacy, and of British imperial and Commonwealth history.[3] Some of these studies refer to the 1938 agreements, but only in passing. The only account that treats the trilateral negotiations in any depth remains R.N. Kottman's dated *Reciprocity and the North Atlantic Triangle, 1932-1938*,[4] which was written primarily on the basis of

American documents, before most of the pertinent British and Canadian papers became available.

More recent scholarship[5] has briefly referred to the negotiations as a way into an understanding of pre-World War Two international relationships. Except for J. L. Granatstein's magisterial biography of Norman Robertson, the chief Canadian negotiator,[6] there has been no attempt to produce an archivally based account of the trade talks. And even Granatstein, because he is concerned to produce a biography of a senior civil servant, presents an account that is brief and incomplete. In our concluding chapter we draw the reader's attention to the major revisions in economic and historical interpretation that we believe to follow from our findings.

The actual trilateral negotiations did not begin until 1938. When they were underway, their course was followed with interest by the press, and by politicians, in all three participant countries, and throughout the western world and everywhere in the British Commonwealth. When the three new trade agreements were signed in late autumn 1938, there was widespread approval.[7] But precisely why were they thought important, and to whom? The question cannot be answered until the details of the negotiations have been explored.

We would agree with the traditional historiography, and with those who conducted the negotiations, that the process and its outcome *were* important, though we find that importance to be not so much for the economic outcome but rather for the indication of attitudes and problems in the international political economy of the 1930s, and as an illumination of certain later developments. More specifically, these negotiations and their outcome cast a valuable light upon Canadian-American and Anglo-American relations at that particular time, and for some years thereafter. In the course of the negotiations the American government came to believe that the Canadians were worthy of encouragement and support. Washington could also recognize that it was possible to negotiate successfully with Great Britain, the perfidious Albion, and thus that the democracies could work together. Here the trade agreements reinforced the impression that had been created in and after 1936 by the so-called Tripartite Stabilization Agreement respecting the management of the exchanges.[8] The British, for their part, had done what they must to keep America sweet—if not for now, for the future. As D.C. Watt has written, "In British political strategy up to May 1940 America figured as the *dea ex machina*, the goddess who would descend from the machine and restore order and harmony in the last act."[9]

We believe that our account will be of interest to diplomatic historians, economic historians, and practitioners, as well as students of the negotiating process itself—a process on which, in the 1980s, more and more scarce governmental energy now has to be expended. We believe that our topic, and our conclusions, possess some contemporary resonance. At a time when the pound sterling and the Canadian dollar are both floating currencies, as they were in the late 1930s, and when Canada and the United States have again carried out tariff-bargaining while the American Congress and administration are regularly raising barriers against Canadian goods, the commercial negotiations of 1938 have considerable relevance. They cast light not only upon the laborious process of negotiation itself, but upon the pitfalls and pressures with which the road toward a final agreement is thickly strewn. Our findings reveal that good will and enthusiasm, even when these feelings are mutual, will not ensure a speedy outcome or a satisfactory one. They also show that when negotiations deal with complex and highly specific topics, they can acquire a momentum of their own, such that they become entirely divorced from contemporaneous developments in the larger world of economics and politics, whether local or international. Finally, we are reminded that, in dealing with the United States administration, there is always the risk of a Congressional stab in the back.

Most important of all, our findings illustrate a transatlantic chasm of ideas and sensibilities, both political and economic, a chasm so deep that it imperilled co-operation among the democratic states of the North Atlantic Triangle. We would not claim that our topic is necessarily the best or only one through which that chasm can be studied and understood. Indeed, one of us has already explored the perplexities of transatlantic monetary negotiations during the same decade, and has found that the same sorts of misunderstandings and mistrusts were rampant in this sphere also.[10] We would certainly claim, nevertheless, that trade negotiations provide an important illustration of the problem. It might be argued that one should concentrate on the "best" topic, eschewing others of lesser importance. But there can be no "best" topic, because all the intergovernmental interactions of the period are relevant to an understanding of the problem of transatlantic misunderstanding. And even if there were a "best" topic, one could identify it only by studying all potential topics in appropriate detail before setting pen to paper. This is not feasible, nor is it the way in which scholarly work proceeds.

We have tried to show that all the participants revealed a mixture of motives. The economic considerations and their concomitant domestic political payoffs eventually predominated for the USA, while on the UK side the dominating considerations were eventually those of international politics, so that in the end the British would certainly not have signed on economic grounds alone, while by that time the Americans had wholly lost sight of the international political motivation that had been present for them, though not dominant, at the beginning. As for Canada, the Dominion government began by sharing the transatlantic vision of a world made peaceful through economic disarmament. Yet it quickly began to seize the economic advantages, and to shun the potential domestic political disadvantages, which presented themselves in the course of the negotiations.

Because our book is about trade negotiations, and because these negotiations were complicated, we have necessarily written a book that is concerned at least on the surface by trade not by politics. In any event, economic issues did determine most of the course of the trade talks, and the direct outcome was economic. The negotiations themselves cannot be understood without some knowledge of the economic circumstances of the time, which, furthermore, were such that one might have predicted a rough and unproductive course for the trade talks. It is not possible to show, on the basis of the archival evidence, any week-by-week or month-by-month connection between the progress of the world political crisis and the course of the trade talks. Similarly, the effect of the economic conjuncture—the gradual recovery from 1933 to 1937, the upward price-movement of those years, and the slump of 1938 that was especially distressing in the United States but that affected Britain also—cannot be traced through the documents in any precise way. That is, one cannot find direct evidence that the demands of the several participants, or the course of events, actually reflected this larger economic conjuncture. One reason, of course, is that because all the participants knew what was happening both in political and economic affairs, they had no need to remind themselves, and one another, of these bigger developments. Nevertheless, as we shall suggest in later chapters, much can be inferred about the connections.

CHAPTER 1

An Unpromising Environment

The trade discussions of 1934-38 took place against a steadily darkening international landscape. When the Americans made their first approaches to Britain in 1934, the authorities in Whitehall certainly did not expect a war in the near future, so that they saw little need to win the good will of the Roosevelt administration, which they regarded as dangerous and thoughtless. The next few years would perhaps not change their opinion of the American president and his government, but the force of events would change their eagerness for American good will. The conquest of Ethiopia, the remilitarization of the Rhineland, the Spanish civil war, the demoralization of the League of Nations, the German annexation of Austria, and finally the Sudetenland crisis of spring and summer 1938, all contributed to London's change of view.

Anglo-American political relations had been intermittently tense and uncertain for many years, and certainly since the Paris Peace Conference of 1919. Efforts at co-operation during the 1920s had not come to much, partly because the United States had not joined the League, although both states had been involved from time to time in such efforts at international tranquillization as the Washington disarmament conference, the Kellogg-Briand Peace Pact, the Dawes and Young Plans for the management of German reparations, and the World Monetary and Economic Conference of 1933. There was, by the early 1930s, a widespread feeling in Britain that the United States had been having a free ride in the international system, and that under the Roosevelt government she intended to persevere in that course. The

---

extraordinary behaviour of the Americans in 1933, when President Roosevelt torpedoed an international economic conference that his predecessor had helped to convene, was a further source of British disenchantment. Conversely, when Britain defaulted on her transatlantic war-loan obligations in the same year, the Americans were understandably annoyed.

By the mid-1930s, all the signs were that the US government was determined to remain in the isolationist redoubt to which it had retreated in 1919. In 1935-37, through a series of Neutrality Acts, Congress embargoed arms sales to belligerents, and provided that warring states would have to pay cash for American goods, carrying them away in their own ships. Other measures forbade Americans from extending credits to nations that had defaulted on their war debts. Therefore, it was reasonable for any European government to suppose that, whatever happened in Europe, the United States would remain aloof, sitting on the sidelines and garnering still larger hoards of gold. Not that American preachment had ceased: as Neville Chamberlain remarked, "It is always best and safest to count on nothing from the Americans but words."[1]

American isolation, therefore, was economic as well as political. In the 1920s, American direct and portfolio investment had been important for some European economies, and Anglo-American cooperation in central banking had been a source of strength to the North Atlantic economy, and to the world. In the early 1930s such things ceased: American capital flowed home whenever and wherever it could, and European capital streamed to the United States in search of security. The American financial collapse of the early 1930s had removed the institutional infrastructure that had facilitated capital exportation in the 1920s, while the European financial collapse made the continent an unattractive place for Americans to lend, and the slump was so severe that few Americans had much to lend in any event. By 1931, America's new foreign investment was negative. The Smoot-Hawley tariff of 1930, and additional tariff increases in 1931 and 1932, were further isolationist elements.[2]

After Hitler's accession to power in 1933, and in light of the fascist and authoritarian movements in other continental states, American isolationism was naturally worrisome to the British government. The memories of the Great War, and of the immense American contribution to it, were anything but dead. The British themselves, with their farflung empire, would have liked to be isolated from Europe, and they were slow to admit that Hitler's policies would eventually mean a continental commitment. The government was convinced that rearmament could only be gradual, and, furthermore, that Britain and France could not hope to win a war against Germany without American goods. And, under the conditions of the mid-1930s, American goods implied American money. Britain's basic economic position was much weaker than it had been in 1914, and this change in circumstances was well understood among Whitehall officials. Although gold reserves had risen since the collapse of the pound in 1931, external obligations had risen also, and the country was running a deficit on its external transactions. Imports and new external lending were financed in part by inflows of hot money from Europe, in part by the depletion of old external assets, and only in part by current export earnings. A war could not be fought without American materials, but Britain's gold and dollar reserves would not finance such imports for long. Under wartime conditions she would predictably sell still less. Yet American legislation closed the American capital market to her. Unless the United States could somehow become more accommodating, Britain would lose any European war.

There was little that the British, if left to their own devices, could do about any of this. There were politicians and officials who believed, in the face of the evidence, that if only Germany were granted better markets and readier access to raw material imports the Nazi regime would become less bellicose. Hence Britain co-operated with a variety of League initiatives, all nugatory, which were meant to ease the German payments position. But Britain herself could not float Germany back to financial equilibrium, whether by importation or by lending, without destroying her own financial stability, although even in the winter of 1938-39 she was willing to extend credits to Berlin.

Such strength as Britain's own export trade possessed came largely from dealings with the Commonwealth, and with certain smaller European and Latin American countries, where preferential and reciprocal trade agreements appeared to be of great importance. Taken together, the Commonwealth and the "Baltic" lands took 58 per cent of United Kingdom exports, and the southern nations of Latin America, with which Britain also had special commercial arrangements, took another 5.4 per cent.[3] Although these agreements annoyed the American government intensely, the United Kingdom could not safely dispense with them: they supported trade with lands that took almost two-thirds of British exports — almost ten times Britain's sales to the United States. The agreements, furthermore, constituted a means of support and encouragement for a variety of more or less democratic European governments that, in their absence, might more readily drift into Hitler's orbit. So far as the American market was concerned, the US tariff wall was an almost insuperable barrier, and no one could be sanguine with respect to American tariff-cutting. In principle, Britain might have made the Americans happier if she had resumed the service of her transatlantic war debts. But her international financial position was not sufficiently strong to make that a reasonable course of action. Furthermore, there was no guarantee that the American reaction would be forceful and helpful enough to make the gamble worthwhile.

There is nowadays a good deal of skepticism among professional economists as to the economic gains from trade liberalization, especially but not only in economically depressed conditions. It is still thought, as in Adam Smith's time, that some trade is better than no trade, and that, under certain carefully defined conditions, general free trade produces an optimally efficient allocation of each nation's resources—labour, land, and capital equipment. Nevertheless, whenever anyone tries to calculate the actual gains from the freeing of trade, the gains appear to be quite small, essentially because there will generally be only a small movement of resources from lower-productivity to higher-productivity uses. Thus a gain of 10 per cent of national output would appear to be high, even if all the displaced resources are quickly re-absorbed into productive work—something which would certainly not occur in a major recession such as that of the 1930s. Furthermore, the smaller the degree of liberalization, the lower the initial trade barriers, and the higher the final barriers that remain after liberalization, the smaller the gains from the freeing of trade. In 1935-37 Britain was still a low-tariff country or a no-tariff country with respect to most of the things that the United States wished to ship eastward, while the United States was a very high-tariff country. Under the American Reciprocal Trade Agreements Act of 1934 US negotiators really had very little that they could offer: they could discuss tariff cuts only if the other partner was the "principal supplier" of a particular import, and they could never cut American import duties by more than a half, so that many American duties, even if reduced through negotiation, would still be prohibitive. In addition, foreign trade was still insignificant to the American economy: in 1936, 3.8 per cent of American output was exported, and only 8.1 per cent of these exports went to Britain, while another 15.3 per cent went to Canada. The US sold Britain a wide range of goods, but most of these were primary products—petroleum, cotton, tobacco, wheat, other temperate-zone agricultural goods, apples, pork products, and lumber. American transatlantic shipments of manufactures, though important for some firms and industries, were less significant in the total flow of trade.

Although no one then described the situation in any such precise way, British officials and politicians certainly began with a reasonable presumption that Anglo-American trade liberalization would do little for the United Kingdom. Nevertheless, it was almost inconceivable that Britain would simply rebuff any American overtures, and it was almost inevitable that, if at all possible, she would contrive to come to an agreement with the Americans on matters related to trade. In 1933-35 such things were less certain, but in later years, as the European scene darkened while the American Congress became ever more isolationist, the British government became more forthcoming. One might overawe the Nazis with the vision of a new Anglo-American entente; if this failed, one might more readily draw help from a friendly USA. Thus in 1936 Chamberlain and his Whitehall officials responded to Franco-American importunities, suppressed their deep misgivings, and made commitments about the management of the floating pound. Thus in 1937, faced with new American proposals in the sphere of tariffs and trade, London did its best to respond creatively.

Britain was much more dependent on trade than the United States, exporting 10 per cent of her output even in 1936. Only 6.4 per cent of these exports, however, went to the USA, while 5.6 per cent went to Canada and another 43.6 per cent to the rest of the British empire. South Africa was a much more significant market for Britain than was the United States, and Canada was very nearly as large; the empire market was almost eight times larger. Hence the importance that British negotiators attached to the placating of the empire's self-governing dominions: it was never reasonable to suppose that they could win enough from the Americans to compensate them for the loss of empire markets, a loss that might very well occur if Britain were to annoy her empire trading partners. The same problem could arise with respect to the Baltic states, which collectively bought more than the United States did; as we shall see, some of the main American demands would have the effect of annoying the Baltic countries, with potentially devastating effects on British exports. These shipments to the Baltic consisted not just of manufactures but also of coal, and it was only too obvious that, if the importing states became annoyed with the United Kingdom, Nazi Germany was ready and willing to supply their needs.

Britain's exports, whether to the empire or to the United States, consisted overwhelmingly of manufactures, although to the Baltic and to some empire markets, such as Canada, coal shipments were not to be ignored, especially when South Wales was so depressed. The American market, however, would never buy British coal. Thanks partly to the US tariff system and partly to the depression, it took small and decreasing quantities of British manufactures, and these tended to be of traditional sorts—textiles, china, Scotch whiskey. The empire markets bought these things also, but in addition they were much more open than the American market to new sorts of high-technology goods—cars and trucks, machinery, telephone equipment, electrical installations—the commodities on which Britain's economic recovery in the 1930s was largely based.

For Canada, by contrast, a satisfactory set of trilateral trade agreements seemed much more likely to produce really useful gains than for the United Kingdom. In 1936 the dominion exported 26 per cent of its output, and 42.4 per cent of those exports went to the United States, while 37.9 per cent went to Britain. Another 9.1 per cent went to other Commonwealth countries; Germany took only 0.7 per cent of Canada's exports—about 0.2 per cent of the nation's output. In relation to the national economy, therefore, little was to be expected from Germany, but the potential gains from trilateral trade-liberalization were comparatively large. The British market took 62 per cent of Canada's farm exports, and another 21 per cent went to the United States, while other significant amounts went to the British West Indies; the Continental markets for such goods had come to be of little importance. Because of the Anglo-Canadian tariff arrangements as embodied in the 1932 Ottawa Agreements, and thanks to American tariff policy, an increasing volume and proportion of Canadian timber exports also went to Britain, inefficient though the long sea haul might appear to be. Of Canada's exports to Britain in 1936, 60 per cent consisted of farm produce, 9 per cent of forest products, and 33 per cent of mineral products. The United Kingdom bought half of Canada's exports of sawn lumber, while the United States—the logical market in the absence of tariff barriers—bought barely one-third. Canada certainly could not forego the British lumber market unless the doors to the American market were to be opened a great deal wider.

Certain Canadian industries had thus become, since the American and Continental European tariff-increases, quota controls, and exchange restrictions of the early 1930s, and since the extension of imperial preferential tariffs in and after 1932, very heavily dependent on the British market, which, in 1936, took 75 per cent of Canada's wheat exports, half of her lumber exports, 96 per cent of her apple exports, as well as 10 per cent of her automobile exports, the balance of which went to other empire countries. No one in Canada had been particularly anxious to bring about this change. For politicians and officials the idea was to sell as much as possible, to anyone who could be induced to buy. Even in the depth of the depression, an "imperial economy" had never made much sense for Canada.[4]

The American economy was a great deal larger than the British, so that for many Canadian primary products, such as forest products and non-ferrous metals, it was inherently much more attractive—if only it could be pried open. For many other goods, however, because

Canada and the United States produced competitive goods under comparable conditions, it was not reasonable to hope for much by way of American sales. Among such goods were wheat and many temperate zone foodstuffs. For these commodities, the main export markets would have to be offshore. The American market remained open to Canadian newsprint, but by 1936 the USA was taking comparatively little Canadian lumber, and barely 21 per cent of Canada's exports of farm products, nor were Canadian-made cars and trucks exported to the USA in any significant quantity. The depression, and the alterations in tariff structures that accompanied it, produced various changes in Canada's trading pattern. The British empire, including the United Kingdom, had become the largest purchaser of Canada's exports.

Nevertheless, in 1936 the United States was the dominion's largest export market, buying somewhat more than the United Kingdom alone, and only slightly less than the empire as a whole. The markets in the other dominions, in India, and in the dependent empire had retained and increased the significance that they had first acquired, so far as Canada was concerned, in the 1920s. The Ottawa Agreements had something to do with this development. But so did the comparatively rapid economic recovery in Australia and the gold-induced boom in South Africa. By 1936, 9.1 per cent of Canada's exports were going to empire countries. Canadians naturally hoped that in due course the European continental markets for foodstuffs, and American markets for lumber, metals, and other primary products, would also re-open. But so far as the European continent was concerned, Ottawa civil servants, while doubtless sharing the popular hope, nonetheless believed that this would not occur—or, at least, that Canada could not hope to do anything that would push the door to Europe much further ajar. As for the American market, after 1934 it was thought that, through mutual negotiation of tariff reductions, Canada might manage to win a larger vent, chiefly for primary products. After all, Canada was the Americans' second-largest export market, and overwhelmingly the largest export market for American manufactures; by contrast Britain, the biggest single export market for the USA, bought mostly primary products. These facts explain the nervousness of the dominion government with respect to the "bound preferential margins" of the Anglo-Canadian Ottawa Agreement: by fixing a minimum preferential margin, the 1932 Agreement limited Canada's freedom to cut tariffs on American goods. Thus, when renegotiating the Anglo-Canadian agreement in 1936-37, the Canadians had made an energetic effort to reduce the number and the rigidity of such "bindings." But even in 1937, not all preferential margins were "bound:" on anthracite coal, for instance, where almost

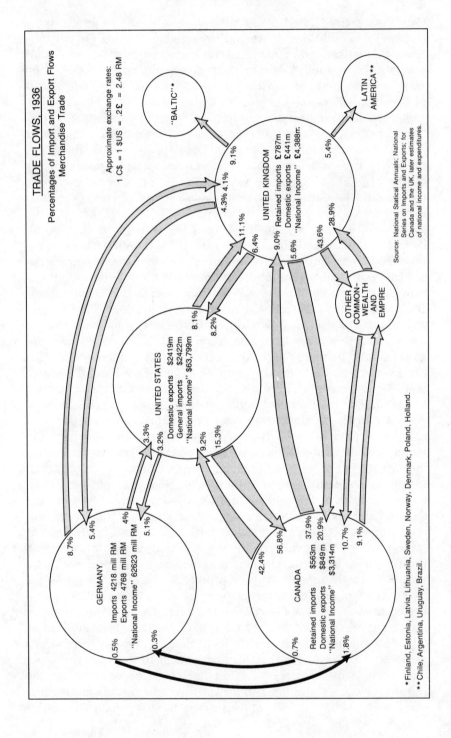

TRADE FLOWS, 1936

Percentages of Import and Export Flows
Merchandise Trade

Approximate exchange rates:
1 C$ = 1 $US = .2£ = 2.48 RM

BALTIC*

LATIN
AMERICA**

UNITED KINGDOM

9.1%
4.3% 4.1%
11.1%
9.0% Retained imports £787m
6.4% Domestic exports £441m
"National Income" £4,388m.
5.6% 43.6%
5.4%
28.9%

UNITED STATES

Domestic exports $2419m
General imports $2422m
"National Income" $63,799m

8.1%
8.2%
3.3%
3.2%
9.2%
15.3%

OTHER
COMMON-
WEALTH
AND
EMPIRE

GERMANY

Imports 4218 mill RM
Exports 4768 mill RM
"National Income" 62623 mill RM

8.7%
5.4%
4%
5.1%
0.5%
0.3%

CANADA

Retained imports $563m
Domestic exports $849m
"National Income" $3,314m

56.8%
42.4%
37.9% 20.9%
10.7%
9.1%
0.7%
1.8%

Source: National Statical Annuals; National
Series on Imports and Exports; for
Canada and the UK, later estimates
of national income and expenditures.

*Finland, Estonia, Latvia, Lithuania, Sweden, Norway, Denmark, Poland, Holland.
**Chile, Argentina, Uruguay, Brazil.

40 per cent of Canada's imports came from Britain, the dominion's preferential concession was an uncovenanted one. And, as we have seen, the Canadian market was important for the depressed mining communities of South Wales. Here as so often the Americans tended to exaggerate the importance of the Ottawa Agreements—and to ignore the domestic political circumstances that tended to support the preferential system.

The Ottawa Agreements of 1932, which had enormously extended and strengthened the system of imperial preferential tariffs, were of considerable importance for Canada's trade, directed as this was to Britain and the empire. The government of Canada had first extended preferential concessions in 1897, and had subsequently negotiated mutual trade agreements, entrenching these concessions and developing them, with such imperial territories as Australia, New Zealand, and the West Indies. The United Kingdom had for many decades been unwilling to negotiate preferential arrangements. In 1919 it did cut its rates of duty on empire goods, but because it then imposed few duties on the sorts of commodity that Canada exported, the concession was of little value to the senior dominion. The automobile industry benefited, but the wheat and lumber industries did not, because Britain imposed no duties on such goods, regardless of origin. These preferential arrangements were somewhat extended in the 1920s, but in ways that were of little importance to Canada. However, Britain's policy changed in the winter of 1931-32, and at the Ottawa Conference, which occurred in the summer of 1932, Canada's Conservative government was able to convince the United Kingdom to impose new or higher duties on goods such as wheat and dairy products from outside the empire, but not on the same products from inside. Britain also gave certain guarantees about the margins between the duties on empire and non-empire goods, and about preferential treatment for empire shipments of various commodities, such as meat, which were thereafter subject to quantitative control. In exchange Canada gave identical guarantees with respect to its preferential treatment of goods from Britain and the empire, in the process raising the duties on many non-empire commodities. The Ottawa arrangements were embodied in a network of bilateral pacts among Britain, Canada, the other dominions, India, and Southern Rhodesia; they also involved the dependent empire. Canada's Liberal opposition, led by W.L. Mackenzie King, objected not only to the higher duties on non-empire goods, such as those from the United States, but to the "binding of preferential margins." This arrangement, embodied as it was in the network of Ottawa trade agreements, limited Canada's freedom to negotiate with third countries, such as the USA, during the term of the agreements, all of which were due to expire, unless renewed, in 1937. The "binding," of course, also limited the power of the United Kingdom, but King's Liberals showed little interest in that element of the Ottawa arrangements. Besides the Ottawa pacts, Canada extended various preferential concessions that were not embodied in the agreements, but which were hallowed by long custom, and which were certainly thought to be part of the "Ottawa bargain." Of these, the most important was that on British anthracite coal, which could and did compete with American coal at least as far as Montreal.

The Ottawa arrangements have often been seen as simple retaliation for the American Smoot-Hawley tariff increases of 1930, and for the further American tariff increases of 1931-32. This interpretation, we believe, is incorrect. The Ottawa conferees were certainly concerned to protect their own economies in the depth of the slump, and if the American economy had remained as open as it had been in the 1920s, they might have gone less far in discrimination against American goods. But it should be remembered that they also discriminated against the goods of other countries. Among the nations that suffered from the Ottawa pacts were the USSR, whose coal and lumber shipments were impeded; the Scandinavian states, whose lumber industries suffered in the same way; Argentina, which faced new barriers in its transatlantic meat trade; and the many small states of northern Europe, all of whom would have more trouble selling meat, butter, bacon, cheese, and ham in the United Kingdom. Furthermore, an important element in the strategy of the United Kingdom government was protection for Britain's own *domestic* agriculture. Empire suppliers, admittedly, were to receive new preferential treatment. Non-empire suppliers were to face higher tariff and non-tariff obstacles, whether or not their governments had raised tariff barriers against the United Kingdom.

It is to be supposed, therefore, that even if there had been no Smoot-Hawley tariff, in and after 1932 American primary products would have faced more severe difficulties at the British frontier. At Ottawa in 1932 Canada had been, in many respects, an accidental beneficiary of Britain's own protectionist evolution. Britain would extend preferential concessions to empire goods—but only if the empire countries, such as Canada, did the same for Britain's own exports. Higher tariffs on American goods were a necessary result, not only at Canada's frontier but throughout the empire.

No one expected Canada to solve the world's commercial and financial ills. Nor would her policies affect the balance between war and peace. Her politicians and officials did not have to worry about defaulted war debts or access to American credit; the national payments position, furthermore, was strong, in that exports exceeded imports and external debt was being repaid. So far as Canadian officials knew, Washington neither knew nor cared about the management of the floating Canadian dollar. Canada was still a member of the British empire, and she gained from the network of preferential tariff concessions that had been elaborated in the Ottawa agreements of 1932. The gains may have been less than Canadians thought. In dealing with the preferential system, however, no Canadian politician could ignore these beliefs. Nor could anyone ignore Canadian annoyance at American protectionism, aimed as this was not only at Britain but also at Canada.

For Whitehall, Canada and the empire would be important elements in the strategies of fighting a war—and of avoiding one. If an Anglo-American entente might impress Hitler, so might the vision of Commonwealth solidarity. Yet no one could be sure just what Canada's position was, or what Canada might do. Isolationism, it seemed, might not be a solely American virus, and Whitehall would have to work to keep the dominions from infection. Canada's leader for most of the 1920s and 1930s, Mackenzie King, specialized in ambiguity and obscurity. The obscurity reflected his own cast of mind; the ambiguity reflected the Canadian reality—American in geography, but British in history. King was desperately anxious to play some role in the great issues of world politics. He was, however, very much aware of local political realities, and their foundation in ever-contradictory perceptions of imperial solidarity, national autonomy, and economic gain and loss. He was therefore anxious to incur no risks.

Germany's economic position was not well understood at the time, and the result was a mixture of optimism and pessimism among observers in London and Washington. Since 1931 Germany had been following a very visible policy of exchange control, and the regulations had become more rigorous with the passage of time. In Britain and France the nature and effect of these controls became well-known to politicians and officials, and even to the general public. Germany had also been "defending" the theoretical gold value of the reichsmark, as fixed in 1924, even though by autumn 1936 Britain, the United States, France, and most of the smaller states of northern Europe had devalued their currencies. In 1931, a dollar had cost 4.196 RM; in 1936, on the average, a dollar cost 2.48 RM, while the price of a pound sterling had fallen from 20.4 RM to 12.35 RM. Germany responded to this situation by inventing a complicated system of multiple exchange rates, so that the cost of a reichsmark was increasingly theoretical, depending as it did on the source of the funds and the purpose for which German or foreign currencies might be sought. Nonetheless, overvaluation of the German currency tended to make

German exportation more difficult, and it certainly increased the need for exchange control. In the United States, remote from central Europe and to some extent isolated from its commercial and financial perplexities, the impact of currency overvaluation and exchange control was correspondingly less clear, so that the distorting effect of purely commercial policy, such as Britain's preferential tariff, could be exaggerated. Like France and most other continental economies, furthermore, Germany extended special protection to agriculture by means of quantitative quotas and mixing schemes. Behind these screens, the Nazi authorities had been pursuing a vigorous policy of economic reflation, first for civil purposes and then for re-armament. The result, by 1936, was full employment plus a chronic shortage of foreign exchange and an almost closed economy: in 1936 Germany exported 7.6 per cent of "national income," as then reported, and imported only 6.7 per cent. Imports of temperate-zone foodstuffs had almost ceased: for instance, in 1936 Germany spent only 0.08 per cent of her import outlays on wheat.

Germany's shortage of foreign exchange was in large measure the result of the domestic reflation, but it was made more severe because Germany's traditional export markets were largely in the depression-damaged lands of Europe and Latin America, where importation was slow to recover from the slump. In 1936, 8.7 per cent of German exports went to Britain, 4 per cent to the United States, and 0.5 per cent to Canada. The national export earnings were depressed by the world slump, while the national need for imports was inflated by the strength of domestic demand, both civil and military. Also, the supply of exportables was itself reduced insofar as Germany's buoyant domestic market claimed ever more of her domestic production. In addition, even after the Nazi government refused to transfer any more First World War reparations, there were financial obligations remaining from the period of heavy external borrowing in the late 1920s, and these increased the need for a stringent rationing of Germany's foreign exchange. Yet it was easy for observers to believe that Germany's foreign-exchange problem was somehow caused by other countries—*their* new tariff-barriers, exchange regulations, preferential arrangements. And Germany's representatives were not slow to urge this view on other nations, especially when demanding "better access to raw materials."

In fact, during the 1930s the producers of raw materials and foodstuffs would have been only too happy to sell. All that the buyer needed was some acceptable means of payment. The problem for Germany was that in many parts of the world, nobody wanted inconvertible German marks, and many nations did not favour the international barter agreements by which, for example, Serbian tobacco was exchanged for Rhenish aspirin, and vice versa. Yet English-speaking observers — especially in Washington — could not readily understand that Germany herself had caused Germany's shortage of foreign exchange. The primary confusion bred secondary errors, and some unfruitful international mediations. Thus the League of Nations, concerned about "access to raw materials," commissioned a serious study of the topic—the Van Zeeland Report.[5]

Another such error, to which Neville Chamberlain, the dominant British politician of the day, himself fell victim, surrounded the German demand for the return of the former German colonies, which the Treaty of Versailles had taken away. It was true that these territories, or some of them, did produce some of the tropical products that Germany needed. It was also true that with intensive development they could and would produce more of such goods — coffee, cocoa, sisal, perhaps even rubber. Any such production would be inside Germany's fence of exchange control, generating no demand for scarce foreign exchange, such as dollars or pounds. Therefore it appeared reasonable, in certain circles, to "appease" Germany economically by returning her colonies to her. But in fact this was not plausible, at least in the short run: the payoff from colonial development, as Britain had learned in the 1920s, would probably not come for many years. Meanwhile, whatever might be done about colonies, if only Nazi Germany could export more, surely she would become less aggressive; after all, she would not need extra territories, because she would be able to buy the extra food and raw materials. Or so it was thought.

It is quite likely that many Nazis believed their own propaganda with respect to food, raw materials, and tropical products, on the one hand, and territorial expansion on the other. Yet it does not follow that, for the Nazis, exports and aggressions were really alternatives. Indeed, before 1939 German expansion did nothing to solve Germany's balance of payments problem. Rather, because the Sudetenland, Danzig, Memel, and Austria were all deficient both in food and in the relevant raw materials, Hitlerite aggression made the problem worse.

Some Americans believed German propaganda too. That eminent free-trade apostle, Cordell Hull, reigned over the State Department, and it was Hull who cast the Roosevelt administration in the role of a crusader for economic disarmament. He brought to that crusade, as Arthur Schlesinger has pointed out, "a peculiar combination of evangelism and vindictiveness, of selflessness and martyrdom. . . . Economic internationalism was not just the way to recovery;

it was the way to peace and salvation. With all the conviction of a Tennessee fundamentalist Cordell Hull was determined to set his country on the glory road." Appearing on the surface to be an elderly, benign and even simple southern gentleman, Hull was that most dangerous of adversaries: a man who knew he was right. His opponents were invariably wrong, and for the most discreditable of reasons.[6]

One of the very proudest of Hull's achievements was the Reciprocal Trade Agreements Act of 1934.[7] It gave the president of the United States authority to reduce tariffs by up to 50 per cent, and to negotiate trade agreements that would involve such concessions. On any particular commodity, rates could be lowered only by negotiating with the foreign country that was the "principal supplier" of the American import market—supplying at least half of American imports of that product. Nevertheless, all trade agreements were to include unconditional most-favoured-nation clauses, so that American concessions granted to any one foreign country would apply to all signatories. Before beginning trade talks, the president was to give notice that negotiations were "contemplated;" he was then to announce that it was his "intention" to make offers on a specified list of goods. Interested parties could make representations to the Committee on Reciprocity Information, a group of officials that would report its findings to the State Department, the agency that carried out the actual negotiations.

In spite of the liberal free-trading rhetoric which surrounded the trade agreements act, it was a resolutely national and nationalist piece of legislation—so it was sold to Congress, and so it operated in fact. "The policy of the proposed bill," said Hull during the Congressional debate, "is to supplement our almost impregnable domestic markets with a substantial and gradually expanding foreign market for our more burdensome surpluses." Francis Sayre, Woodrow Wilson's son-in-law, was brought in to help win public and political support for the bill. Sayre was an internationalist of impeccable credentials, but he too argued that the bill's real purpose was to generate extra American exports. "The very foundation of such a program must be avoidance of undue injury to American producers." Trade, after all, was the principal index of a nation's prosperity, and had been since long before the Industrial Revolution.[8] Sayre stayed on in Hull's service after the bill's passage, as assistant secretary of state for trade agreements, and his views did not alter. Nor, paradoxically, did his idealism waver.

The trade agreements act did not remove politics from the American tariff, or from proposals for tariff change. It simply changed the way in which politics impinged on tariff-making. Given the full panoply of administrative and Congressional restrictionism, and the actual behaviour of the State Department's negotiators, the Americans were far from "free traders," and suggestions that Hull was committed to free trade, or was anxious for it, are wide of the mark. When negotiations took place under the act, they could not reduce positive rates of duty to zero, and rates might still be very high by international standards. If, for example, a duty of 110 per cent *ad valorem*[9] was reduced by 50 per cent, the new duty would still be 55 per cent—no small hurdle. Furthermore, the American negotiators were not obliged to offer a reduction of 50 per cent; they could and almost always did offer considerably less. Although it did not directly intervene in such trade negotiations, the United States Congress could impose new duties or duty-like charges, as well as non-tariff barriers such as quotas and "marking regulations." Congress could also threaten, if significant concessions were not seen to be won, to repeal the act itself, or not to renew it beyond its three-year term.

Hull was nevertheless devout in his desire to banish American economic isolationism—he had described the tariff as the "king of evils" in his maiden Congressional speech three decades before[10] —and to bring world peace through increased commerce. "Economic appeasement" had a widespread and powerful appeal. If nations and individuals could only somehow be made prosperous, political well-being would follow; there would be no pent-up feelings of frustration and anxiety to be released in a moment of international crisis. As Hull put it, if goods could not cross international boundaries, armies would.[11] He assigned the highest priority to enlisting Great Britain under his banner of non-discrimination, and in 1936 he shifted his rhetorical campaign against British economic policies into high gear. As he explained in his memoirs, the British ought to take the initiative because of their movement "in the opposite direction, towards economic nationalism, and because her commercial relations with most of the nations of Europe were closer than those of other countries."[12] In Hull's mind an Anglo-American agreement would lead inexorably to others. Pressing for such an agreement, he made no allowance for the deterioration in Britain's basic balance-of-payment position, or for the troubles in her export industries. Both circumstances would naturally make Britain nervous about any "adventurous" trade agreement. The same factors would be present for many other countries that had balance-of-payments problems—in other words, for most of the states in the western world.

Hull's thinking, in fact, was anything but clear. The American secretary of state appears in theory to have taken the "all-inclusive" approach to economic appeasement, believing in "a strenuous effort to bring in the Dictators right from the beginning, instead of trusting merely to the force of example, which often in the field of international affairs worked too slowly."[13] Often, however, Hull seemed more interested in a "general lead" than specific actions. He seemed to feel, says Schlesinger, "that the enunciation of a lofty principle was three quarters of the battle."[14] In practice he therefore talked a great deal and concentrated, after 1936, on an accord with the British.

Although Great Britain and the United States had been signing commercial treaties since the early nineteenth century, until the 1930s neither had much experience with tariff negotiation. Before the passage in 1934 of the Reciprocal Trade Agreements Act, most countries believed that it was pointless to discuss tariff rates with the American government. After that year the Americans admittedly learned fast: they negotiated some twenty agreements in short order. Nevertheless, they were slow to develop the administrative infrastructure—or the filing system—to support the process.

Canada, which rapidly became an important part of the Anglo-American discussions, had a more substantial background in such matters, and considerable incentive to pursue trade liberalization. Hard-hit by the depression, which both contracted and closed so many of its export markets, the dominion made much of its living as a trading nation, and it had been negotiating about tariffs since early in the century. It ran a large current-account deficit with the United States, but in the 1930s this was more than covered by surpluses in other directions. Because of the severity of her domestic slump, which depressed the nation's demand for imports, Canada was in overall surplus, so that Ottawa would not have to calculate the balance-of-payments effect of every trade concession. Both the Conservative government of R.B. Bennett, which held office from 1930 to 1935, and the succeeding Liberal government of Mackenzie King, were anxious to negotiate about trade, primarily so as to increase the vent for Canada's own exports. King, a philosophic free-trader, in addition, had some interest in cutting Canada's own tariffs for the sake of the dominion's own consumers. Bennett took speedy advantage of the opportunities that the American trade agreements act provided. The negotiations for a Canadian-American agreement that he began were carried to completion by the King government immediately after its election in 1935.

In Canada, a federal country where the provinces controlled most aspects of property and civil rights, it was thought that the nation could not control agricultural production, and neither the national nor provincial governments had sufficient resources to subsidize farmers. Canadian authorities, nevertheless, were as anxious as the

British and Americans to help their distressed farmers. One way was to bargain for new or better external markets. Hence the Canadian demand, first voiced in the 1890s but renewed by Prime Minister Bennett in 1930, for preferential protection in the British market for imported foodstuffs.

Any trilateral trade discussions were bound to involve the interlocking set of Ottawa Agreements, signed among Britain, her dominions, and India. Britain imported enormous amounts of food, and the Ottawa Agreements naturally annoyed other exporters of foodstuffs, such as the United States. Indeed, by 1931 the British had been the only remaining food importer of any size; larger continental countries such as France and Germany were closing their markets, so far as they could, to foreign meat and grain. Among the major suppliers of the British market were Holland and the Baltic states, Argentina, and the United States. Some of these countries also imported North American grain, but compared with the British market or the German one, their potential was limited because their economies were so small, and because some of them, such as Argentina, were also exporters of the wheat that Canada and the United States were so anxious to export. So far as her European and Latin suppliers were concerned, Britain followed the Ottawa Conference with a series of trade agreements, each providing certain guarantees. Basically, these smaller suppliers were promised that Britain would not further raise her duties against their products, and that they could share in the assigning of quotas for such products as ham and bacon.

It was certainly true that the Ottawa Agreements seemed to discriminate particularly against non-empire exporters of such goods: Argentina, the smaller Continental nations—and the United States. American exports to Britain consisted largely of primary agricultural products. With respect to empire tobacco the Ottawa Agreements extended and refined the preferential system, although they did nothing for empire cotton. Of Britain's total imports in 1929, at least 27 per cent by value were affected by the 1932 changes in tariffs, preferences, and quantitative controls.[15] On the American side, half of the nation's 1929 exports to Britain consisted of crude materials and foodstuffs, most of which, the chief exception being raw cotton, were affected by Britain's new tariff regime.[16] America's share of Britain's import market, furthermore, had indeed been reduced— from 16.5 per cent of total imports in 1929 to 11.1 per cent in 1936. Hull, it might appear, was not far wrong.

Nevertheless, British officials were right to think that the Ottawa system of preferences had not done much harm to American exporters. Canadian timber, for example, had won some ground in the British market at the expense of the American, but in the US home market the opposite had happened, so that the position of the American producer cannot have been much affected. Cotton still entered Britain duty-free. If America's market share had diminished, the culprit was her own Agricultural Adjustment Act, which artificially raised the price not only of home-grown cotton but of many other American primary products. Britain levied a heavy duty on tobacco, and ever since 1919 she had charged a much lower duty on "empire tobacco." The prosperity of Southern Rhodesia was based on that tobacco preference, which Britain promised in 1932 to maintain for ten years. Yet American sales rose steadily throughout the 1930s, in spite of the price-raising efforts of the Agricultural Adjustment Administration. In mid-decade American tobacco continued to supply over 80 per cent of the British demand—much the same share as in the late 1920s, when preferences were lower and the Rhodesian industry was less extensive.

Britain had also imposed a preferential wheat duty in 1932, taxing non-empire wheat while admitting empire wheat free, and she had made arrangements to subsidize the domestic production of a certain quantity of the grain as well. The domestic subsidy certainly reduced Britain's total wheat imports, although until the domestic quota was raised in 1937 the effect cannot have been great. The preferential wheat tariff may well have affected the world pattern of wheat marketing, but it cannot have affected America's market prospects, whether in volume or in price terms, although the Americans would never have admitted as much.[17] The empire produced more exportable wheat than Britain consumed. If the preference drew more imperial wheat to Britain, there would be less of it on other markets; foreign wheat would take up the space that the empire wheat had vacated. Prices in British and foreign markets would be the same whether or not a preference existed. The Ottawa Agreements themselves provided that the preference was conditional on the absence of price differentials. Empire producers in general, and Canadian producers in particular, were not to be allowed to exploit their British customers. In any event, it was drought and dustbowl conditions, not imperial preference, that reduced American wheat exports to the vanishing point for several years in the 1930s.

The Ottawa Agreements also involved preferential concessions on empire softwood timber and lumber. Although more than 90 per cent of British softwood imports came from the Baltic states, Scandinavia, and the Soviet Union, Canadian producers were anxious to find new vents in Britain because the increase in American duties had shut them out of that much more convenient and natural market. Non-ferrous metals were also covered by Ottawa, and for the same reason: American tariff increases were causing pain not only for Canadian producers but for the newly-emerging copper mines in another part of the empire, Northern Rhodesia. In this instance conditions were attached, and because these were not satisfied, the preferential duty structure never came into force.

Because most of America's primary products were consumed at home, the troubles of US farmers and lumbermen primarily reflected the nation's own slump, not the growth of protectionism and tariff discrimination that the Ottawa Agreements embodied and symbolized. And for some American export commodities, such as cotton, the world-wide depression was to blame. For instance, because Britain's own cotton exports had collapsed, Britain was naturally buying less raw cotton from the United States. And Japanese mills, whose export trade was doing rather better, depended more heavily on Indian cotton than on American. Nevertheless, it was hard for primary producers and politicians, especially in the New Deal administration that took office early in 1933, to avoid the suspicion that "Ottawa discrimination" had caused the trouble, or had made things worse.

In the United States, as in the United Kingdom and to some extent in Canada, the depression was often blamed on the collapse in the prices of primary products. Although that was at least as much the effect of the collapse as its cause, governments did what they could to raise prices. The British placed heavy emphasis on limiting not only domestic production but also imports. The Americans reduced agricultural production, by means such as the Agricultural Adjustment Act of 1933, while at the same time compensating farmers. For many field crops, drought quickly converted surplus to shortage. But for some this did not happen, and it was these products—apples, citrus fruits, tobacco, pig products, lumber —which figured prominently in the Anglo-American trade discussions that form a large part of this book. Furthermore, the Agricultural Adjustment Act was declared unconstitutional in 1936, and Congress provided a general replacement only in 1938. Export markets must have seemed even more important for the American primary producer in the years between 1936 and 1938, the years in which the trade talks were being conducted in earnest.

Hull detested the Ottawa Agreements, claiming that 40 per cent of American trade with Great Britain had been affected by these unfair arrangements,[18] and he fretted about the discriminatory features of certain other British trade agreements, such as those with Argentina and the Baltic states. He wanted the British to buy more of America's surplus agricultural goods, although he was not at all anxious to buy more from Britain. These demands were reasonable enough in many respects, and there were plenty of civil servants in Whitehall who disliked the path that Britain had been obliged to tread since 1931. But the United Kingdom had a very large deficit on visible trade, and a smaller but still significant deficit on her current international transactions as a whole. This current-account deficit had appeared in 1931, and continued year after year. We now know that 120 years of British surpluses, interrupted only in the last year of the Great War and in 1926, had come to an end. Worse still, much of Britain's trade was with countries such as Argentina whose current accounts were in an equally precarious condition. In these circumstances the British could hardly leave the Argentines free to spend their sterling earnings as they liked. Nor could she follow that line with Germany, which still owed a great deal to Britain's banks. The United States, in surplus overall and with almost all countries, could allow her trading partners to spend their dollars as they liked. The British authorities would have liked to do the same, but could not treat all their trading partners in that way.

There were many domestic primary producers whom the American government could placate by winning British concessions, whether on tariffs, on preferential margins, or on quantitative controls. Among the most important were the hog raisers, the citrus growers, and the producers of fresh, tinned, and dried fruit. Some of these, indeed, may have actually suffered loss from the Ottawa system, and others had been suffering ever since Britain first introduced preferential concessions in 1919. All these interests faced competition in Britain, sometimes from empire suppliers, sometimes from home producers, and sometimes from nations in Northern Europe and Latin America that Britain was anxious not to annoy. The same was true of lumber. Observing that the Ottawa preferences had drawn some Canadian lumber to Britain, American sawmill owners called for "tariff parity." For all these products, as for tobacco, any British concession would help to raise American prices, thus making life easier for the farmers and the bureaucrats, not to mention the politicians.

If the Americans were to be satisfied, Britain would have to renegotiate or denounce a whole network of commercial treaties and trade agreements, both in the British empire and outside it. She would also have to change her own arrangements for collecting customs revenue and for agricultural subsidy. The implications would be unpleasant, especially for a "National Government" that was pledged to fiscal rectitude, a balanced budget, and a better deal for Britain's own farmers.

There could be no question, from Washington's point of view, of accepting British protestations regarding the nature of treaty commitments, the problems of renegotiating agreements with five dominions and more than twenty foreign countries, and the domestic problems—parliamentary, financial, and administrative—that the American demands could create. The United States was presumed to be pure in heart, notwithstanding her own protective tariff and preferential arrangements with Cuba and the Philippines. Britain, in spite of her lower tariff, was judged in Washington to be not merely ingenious in negotiation but also dishonest in argument. Not for the first time, and not for the last, one side was assessing the other in terms that might more appropriately be applied to itself.

So far as the British were concerned, it was the Americans who were the chief sinners, not in tariff matters alone, but in the general disruption of the international economy. The United States ran a balance-of-payments surplus, yet she refused to lend abroad. The Americans demanded payment on Great War debts while refusing to accept any more imports than were absolutely necessary. Great Britain bought far more from the United States than she sold there. Most British tariffs, which officials tended to see as an outgrowth of the depression, began in 1932 at very moderate levels—generally at 10 per cent *ad valorem*. Even though they tended to drift upward, they were in general far lower than American tariffs. Britain, in addition, was more restrained in her use of quantitative import-controls. There was therefore real anger when Hull directed his rhetorical thunderbolts against Britain's tariffs and quotas.

In Whitehall there was much concern, both in the Board of Trade and in the Treasury, about Britain's immense trading deficit with the United States. Washington, if pressed, would respond that one should also look at the American deficit with the overseas sterling area,[19] from which the United States bought wool, rubber, and tin. Whitehall was not impressed. The Board of Trade believed that Britain's record as a free trader was at least as good as the American, and that her transatlantic trading deficit was proof of this fact, so that in any discussion about trade it would soon become apparent that Britain had nothing to give: her own imports from the United States were largely duty-free, or, if taxed, paid only "revenue duties," not protective levies. In the Treasury, Sigismund Waley summed up the situation: "The United States do little or nothing to reduce tariffs and by keeping out foreign goods they drain gold from the rest of the world and make it impossible to contemplate any stabilisation of currencies. . . . It is difficult to commend what Mr. Hull preaches without at the same time condemning what the United States in fact practises."[20]

In the economic theory that was accessible to Cordell Hull and to his fellow-thinker, Mackenzie King, it was normally argued that free trade was better than protection, with the implied corollary that tariff reduction was always advantageous. Admittedly, there was already in existence a body of thought which demonstrated that, in certain circumstances, a country could increase its gain from trade if it imposed tariffs of just the right height on the precisely appropriate goods. No one, however, would claim that the existing tariff structures of Canada, the United States, and the United Kingdom were "optimal" in that rather special sense. Nor could it be shown that the real world corresponded to the abstract one in which the "circumstances" were just right. The theory of customs unions, which has been developed in the past thirty-five years, has given economists a much clearer understanding of the ways that tariffs work. In the process, analysts have uncovered some cases in which tariff cuts make things worse, either for the tariff-cutting country or for the world at large. The case for freer trade, in other words, is now understood to be somewhat weaker than the statesmen of the 1930s commonly believed.

In the traditional theory, however, free trade was thought to produce a high level of economic efficiency. Individual countries benefited because they concentrated their productive efforts on the things they did relatively well, so that their supplies of labour and raw materials could generate a higher level of consumer satisfaction through trade. The whole world would then be better off than if the various countries did not trade, because every country would be using its resources in the most productive way. The theory assumed that inputs which are displaced from one sector would find other work reasonably quickly, either through the growth of other industries or through a change in the techniques of production within the surviving industries.

If we apply this theory to the case of a tariff cut that applies to any one product, we can identify several separate effects. First of all, the domestic price will probably fall by the amount of the tariff cut. Secondly, domestic consumption will rise. Thirdly, domestic production will fall, perhaps to zero. Fourthly, imports will rise. Underlying these obvious effects are several that are less so. The surplus revenue of producers will decline. There will be a net release of resources from the contracting industry. Revenue from customs duties may or may not fall, but consumers are unequivocally better off. In principle, the improvement can be measured by calculating the increase in consumer satisfaction minus the decrease in producers' surplus revenue and the loss of tax revenue on the old level of imports. It can be shown that the result is always a positive figure, although it may be a small one; the amount varies directly with the size of the tariff cut, the reduction in domestic production, and the increase in consumer purchases.

This approach is very different from the "game-playing approach" that tariff-bargainers generally adopt, and that we describe more fully in Chapter 9. In that approach, the aim is to cut one's own tariffs as little as possible, thus minimizing the possibility of gains from trade. Furthermore, the game-playing negotiator is likely to think that he has "lost" if he concedes anything which involves a fall in domestic production. But the economists' traditional theory recognizes that, in order to extract significant gains from trade, a country has to be willing to contract production. More cannot be exported unless more is imported. The solution, for the game-player, is likely to be the following: he will offer tariff cuts on things his country does not produce at all, and he will try to minimize the resistance of the "other side" by pressing for tariff cuts which will be at the expense of third countries. He will do this because he knows that such reductions will produce the least resistance on the other side.

In pressing their own demands on the United States, the British negotiators would have little opportunity to gore the ox of some third country. It was clear to everybody that American factories, not Brazilian or French ones, would lose any extra sales that Britain would gain. The exact impact on American factories is in fact impossible to deduce: lower prices mean higher total sales and increased imports, but American market structures—cost patterns and the degree of competition—will affect the United States outcome in terms of employment and output. Nor could Britain exploit all the possibilities for increased exports. Under America's Reciprocal Trades Agreement Act, as we have seen, Britain could press for concessions only when she was a "principal supplier" of American imports.

There was a further problem. Many of the relevant British exports were "intermediate goods" rather than "final products." That is to say, Britain's exports tended to be bought by American manufacturers for further processing, not by final consumers of finished manufactures. Textiles were an important example. By 1938 most cottons were worked up in the "rag trade," not in households. In the event, therefore, the demand for such goods must have been relatively insensitive to the price of the goods. Consider an American tariff cut on Levers lace. The cut would lower the American price. The lace was used to trim nightgowns. Cheaper lace might somewhat increase the yardage of lace per nightie, and would permit a lower nightie price. Both developments would increase total sales of lace, but both effects would likely be small. For Britain, the only important exception in her transatlantic export trade was whiskey. But whiskey was not a subject for negotiation.

In short, the character of the Reciprocal Trade Agreements Act combined with the character of Anglo-American trade to produce the maximum amount of resistance on the American side, and the minimum realistic expectation of British gain. It also affected the nature and distribution of the gains from tariff reduction. Final consumers of nighties, for instance, would hardly notice the resultant price decline from a tariff cut on Levers lace, because it made up only a small fraction of the cost of production. Because nightie sales would rise very little, virtually all of the net efficiency-gain to the US economy would have to come from the contraction of the American lace industry. The losers would be a small but vocal group of factory owners. Factory employees were also likely to think of themselves as losers, and in the depressed conditions of the late 1930s, it would be difficult to blame them. The winners, on the other hand, are the buyers of lace-trimmed garments, who face slightly reduced prices, and the American population at large, who benefit from the more efficient allocation of resources within the USA. Neither group is likely to be loud in its praise of the government; neither is likely to take note of its good fortune.

On the British side the situation was really quite different, although here too the domestic situation with respect to cost and market structures would determine the actual effect, industry by industry and product by product, from a tariff cut. First of all, in manufactures the Americans wanted concessions on finished products—typewriters, peanut butter, motor cars—not on intermediate goods such as yard goods or lace. Retail prices, therefore, would fall quite directly as a result of a tariff cut, and with any luck the price decline would equal the full tariff reduction, producing a perceptible increase in consumer purchases and in American sales. Precisely because British tariffs had been low or non-existent until the winter of 1931-32, there had been little chance for really high-cost, inefficient production to develop. Those industries which had been protected at substantial rates since 1915 under the McKenna Duties were obvious exceptions, but in general the American proposals were not aimed at this group of industries, or where a "McKenna industry" was a target, as in the case of the motor industry, the Americans were concerned with a segment of the market where British sales were small and where British firms were ill-represented in any event. British industry was thus much less exposed than American. There was a real chance that tariff cuts would create new trade without producing much reallocation of domestic resources, because they would have a more expansionary impact on sales and because a smaller fraction of British production was grossly inefficient at the tariff rates of the mid-1930s.

The United States also wanted to win concessions on natural products. Many of these were consumed directly by ordinary households. For all these goods, there was competing supply from third countries, either inside the British empire or outside it. Britain's own production of such things as wheat and hog products was managed in quantitative terms: domestic production would not fall in the face of a tariff cut, although the government might have to raise its subsidies. In terms of negotiation, therefore, Britain could make concessions without the usual domestic repercussions; yet, because domestic production was regulated, there would be no British gains as a result of the internal reallocation from inefficient to efficient industries. British farmers would grow just as much wheat, and raise just as many hogs, whether or not the lard duty and the wheat duty were reduced—so long as subsidies were increased sufficiently. Because ordinary people ate the tinned fruit and bought much of the lard, tariff cuts on these products would be transmitted full force to retail prices. However, because such things were not large elements either in the diet or in the spending patterns of British households, the consumption response to a price cut might not be very large. In other words, if the Exchequer could stand the extra subsidies, Britain might find it easy to concede lower tariffs on such food products, but there would be little or no gain from reallocation of resources, and against the gain in consumer satisfaction we should have to set not only the loss of tariff revenue but also the extra subsidy. If purchases do not rise by very much, the subsidy can be larger than the apparent gain to consumers, especially if domestic production contributes a big share of domestic consumption. If our standard is the welfare of the British household and the British economy, a tariff cut then makes no sense at all, and the UK's concessions involve a net loss to that economy.

The situation is amusingly paradoxical, unless one lives in the United Kingdom. Production-control and subsidy shield the British economy from what the game-playing negotiator regards as the bad effects of a tariff cut, but they also prevent Britain from maximizing her gains from trade.

The timber and tobacco duties were very different. Both products were intermediate goods, like Levers lace. Neither, however, was produced to any interesting extent in the United Kingdom. Thus in making a tariff concession, Britain could not expect to gain anything from any internal reallocation of her own resources. All the gains would go to households, and against these gains would have to be set the loss of revenue from the reduction of duty on the old level of imports. Tobacco was an important element in the cost of cigarettes; in construction costs, softwood timber was a much less significant element, although it counted for more than Levers lace in the nightgown industry. Thus a tariff cut on timber would have a comparatively small effect both on the price of housing and on the demand for timber, while a tobacco reduction might have an enormous impact on the price of cigarettes, and so not only on smoking but on tobacco imports.

The conclusion of this sort of analysis is a dismal one. Given all the circumstances, the Anglo-American trade talks could not possibly produce much of a real gain for either party. Although nobody carried out any such analysis at the time, the instinct of the British officials was sound: from the economic point of view, the whole exercise was a waste of time. In fact, it was entirely possible that a trade negotiation which the Americans would regard as "successful" might actually involve a loss of economic welfare, so that the new and lower set of tariffs would find the British population worse off than it had been before. Britain's timber tariffs provide a case in point. Let us suppose that, through a mixture of selective tariff reduction and careful tariff subdivision, Britain came to import less from low-cost suppliers such as Sweden, and more from high-cost suppliers such as the United States. Suppose that by applying the new and lower duty to the higher American price we get the same British price as we had before the new tariff structure was introduced. Swedish timber, we suppose, does not pay the new and lower rate because the British and the American negotiators have worked out an ingenious system of tariff-classification. Swedish, Canadian, and American timber now compete "on equal terms." Because the British price has not changed, Britain buys the same quantity of sawn lumber as before, but the Exchequer collects less revenue, because some of the timber is American, which pays a lower duty. Trade is diverted from low-cost Swedish suppliers to high-cost American suppliers; within the British economy, there are no gains to set against the loss of customs revenue; the world economy becomes less efficient, because more of its timber needs are supplied from high-cost American sources.

Although they did not think about trade diversion in very rigorous terms, it was precisely that sort of distortion which annoyed the State Department in general, and Cordell Hull in particular, about the Ottawa Agreements. By widening the scope for tariff-differentiation, the agreements seemed, in Washington, to have diverted trade from low-cost *American* exporters to high-cost empire countries. Surely, therefore, the removal or reduction of preferences would make sense? Surely that removal or reduction would simply return the pattern of world production and trade to a more efficient and "natural" course? Perhaps. The situation, however, was complicated. Consider the timber problem, where the Americans thought that British preferential concessions had diverted trade from US to Canadian mills. Who is to say that the Canadians were higher-cost producers? Wages were lower in Canada, and the value of the standing timber, the only other important element in cost, has to be calculated backward, or "imputed," from the final selling price; it does not have any independent existence as a determinant of cost. As for transport costs to the British market, there was little to choose between British Columbia mills and those of Washington or Oregon. The timber preferences must have diverted some trade to Canada from Scandinavia, and that would certainly have been wasteful, because wage rates were much lower in Scandinavia and because transport charges to Britain were lower too. Yet Scandinavian timber retained its dominance in the British market.

For tobacco and for many other American natural products, the situation had become more complicated because it was government policies, not supply and demand, that fixed the domestic price levels. In 1932 there were no such governmental influences; by 1938 price support programs had enjoyed some years of vigorous and increasingly expensive existence. As the whole point of these supports was to keep farm-door prices above their natural levels, for such commodities the domestic price level was often considerably higher in the United States than in such countries as Canada, Denmark or Holland, where such arrangements had yet to be introduced. On the other hand, American price support agencies were already following policies by which "excess" production was dumped abroad—sold for whatever it would bring. Tariff reductions in export markets, such as the United Kingdom, could generate some extra sales and might even raise prices, especially if trade could be diverted from third-country suppliers. Subsidized export by the Americans would obviously help consumers in the United Kingdom, whose government would need strong reasons to reject such largesse. Among these reasons were empire solidarity and prior commitments in the trade agreements of 1932-34, the precise period that saw the very beginning of America's commitment to price support and export subsidy. Because no one knows what the extra exports actually cost to grow, no one can tell whether the world would be well or ill-served by a diversion of demand from third country suppliers to subsidized American goods. But economists will always be suspicious of this sort of subsidy-induced trade-diversion, whether in 1938 or fifty years later.

It would be hard to have devised a more unpromising environment for transatlantic trade talks. The Americans, with their enormous trade surplus, wanted to push the surplus still higher by extracting concessions that Britain could grant, if at all, only by antagonizing her other trading partners in the empire and outside. These markets were far more important to her than the American one, which in the mid-1930s was taking only 6.4 per cent of Britain's domestic exports—less than Australia was buying, and less than the Baltic was absorbing. The British could have no hope that negotiations would reduce their trade deficit overall, or with the Americans; indeed, the results would almost certainly increase that deficit. They might hope to win some additional sales, and thus absorb a few jobless workers into employment, by winning concessions on specialty items such as some textiles, boots and shoes, and china. There was, however, only sporadic and short-lived optimism about the chances of any real concessions, even on goods such as these.

But trade talks—and a trade agreement—there would have to be. It was the economic arena, and this arena alone, that provided an opportunity for Anglo-American co-operation in the middle and late 1930s. In 1933-35, Washington was annoyed because the British had refused to talk seriously either about war debts, exchange rates, or trade.[21] London was repeatedly upset because the United States acted, in the British view, capriciously and foolishly in the management of international trade and finance. In 1936, however, Neville Chamberlain, the UK chancellor of the exchequer, and Henry Morgenthau, the US Treasury secretary, successfully contrived the Tripartite Stabilization Agreement—three declarations committing Britain, France, and the US to refrain from competitive devaluations of currency and to co-operate in the management of the exchange.

A process of political rapprochement through economic means had thus begun, and both sides now wanted to carry it further with discussions on trade. As Norman Davis, one of Roosevelt's unofficial diplomats, told British Foreign Secretary Anthony Eden in early 1937, it was unlikely "that the United States would ever come into a political settlement, however desirable this might be." The United States might be persuaded, however, to involve itself in Europe by means of an economic agreement. As Davis explained, "one could get away with murder under the name of economic appeasement in the United States today." The Roosevelt administration, he said, "was most particularly anxious for a trade agreement between Great Britain and the United States."[22] There was something for everyone: the prospect of securing new advantages in a major market; keeping up the momentum of the Hull programme; winning something for the farmers, who had felt left out of earlier agreements; and giving an example to the world of North Atlantic peacefulness.

The British Foreign Office was just as committed to the economic approach. Shortly after the Davis visit, Anthony Eden put his department's case forcefully in May 1937:

What means have we at our disposal to maintain and improve our relations with the United States? The political approach is closed. Of that there is no question. There are, of course, always matters of minor significance on which we can avoid unnecessary friction, though by this is not implied anything in the nature of obsequious acquiescence on any question. But the major approach quite clearly lies in the economic sphere. In this connexion should be mentioned the cordial co-operation now persisting between the United Kingdom Government and the United States Government on financial and currency matters. That is excellent as far as it goes. But special attention should be given to the persistence with which Mr Cordell Hull has for four years been pursuing his policy of breaking down the barriers to international trade. To him it is a matter of faith. He believes it to be the one method of avoiding war and I should be the last to dispute his diagnosis. But his movement can only live on successes. He has hitherto been able to make about sixteen trade agreements, but now he has reached the point where, if he is to go forward, he is faced with the necessity of negotiating with the United Kingdom. It is not too much to say that the future of his policy depends on his success or failure in that respect.[23]

If peace was the aim of diplomacy, said Eden, "no greater task lies before us than to retain the goodwill of the United States." The appearance of Anglo-Saxon solidarity was already making an impression on the dictators, and not just in Europe. If war should come, the importance of a friendly US could hardly be over-estimated. A member of Eden's economic relations department, Gladwyn Jebb, wrote that "to keep the United States well disposed towards us in the economic sphere may well, in the present unfortunate condition of the world, be a question of life or death to us in the coming two years." For this reason if no other, "I think that we should pay the most lively respect to the susceptibilities of Mr Cordell Hull, however prosy and illogical (given the height of the American tariff wall) his lectures to us often seem to be."[24]

It was one thing, however, to want or to need a trade agreement, quite something else to find a way even to the negotiating table. Our tale cannot be other than a long and tangled one.

CHAPTER 2

Talks about Talks

September 1934 - April 1937

Shortly after the passage of the Reciprocal Trade Agreements Act, the American government began to explore the possibility of an Anglo-American trade agreement. Francis Sayre set his State Department officials to work in the summer of 1934. The result of these labours was the creation of a "British Empire Committee" whose mandate was to find ways and means to undermine the system of imperial preferences. That network, however, was complex and deeply-rooted. A thoroughgoing Anglo-American agreement was unlikely precisely because it would necessarily involve a substantial modification of empire preferences. The committee recommended instead that the American government approach Canada, the only one of Britain's dominions to offer an immediate prospect for profitable change. Perhaps Canada could gain enough in a comprehensive trade agreement to make it abandon the Ottawa accords, thus forcing the issue with the rest of the empire.[1]

In September 1934, even so, Sayre spoke with Sir Ronald Lindsay, the British ambassador in Washington. Anxious for Anglo-American rapprochement, and somewhat unversed in economic matters, Lindsay had already taken up the subject with Walter Runciman, president of the United Kingdom Board of Trade, earlier in the summer. Whitehall took the matter seriously, but no one apparently shared Lindsay's optimism or Sayre's enthusiasm. Runciman had "no constructive suggestions to offer" to Lindsay and the Americans: his attitude "was not to take the initiative himself but to entertain sympa-

---

Reference notes for Chapter 2 begin on p. 171.

37

thetically any approaches." The ambassador continued to hope. In April 1935, he wondered aloud to the Foreign Office whether Britain could not "produce an echo" to Hull's calls for the reduction of trade barriers, even if "any response such as I have suggested may provoke an invitation by the United States to negotiate a trade agreement and land us in a whole mess of trouble."[2]

The matter was pursued by Oscar Ryder, a member of the United States Tariff Commission, who visited London in May 1935. The commission was an advisory body, established years before to measure and fix "scientific tariffs" which would give no more protection than necessary. Few American tariffs were, by any definition, "scientific," but the commission was one of the few places in Washington where tariff expertise lurked. On 22 May, Ryder spoke to Sir Frederick Leith-Ross of the Treasury, Sir William Brown and John Stirling of the Board of Trade, and other British officials. Washington believed, Ryder explained, that Britain had violated most-favoured-nation principles in some of her trade agreements. The British were not forthcoming. They explained that these agreements, plus the Ottawa arrangements, prevented Britain from doing anything for American bacon, ham, fruit, tobacco, and motor cars. Ryder responded that there was perhaps still some scope for an agreement. The United States *might* help British china clay, whiskey, woollens, linens, leather, pottery, iron and steel. On his return to Washington Ryder lunched with Sayre, Henry F. Grady, chief of the Division of Trade Agreements in the State Department and H.O. Chalkley, commercial counsellor at the British Embassy. Chalkley did not have the impression that the Americans wished to make haste; he reported to Whitehall that there was "no early prospect of my being asked to continue the discussions." Given the length and complexity of the procedures that Hull's Act required, there would certainly be no accord in 1935.[3]

The Americans, however, were encouraged. They understood Chalkley to say that, although Whitehall had hitherto been skeptical "as to prospects of a successful trade agreement with the United States," London now wished to look into the matter "more carefully and sympathetically."[4] If Chalkley really did say as much as this, he was certainly going beyond the brief that the Treasury and Board of Trade had prepared for him. And it appears that he did go further: Grady agreed to a preliminary survey by an American committee, indicating what concessions might be asked and offered, and Chalkley said he would try to get his superiors to reciprocate.

The State Department's Committee on Trade Agreements proceeded to set up a "Country Committee on the United Kingdom"—a departure from usual practice. Such a body was not ordinarily created until after a formal decision to negotiate a trade agreement. The trade agreements committee, however, felt that the Anglo-American relationship was a special one, justifying extraordinary measures. The United Kingdom subcommittee, under John Hickerson's chairmanship, found many "difficulties to be surmounted"—the Ottawa Agreements; dominion farm surpluses; the agricultural protectionism of the United Kingdom herself; Britain's "protectionist commercial policy;" the difference in tariff levels; the balance of trade; the currency situation; and competitive products.

The subcommittee framed its proposals "on the basis that the Ottawa Agreements will be modified." If Britain could not arrange this, there might be no sensible basis for negotiation at all. The United States, the committee argued, should seek concessions on lard, tobacco, barley, oranges, grapefruit, but not wheat or flour, on both of which concessions were later demanded. The list of industrial products included doors but omitted products such as lumber, motor cars, and many electrical items that were to become important American demands. As for enticements that might be offered to Britain, seventy-six items were identified, and "major concessions" were proposed for china clay, pottery and china and various cottons and woollens. On these items, the weighted average of *ad valorem* duties had been 21.5 per cent in 1920, 42.5 per cent in 1929, and 55.6 per cent in 1933. Even if all these rates were to be cut by the full amount that the Trade Agreements Act allowed, the average rate would still be 27.8 per cent.[5] Detailed studies were to be ready in September 1935, but in mid-October they were still not done,[6] and it appears that the work lapsed until well into 1936.

Nineteen thirty-five did see the successful completion of the Canadian-American reciprocal trade agreement, which was one of the first fruits of Hull's policy of reducing tariffs and discrimination in the world economy. This, *inter alia*, reduced the US whiskey duty by 50 per cent, the maximum allowable cut. By devising subclassifications of the tariff headings, it would have been easy for Washington to exclude Scotch whiskey, restricting the benefit to Canadian rye. On 15 November, however, US officials told Chalkley that the concession would not be limited through subclassification. It would be extended, under the most-favoured-nation principle, to Scotch. Chalkley had apparently not expected the Americans to do this; the officials told him that the provision was a deliberate and unilateral "gesture toward better trade relations" with Britain.[7] Of course, the concession could be withdrawn at any time. Whitehall received it gratefully, but more would have to happen before London could be persuaded that Washington really wanted to talk seriously about trade.

Sir Ronald Lindsay believed that, because Roosevelt was at odds with America's industrial tycoons, Washington would pay generously in industrial concessions for whatever agricultural offerings Britain might make. It is doubtful whether anyone in London shared this belief. "The Ambassador," a Board of Trade official minuted in early 1936, "thinks commercial negotiations are easier than we think they are."[8] It was assumed in London that the Americans would have to make the running, because Britain had little to offer and because US tariffs were so high.[9] The British therefore played a waiting game, and did little by way of formal preparation of lists or negotiating positions. It would be, wrote a member of the Treasury department, Sigismund Waley, "a mistake to be too fast about this."[10]

The Americans, for their part, slowly moved ahead, arguing that discussions ought to be continued until it was reasonably certain that a satisfactory agreement could be achieved. They told the British so in April 1936.[11] In June Chalkley was informed that State Department studies "had progressed to the point where we believed that a comprehensive trade agreement of great value to both countries could be consummated." The Americans, however, again warned the commercial counsellor about empire preferences. Britain would have to "be prepared to consider modifications of imperial preferences affecting a very substantial portion of our export trade with the United Kingdom."[12]

On 24 June 1936, Chalkley met with American officials once again, a meeting that the Americans regarded as the first occasion on which the concrete lines of a trade agreement were discussed.[13] Chalkley delivered a tentative list of British demands and explained the UK position to the Americans as clearly as he could. Imperial preferences had little effect on America's trade, and in any event "effective argument against them was difficult except in very exceptional circumstances." It was most unlikely that Britain would reduce her own duties or preferences; that could happen only if the affected dominions did not resist, and only where the United States could make a strong case for injury through trade diversion. The United States should get in touch with the Canadians "in an effort to come to some agreement about preferences of major importance to the United States."[14] The Americans, however, already found this arrangement unattractive. They had just completed a trade agreement with Canada, and there were other agricultural countries that wanted to negotiate with them. Because the negotiating machinery was so cumbersome, the State Department was reluctant to undertake many simultaneous talks. Nor did they want to "pay twice" for any concessions Britain might give them.

Early in 1936, to the intense annoyance of Whitehall, Hull had begun to wage a vigorous public campaign against Britain's commercial policy. Diplomatic channels were assiduously used as well. Some of the ideas came from Dr Herbert Feis, the chief economic advisor in the State Department. In January 1936 he had told Hull that Britain "continues to pursue a search for special advantage wherever such is obtainable." This was done through clearing agreements, imperial preference, and quota plans that were forced on "certain small European countries." Each instance, Feis said, was "costly to American trade and financial interests." Britain should be induced to abandon such arrangements.[15] Nothing was said about the larger political significance of "economic appeasement." Hull rehearsed these arguments with Lindsay shortly after reviewing the Feis memorandum, and soon thereafter he asked Ray Atherton, the American *chargé d'affaires* in London, to make sure that Anthony Eden, the British foreign secretary, and Walter Runciman were "aware of the divergent trends of policies of the two nations." Could they not jointly "go forward on a broad and farsighted commercial policy?"[16] What Hull wanted at this stage was not a discussion of particulars but a public commitment by the United Kingdom to a "broad program" of economic disarmament—more or less what he and Lindsay had discussed the year before. Eden told Atherton that he did not want conflict with the United States over trade, but Britain might find it hard to fall in with Hull's wishes: "British officials were averse to mere empty declarations," and so were British statesmen.[17]

Whitehall officials felt that Hull's preaching, to which they had to draft mollifying responses, was discourteous and intolerable. "Our feeling here," wrote J.M. Troutbeck of the Foreign Office, "is that we cannot lie down under Mr. Hull's accusation and that it is time he was courteously and amicably shown that there must be limits to his lecturing."[18] In the Board of Trade it was admitted that Britain believed it quite proper to bargain from strength, where strength existed, in order to maintain her export trade. One official wrote: "I cannot discover that in practice American aims are different from ours; namely to get all we can (with a reasonable prospect of maintaining the position for a sufficiently long period). Our common interest is self-interest." Nevertheless, "as a great trading nation it is our interest that barriers to international trade should be broken down, and we believe that our most-favoured-nation policy tends in the long run to that result."[19]

Treasury officials naturally concurred, but it had to be admitted that there was something in Hull's charges. As Waley wrote, "there is a real disagreement between us and the United States Government, since they are in favour of unilateral economic disarmament in the sense that they think it wrong that we should expect countries from which we buy to maintain or increase our purchases from us." Although he did not think that Britain aimed *in general* at an equal balancing of trade, he agreed that "this is our policy" with respect to Argentina, Denmark, Germany, and the Baltic. "It is natural," he went on, "that the United States should adopt a more liberal policy because there are only one or two countries, e.g., Brazil, where a less liberal policy would be of any use to them. In any case . . . we shall continue to do things of which they the Americans disapprove, and in these circumstances the longer we can avoid any detailed arguments with Mr. Hull, the better."[20] After all, although both countries had a serious unemployment problem, the US had a big trade surplus. And, throughout the decade, as we observed in the previous chapter, the British had a large and chronic deficit.

Hull's pressure—and British resistance—continued into the fall of 1936, as did the State Department's studies. On 21 September Chalkley politely (but firmly) inquired about American intentions, an action that brought a very quick response. By the end of September Chalkley and the Americans had agreed to exchange lists of demands on 16 November. Indeed, the American documents suggest that Chalkley was told to have the British list ready by then.[21] This "sudden" demand seems to have surprised British officials.[22] Meanwhile, the Americans supplied a list of one hundred commodities of which Britain was the principal supplier, and asked Whitehall to arrange the British list of desiderata in accordance with the American classification.[23]

Neither side, however, thought the prospects bright in autumn 1936. In Washington Feis told Hull that it would be hard for the United States to offer any substantial tariff concessions, although the question had not yet been studied. He foresaw that "because of the position of the bilateral trade balance" Britain would expect "the bulk of the concessions would come from ourselves."[24] A.E. Overton at the Board of Trade thought the United States might have useful things to offer, but that, partly because of the Ottawa Agreements, "the main difficulty will no doubt be to find anything to offer in return."[25] One extremely important matter for Whitehall to consider was the question of Britain's customs revenue, a factor which haunted the British throughout the trade talks and which the Americans always signally failed to appreciate. The implicit assumption on the British side was that one could not or would not raise other tax rates so as to produce a compensating increase in revenues from other sources. Tobacco, lumber, and pork products all yielded large sums to the Exchequer. Describing the tobacco duties, Customs officials wrote that their importance to revenue was so great that the United Kingdom would not dare grant conventionalization—a fixing of the duty for the term of a trade agreement, so as to prevent later increases in rates—much less reduction. Nor could she allow the present duty on non-empire tobacco to be cut, so long as Britain was committed under the Ottawa pacts to maintain existing preferential duties—a commitment that would expire only in August 1942. Significantly, Sir Warren Fisher, head of the Treasury, agreed with the Customs view.

On 16 November, in the wake of Roosevelt's immense electoral victory, Chalkley presented the British list of desiderata, which emphasized textiles, and received the American list, which was soon to be known as the "must list." This consisted solely of goods— agricultural products and lumber—on which the Ottawa Agreements prevented Britain from granting concessions without dominion consent. Of course the Americans knew that these agreements expired in August 1937, and that negotiations with Canada and other dominions were already in train. The agreements could be modified, denounced or simply allowed to lapse. If the Americans insisted on their "must list," Chalkley was quick to explain, they would get no trade agreement, and he observed that the United Kingdom had no essential items in its list. Harry Hawkins, Grady's successor as chief of the trade agreements division, explained that the current list was not the final one, but Britain should expect the American list of essential demands to grow, not to shrink! Neither side said what it might concede.[26]

In London no one outside the Foreign Office greeted the prospects of impending negotiation with joy. The Treasury officials regretted that discussions were in train at all, just when they were "getting on so nicely" with American secretary of the Treasury Henry C. Morgenthau, Jr, with whom there had been co-operation on currency management since September. Waley observed that the American behaviour, in asking for concessions not only on imperial preference but on tobacco, "does not seem to confirm Sir R. Lindsay's view that the United States Government have all along understood that we have little to offer but were at the same time prepared to make us substantial concessions."[27] When an interdepartmental meeting was convened in early December 1936 to discuss the American list of essentials, only Frank Ashton-Gwatkin of the Foreign Office spoke warmly of an agreement. Sir William Brown explained that the Board of Trade still did not attach "very great importance to an agreement with the United States;" there was not much hope of selling more to the Americans as a result, and certainly it was "not worth our while to quarrel with other countries, particularly the Dominions, in order to do a deal with the United States." A Dominions Office representative observed that the United States was asking for concessions that cut right across the Ottawa Agreements, and claimed that Australia, at least, would not be willing to negotiate with the United States, having already been themselves rebuffed several times. Gwatkin, however, wanted to bring the dominions into the negotiations.[28]

Later in December Walter Runciman told R.W. Bingham, the American ambassador in London, that he thought there was hope for an Anglo-American accord so long as the Ottawa Agreements did not have to be discarded.[29] A few days thereafter Bingham reported to President Roosevelt that Prime Minister Stanley Baldwin, Anthony Eden and Runciman were all committed "in principle" to a trade agreement. Runciman's support, Bingham continued, "would not have come . . . without the approval of the financial and commercial influences in the Government, which has hitherto been holding out on us, so that this marks concrete progress toward some form of trade agreement."[30]

Chalkley had meanwhile told Hawkins and Hickerson that the American "must list" was unacceptable. Britain would not risk antagonizing the dominions, whose supplies would be essential in case of war; the Americans would have to negotiate with the dominions for the relinquishment of their preferences in Britain, and would have to offer an adequate *quid pro quo*, as Britain had nothing to offer them. Certainly a tripartite agreement on timber would be required.[31] An official reply to the American demands reached Washington on 29 December 1936.

In January 1937 Hull's oracular pronouncements and flinging of thunderbolts continued,[32] and there were new talks in Washington, occasioned by the visit of Walter Runciman, the president of the Board of Trade, to the American capital. Runciman's conversations were meant to be general and informal. He did not go to Washington to negotiate anything. Francis Sayre, nevertheless, reviewed the whole Hull package for him, later reporting that "Mr Runciman seemed to have but a foggy and hazy notion of what I was driving at." Sayre explained that, without British concessions on hog products, barley, rice, fruits, tobacco, lumber and leather, "it would be most difficult to obtain political support for the agreement." He did not say why political support was necessary at all, given the fact that Congress did not have to approve its terms.[33] Doubtless Sayre was thinking of interest groups and their Congressional champions. Presumably he was also worried about the fact that the act itself would have to be renewed in the course of 1937. Runciman reported that Hull and his officials "reiterated their dislike of the preferential system of the Ottawa Agreements. I told them that just as we the UK accepted as an awkward fact the high tariff system of the USA even when it was the subject of modification by agreement, they in the US must accept the fact that we could not go back on the principles of preference which are embodied in the Ottawa Agreement even though the details were always capable of discussion and readjustment. . . ."[34]

In the course of the discussions the Americans stressed the "political reasons for such an agreement." They were not specific about these reasons, but later events would show that Roosevelt and some other members of the cabinet, their eyes fixed on the domestic scene, were anxious to solidify their support in the middle-west farm communities. They may also have been thinking of the European situation, although the texture of these particular discussions suggests the contrary. The Americans explained, however, that they could not reduce tariffs unless Britain cut some of hers too, even if in so doing there might be some damage to the preferential system, which they recognized Britain would have to maintain. They were not prepared to compensate the dominions, as Britain had suggested, although they thought that "it was for the United Kingdom to represent to the Dominions the desirability of the conclusion of a Trade Agreement between the United Kingdom and the United States, both as a means of promoting Anglo-American economic co-operation and, thereby, world peace and prosperity, and as a necessary preliminary to subsequent trade agreements between the United States and the Dominions." [35]

By this time the situation ought to have been clear enough. The United States wanted to find a outlet for its primary products in an industrial country, and the United Kingdom was the only plausible candidate. American opposition to imperial preferences was absolute on principle, as it had been in the nineteenth century, and that opposition was not diminished by the facts. Not only was Britain the centre of the preferential system, but she was also the only available market for American agricultural surpluses. One way or another, the Ottawa Agreements would have to be substantially modified.

To an outsider, the Runciman visit might seem the beginning of serious Anglo-American trade talks.[36] Yet Whitehall still had no idea how, when, or in what manner the United Kingdom government could approach the problem. It had long ago been decided that the forthcoming Imperial Conference would not be used for trade talks. The dominions might well concert their efforts, and empire primary producers would combine with British industrialists to exert strong pressure for new protective measures. Everyone in London, moreover, remembered the strains and humiliations of the Ottawa Conference. Bilateral discussions, not a conference format, were to be preferred. Indeed, recent talks with Canada and the Antipodes had been conducted in accordance with this bilateral formula, which would soon be used for India and Burma as well. The Dominions Office pointed out, nevertheless, that the Americans were clinging to their belief that the empire would settle its attitude to preferences and the United States at the Imperial Conference. The example of Ottawa was necessarily in the Americans' minds, and understandably so; Washington cannot have known how little the coming conference was actually meant to do. One Dominions Office official minuted: "I cannot conceive that it will be decided to raise the question at the Imperial Conference. This would have the effect of lining the Dominions up against us."[37] Fair enough. But if not there and then, where and when?

As expected, on 2 March 1937, the Americans provided a refined "list of products subject to the Ottawa Agreements . . . on which an improvement in the treatment now accorded by the United Kingdom to the United States is deemed essential." Sir Ronald Lindsay gave a copy to the Canadian minister in Washington, Sir Herbert Marler.[38] The new list of essentials was shorter than that of the previous November. Thus it reflected the American "understanding that the problem of finding a basis for negotiations arises largely, if not entirely, from the commitments of the United Kingdom to the Empire countries." If the Americans eventually decided that there was a "satisfactory basis for negotiation," they would proceed to bring forward other products where "no such contractual obligations exist." For the time being they provided only two lists of products which the Ottawa Agreements affected. One list grouped those products on which Britain would simply promise not to increase the most-favoured-nation duty or the margin of preference—in short, conventionalization of duties and "binding" of preferential margins. The other list was made up of products where "improvement of present treatment is essential." On the first list were wheat, barley, cornstarch, linseed oil and meal, canned pigs' tongues, fruit juice, pig casings, canned salmon, canned fish n.e.s., oleo-margarine and oleo-oil and refined tallow, plywood faced with Douglas fir, paraffin wax, reptile leather, glacé kid, and miscellaneous dressed leather. Such "binding of present treatment" would not worry the dominions or upset Britain's own producers. It was the other list—the "essentials"—that would cause trouble. In this category were rice, raw apples, grapefruit and pears, dried prunes, apricots, raisins, apples, pears, peaches, nectarines, tinned and bottled apples and other fruits, honey, unmanufactured tobacco, patent leather, softwood lumber, sawn or dressed, Douglas fir and southern pine. There was also a short third list of products on which improved treatment was essential but which might or might not be bound under the Ottawa

Agreements. These goods were Douglas fir doors, preserved logan-berries, and sugarless tinned or bottled apples.[39]

For each product where improvement was "essential," the Americans proposed the duty they desired. The cuts were substantial, ranging from 30 to 100 per cent of the existing *ad valorem* and specific duties. Lumber, which was taxed at 10 per cent, would come in free; apples would pay two shillings and six pence (in the notation of the time, 2/6)[40] per hundredweight (or cwt)[41] instead of 4/6; honey would pay 3/6 per cwt instead of 7 shillings; and so on. Because all these products were ones in which American and empire producers shared the British market, and as in many instances there was British produc-tion also, a cut in the mfn duty[42] would reduce the returns to empire and United Kingdom producers by the full amount of the cut, at least in the short run. With respect to the apple duty, there were special and additional worries for Britain's own producers and for Canadian exporters, especially in the Annapolis Valley of near-bankrupt Nova Scotia. American apples entered the market at the wrong time of year, just when British and Canadian apples were being marketed. If American trees produced a bumper crop, it was suspected that the surplus would be dumped into export markets regardless of the price. To regulate the flow to Britain there was a cartel, the Empire Fruit Council. Would American growers join?

As for timber, the 10 per cent duty on US softwood had diverted some British purchases to Canada; more importantly, it increased the return to Canadian producers. Washington argued that "the only step which would be effective in meeting this situation would be the complete abolition of the preference." The Americans neglected to point out that Canadian producers had sought a new vent in Britain precisely because America's own tariff increases had shut them out of the US market. Nor was it noted that it was Scandinavia, not North America, which supplied most of Britain's softwood. If the Swedes and the Finns and the Russians could swallow a 10 per cent tariff and still provide more than 80 per cent of the softwood that Britain used, what was wrong with American exporters?

At the Foreign Office Frank Ashton-Gwatkin reflected on Brit-ain's immense negative trade balance with the United States. From "the purely economic point of view," American pretensions were "ridiculous." Moreover, unless the US were to offer very large tariff concessions both to the United Kingdom and to the dominions—a most improbable event—the empire would find it extremely difficult to give as much as the Americans wanted. Gwatkin continued:

> In short only the most pressing political considerations justify any
> commercial negotiations with the United States on their present

assumptions, except as part of a general relaxation of trade barriers. The fact that these political considerations do exist, and that the relaxation of trade barriers may at least be encouraged should not, however, blind us to the fact that American commercial, financial and shipping policy has, since the war, been one of the major causes—possibly the principal cause—of economic strain (and sometimes of political tension as well). The United States have immense economic influence on the rest of the world—as great as our own. They have used this influence with heedless irresponsibility, giving loans where no loans should have been given, and then withdrawing their money at precisely the wrong moment. And always the tremendous height of the United States tariffs has kept out imports from debtor countries—except the imports of capital for gambling on Wall Street.[43]

Gwatkin's concern about transatlantic co-operation was an attitude most strongly held in the Foreign Office.[44] His words about economic affairs, on the other hand, would have found a ready echo in the Treasury. They remind us that Whitehall had no illusions about the character or direction of American economic policy. But there were good reasons why neither officials nor ministers found it politic to say such things in public, or loudly, or at all. As the international tensions accumulated, Britain had ever more reason to avoid controversy with the United States. And so the trade talks had to go forward. Furthermore, as we shall see, for a time during the spring of 1937, Whitehall had reason to think Sir Ronald Lindsay might be right, and Gwatkin wrong. Perhaps, after all, the United States might be willing to make really generous concessions—concessions of genuine value.

As for America's demands with respect to industrial products, concessions in Britain's market would certainly be asked, but as yet no one knew what they might be. Whitehall already knew, or could guess, that as part of the bargain Canada would also ask for some release of the preferential rates and margins that were still "bound" in the Anglo-Canadian trade agreement of February 1937. The Americans, however, had just begun to formulate their industrial demands. Only in mid-1937 were the American consul general in London and the other commercial representatives throughout Britain asked to suggest the industrial goods on which concessions might usefully be sought. The consul general's list was not a long one, and it included some commodities, such as tracklaying tractors, that were admittedly of interest as much in the dependent empire as in Britain itself. A good deal of attention was devoted to machine tools and typewriters; "McKenna goods,"[45] such as cars, were not considered on the ground that no United Kingdom concessions on such goods were at all likely. It is not without interest that, when the American negotiators finally did transmit their industrial demands almost a year later, such things as tractors, typewriters, and machine tools figured largely among them. But so did cars.

In spite of the rather tattered cloak of secrecy with which the State Department sought to hide these Anglo-American preliminaries, it was widely known that talks about talks were taking place. The result was a considerable number of unsolicited inquiries or representations from a wide range of firms and associations that hoped to sell more in Britain. It is hard to find any precise relationship between these letters and the actual American demands, although sometimes the latter apparently reflected the former.

Much more significant, and already reflected in the American position, were representations from the International (that is, American) Apple Association and the associations of lumber producers and exporters. By mid-1937 the State Department had been put on notice that both groups of primary producers expected great things. And in the later course of negotiation the department's negotiators did their best to oblige.

The American government set the question of trade talks in the context of general "economic appeasement." What, one might ask, had the United States' desires on specifics have to do with this broader question, this larger aim? Regrettably, the answer must be, "Nothing." Truckloads of canned cherries, boatloads of dried prunes, and vanloads of unmanufactured tobacco were not waiting at the German frontier to surge across the Channel the moment British duties were lowered. Balkan tobacco would continue to move to Berlin not to Bristol. Hungary and Romania would not solve their foreign exchange problems by flooding the British market with rice, honey, or dried nectarines. If *American* mfn tariffs were reduced enough, and if the network of trade agreements were to extend these duties to the exchange control countries as a consequence of the Anglo-American discussions, "economic appeasement" might make some headway. Not otherwise. The Americans, however, had not yet said what they might concede, and if they had such things in mind they would have done better to negotiate directly with Germany, Italy, Poland and Yugoslavia, not with the United Kingdom. On the other hand, if Britain were to make concessions to the United States on manufactured goods, the existing network of trade agreements would automatically extend these to some exchange control countries — most importantly Germany. Strange to say, at no point in the documents can one find the slightest sign that the Americans were aware of this possibility, except in connection with lumber. The British, however, constantly thought of it.

It might be argued that these remarks are unfair to Hull and Roosevelt in one important respect. Although the president had just been re-elected with an immense majority, he could not be sure that Congress would renew the Reciprocal Trade Agreements Act, which was due to expire in 1937. If the act were not renewed, Hull would be unable to negotiate new agreements with additional countries, such as Germany and the other exchange-control states, where an economic initiative might yield the peaceful dividends about which Hull dreamed. There was even reason, one suspects, to fear that the existing agreements of the period 1934-37 might evaporate, causing American tariffs to revert to the Smoot-Hawley level at which the general tariff law still fixed them. If the president could claim that the trade agreements program had won important gains for American primary producers, perhaps the relevant legislators—representatives and senators from the hog areas, the lumber regions, the corn states, the cotton and tobacco districts, and the apple and citrus zones—would support the renewal of the 1934 law. Roosevelt and Hull could have plausibly argued that way before the actual renewal of the Trade Agreements Act, but after Congress renewed and extended the measure the administration continued to press Britain hard—indeed, harder than ever—on the agricultural front. Eyes were firmly fixed on the polls of agricultural opinion, which showed substantial unease about the trade agreements agenda, even after a "concerted effort to educate farmers in the advantages of the reciprocity program in general and the Anglo-American pact in particular."[46] Real benefits for the farmers would have to be won.

As yet London had the list of American "essentials," but little further information. Officials and ministers, especially but not exclusively in the Ministry of Agriculture and Food, thought this a most unsatisfactory basis for real discussion. As we have already seen, however, there were considerations of international politics that could not be overlooked. The Foreign Office believed, as Gwatkin put it, that an agreement with the United States was becoming not merely desirable but necessary. Runciman's visit to Washington in early 1937 had raised expectations. Failure to reach an understanding would be more than a commercial disappointment; it would be a political blow to British diplomacy in Europe and the Far East. There was "an appearance of solidarity between British & American policy, which is having its effect in curbing the Dictators and in keeping up the spirits of Central Europe; it also must be affecting the Far Eastern situation, where good Anglo-American relations are an essential check on Japan."[47] If diplomacy should fail, a trade agreement would take on even more meaning. There was a limit, however. Anthony Eden minuted that the "U.S.A. really do not make this easy for us. They almost seem bent on destruction of Imperial Preference. This we could not accept."[48]

In March 1937 Whitehall instructed Chalkley to ask again what the Americans might do for British trade. It should be remembered that Washington had had Britain's list of desiderata for many months. Chalkley asked the State Department whether any of the British desiderata were hopeless, where the maximum reduction of American duty might be expected, and what "non-Ottawa products" the United States proposed to add to its own list of essential demands.

The result was heartening. Shortly after his request, Chalkley was told that about 125 tariff rates might be cut on about 100 customs paragraphs, and that none of Britain's desiderata were impossible. Of the 125 rates, some 60 exceeded 40 per cent, and of these, cuts of one-half appeared possible on nearly half, while "substantial reductions" might be expected on most of the remainder. As for new essential demands, the Americans would ask for better quota treatment on some hog products, especially ham.[49] And two weeks before, Sayre had told Chalkley that he would very much like a reduction on the wheat duty—"even a slight reduction . . . would aid us very greatly from a political and psychological standpoint."[50] This was a verbal suggestion only, and had not yet been embedded in America's demands.

The American response of 17 March encouraged Runciman and officials at the Board of Trade to believe for the first time that the United States might actually do something useful for Britain's export trade. W.S. Morrison and his officials in the Agriculture Ministry, however, were terrified of any agricultural tariff cuts, while from the Dominions Office and its young secretary of state, Malcolm MacDonald, came nervous quiverings regarding empire reaction to American importunities. Runciman made it known that he wanted to discuss these with the dominions, one by one. Aware that questions of high policy were involved which only ministers could settle, he asked his colleagues on the Cabinet Trade and Agriculture Committee to approve definite offers on certain fresh and preserved fruits, "on which the Departments have been unable to reach agreement." The foreign secretary circulated a despatch from Sir Ronald Lindsay in Washington, emphasizing the general international political climate which made Anglo-American rapprochement so desirable. The ambassador also argued that Washington would certainly concede far more than she would demand. Lindsay explained why Hull had to get something for agriculture, but repeated his claim that American industrialists were so alienated from Roosevelt that the American government would not have to worry about them. Thus it would be able to "offer abundant compensation, pressed down and overflowing, for any concessions" Britain might grant to—or extract from—the dominions.[51]

When the cabinet committee considered the issue further on 12 April, opinion flowed strongly in favour of trade talks, despite the agriculture minister. Morrison argued strongly against any acceptance of the American proposals; they implied a "political" agreement, devised to satisfy American domestic interests, not a "commercial one intended for the benefit of their trade and industry." He was especially agitated about apples and hogs, where Britain's own agriculture would be affected, and he did not want anyone to approach the dominions. No one agreed. MacDonald thought that the dominions would be difficult, but Britain should try to bring them around. Eden stressed the great advantages of victory and the consequences of failure. Runciman argued that Britain could secure not only political advantages but also economic ones. Neville Chamberlain, the chancellor of the exchequer and one of the architects of the 1932 Ottawa Agreements, said that Hull must not be allowed to break the system of imperial preference. But the agreements could be modified, given the possibility that a trade agreement would be genuinely valuable. The terms, he said, were "far better than he had previously believed to be within the range of possibility." The Americans were still pressing demands which the British had already rejected. Now, however, the United States seemed to be making offers which were genuinely attractive and valuable. Surely it would be wrong not to continue. The committee decided to forward proposals to the Americans "which we are prepared to communicate to the Dominion Governments 'as a basis for consideration'."[52]

On 13 April, therefore, London sent its reply to Washington. It was explained that there was no point putting the American proposals to the dominions and India because these governments would reject them: "There is little, if anything, which they could offer to the Dominions etc, by way of compensation. . . . Dominion goods already enjoy free entry into the United Kingdom . . . consequently the field in which the Dominions concerned would probably seek compensation consists of further preferences, i.e., increased duties on imports from foreign countries. . . . The United Kingdom Government believe that on general grounds the United States Government would share their desire to avoid any such result." In addition, Whitehall observed, such duties as that on fresh apples were protective, and would have been imposed "even if there had been no Ottawa Agreements." Nor could the United Kingdom agree to bind "existing revenue duties," such as those on tobacco and sugar. Nevertheless, London was prepared to suggest reductions in mfn rates on fresh pears, apples, grapefruit, some but not all dried fruits, tinned apples, honey, patent leather, and Douglas fir doors, as well as some classes of softwood. With respect to the binding of duties it was prepared to meet American demands on everything except barley and glacé kid. As for tobacco,[53] the duties and the preferential margin could not be reduced, but Britain was willing to promise not to increase them. Nothing more could be done for rice, some dried fruits, most tinned fruits, or Douglas fir, but London would test the waters with the dominions on apples, grapefruit, pears, dried and tinned apples, tinned cherries and fruit salad, honey, Southern pine, patent leather, and Douglas fir doors. This listing ought to suggest that, if considered from the perspective of the larger economic welfares of the two countries, the prospective negotiations would have their frivolous side.

While recognizing that there would be great political value to a trade agreement, the British government informed Chalkley "that the present United States proposals go far beyond what is politically and economically possible both here and in the Dominions. . . . " No doubt the government was thinking of domestic political pressures. Dominion representatives were beginning to arrive for the 1937 Imperial Conference, and "it would be helpful if we could as soon as possible have the United States replies on the matters on which further information is sought and learn whether they would desire us to approach the Dominions on the lines we now indicate."[54]

On the eve of the 1937 Imperial Conference, the British government was at last sanguine about the economic prospects of an Anglo-American trade pact. It would not abrogate the Ottawa Agreements, and with respect to many of the commodities the Americans thought "essential" it would not make proposals, but it was willing to discuss possible options with the dominions. The Imperial Conference, it seemed, would have an important economic dimension after all. This had been the Americans' hope, and their expectations, if anything, were on the rise in the spring of 1937. To understand why, the role of the United States' neighbour and close trading partner must be explained more fully. A new character must be brought out from the wings and placed at the centre of the stage. The country is Canada, Britain's senior dominion; the character is the wily and complex William Lyon Mackenzie King, already in his second decade as Canadian prime minister.

CHAPTER 3

Mackenzie King and the British

January-June 1937

Canada was important in the emerging picture of Anglo-American trade negotiations in two respects. First of all, in the winter of 1936-37 Canada was re-negotiating its own trade agreement with the United Kingdom. Secondly, Washington seems to have hoped that Prime Minister King, whose tariff-cutting propensities were well known, could be enlisted on the American side, so that he might mine the structure of imperial preference from within. King's theoretical view of international relations, political and economic, was deeply felt, idealistic, and often downright naive. As a woolly-minded dreamer King often seemed to rival Cordell Hull himself. In the cut and thrust of tariff-bargaining, however, King and his officials revealed a hard-headed pragmatism which proved to be fully the equal of anything to be found in Great Britain or the United States. Whatever role the Americans might have hoped that King would play, his realism always got the best of his romantic internationalism. Canada became absolutely central to an Anglo-American agreement, and it proved to be the stumbling-block on which the entire enterprise was almost destroyed.

King had been opposed to the 1932 Ottawa Agreements. Leader of the opposition at the time, he had argued that it was wrong for Canada's Parliament to make such firm commitments with respect to preferential margins and, by implication, on mfn rates. If Canada was

Reference notes for Chapter 3 begin on p. 173.

55

to negotiate successfully outside the empire, he said, it needed the power to manipulate both mfn rates and preferential margins. This did not mean that King was against the preferential system. In 1930, when he was prime minister, he had taken considerable pride in the measures by which Charles Dunning, his minister of finance, had increased preferential margins. But he did not like explicit imperial convenants. To him they smacked of old proposals to federate the empire, which he had opposed throughout his political life. Nor did King like rigidity. The most flexible of men, in trade negotiations as in other respects, he sought as much freedom of manoeuvre as possible. Unilateral preferential concessions were one thing; intra-imperial trade agreements were something else again.[1]

King took great pride in the Canadian-American trade agreement of 1935. He had given the highest priority to the matter when he returned to office in October 1935, and within a month he had achieved success. In addition to the immediate and undoubted domestic political, economic and rhetorical gains, King thought that it would strengthen Canadian-American ties, and he hoped that it might help to improve relations between Great Britain and the United States. Like Hull, King believed in the power of example: one agreement would lead to another; the whole regime of economic nationalism would be challenged. This was the right and wholesome course, and it would be profitable in the bargain.[2]

King luxuriated in the warm glow of the easy relationship he believed he had rapidly established with the American president and secretary of state. It was easy for King to over-estimate his impact on F.D.R., who could say "my old friend" in a dozen languages.[3] But Hull and King, sharing so much in outlook and technique, obviously took to one another.[4] King's Canada, nevertheless, looked primarily to its own interests. His occasional effusions to the contrary, the prime minister had no desire to travel the "American road" if it meant foregoing the warm embrace of the British empire.[5]

When Anglo-Canadian trade talks began in 1936, King was determined that Canada keep the maximum control over her own tariff structure. "Bound margins" should be reduced, or if possible eliminated. To the American State Department these views were welcome indeed, but Washington was less apt to notice King's continuing attachment to the preferential system, his remarkable imperialist longings and sentiments, or his unwillingness to sacrifice hard-won economic advantages.

Intra-imperial conversations were, of course, no business of the United States. Nevertheless, when the State Department heard that Anglo-Canadian talks were in prospect, they became exercised at once. They "pointed out that we would regard it [as] unfortunate if these conversations should result in commitments to the Dominions which would make it impossible for the British Government, later on, to entertain our requests in respect of particular products of interest to us which are now covered by the Ottawa Agreements. . . . "[6] Cordell Hull may or may not have been trying to delay the talks, but it appears that he was anxious to ensure that any new Anglo-Canadian agreement would not prejudice the chances of successful negotiation with the United Kingdom.

John Hickerson, the State Department's expert on Canada and a negotiator of the 1935 Canadian-American agreement, came to Ottawa in June 1936. He told King that it was the secretary of state's "feeling that nobody could question the legal or moral right of the various parts of the empire to grant nominal preference to one another to demonstrate to the world their political solidarity." It was, however, not only unsound and unwise but also in the final analysis would reduce the sum total of world trade when preferences were "substantial enough to cause an artificial diversion of trade."[7]

As the year passed, Washington increased the amplification. In November Hull told Sir Herbert Marler, Canada's earnest and none too swift minister in Washington, that he knew King was as interested in the program of economic liberalization as the secretary of state himself.[8] At the same time Norman Armour, the American minister in Ottawa, asked O.D. Skelton, King's principal adviser, to pass on certain information. The secretary of state was anxious that Canada should realize the ways in which Britain was using certain clearing and payments agreements for its own commercial advantage. Canada had also sinned in this regard, having recently signed a bilateral clearing agreement with Germany.[9]

In January 1937, just as the new Anglo-Canadian agreement was about to be signed, Hull pressed King to make a statement about the evils of economic nationalism and the glories of freer trade. King believed that Hull wanted this because "the British are playing the old game and stating to the States that they cannot lower duties because of the opposition of Canada."[10] During December 1936, when King had brought the Anglo-Canadian trade negotiations to a screeching halt by insisting that Britain should allow Canada to "unbind" most of the surviving preferential margins, he found that Whitehall was not willing to go as far as the prime minister desired. Can that be what King had in mind? In an economic sense, there was no "old game" to be played: game and rules had been invented in Ottawa in 1932, so that in 1936 and 1937 only the players were elderly. Britain, furthermore, was as ready to plead contractual obligation as dominion intransigence.

Politically, however, it undoubtedly seemed to King (who was given
to such reflections) that he had been there before: little Canada and its
prime minister were being used and abused yet again.

From Washington Sir Herbert Marler dutifully conveyed American nervousness. With no information at hand about the actual content of the Anglo-Canadian agreement, Marler sent excited messages
about the Hull-Runciman talks, the threat to the Ottawa Agreements,
and the possibility that the pending Anglo-Canadian accord might
block the path to an Anglo-American one. Marler reported in early
1937 that, in British Ambassador Sir Ronald Lindsay's view, the new
Anglo-Canadian agreement might be an obstacle in the Anglo-
American talks. Lindsay explained that he thought Hull objected to
the agreement because, to maintain the momentum of his commercial
policy, the secretary of state would have to make an agreement with
some big industrial country, such as Britain. Marler did not know
what the United States was demanding of Britain; he conjectured that
lumber, apples, and pears would be among the products on which
concessions would be asked, but that wheat would not. "There is
some danger," he wrote, "that Mr. Hull and his advisors are coming to
regard Canada as the obstacle to what they look upon as a vitally
important step in economic disarmament."[11] In February Marler had a
long talk with Hull, who again mentioned his worries about the
Anglo-Canadian agreement.[12] What Hull appears to have wanted were
unilateral concessions by Canada, or by Britain, that would facilitate
an Anglo-American accord. Ottawa responded by briefing Marler
with respect to the actual content of the new Anglo-Canadian agreement, explaining that "it should be clearly understood that throughout the negotiations which resulted in the present Agreement the
Canadian government have insisted on the progressive liberalization
of the preferential system and have endeavoured to apply within that
system the principles of commercial policy which they hope to see
realized in international economic relations."[13]

London had already informed Washington that its concerns were
without foundation. The new agreement was not a barrier to anything;
there were no increases in fixed margins; in fact, many such rigidities
were reduced or abolished. The Americans were told that the Ottawa
Agreements would not prevent the liberalization of world trade: Britain was quite prepared to discuss "modifications of certain margins
of preference fixed on certain imports," so long as the dominions
would agree.[14] This did not dissipate Washington's concerns, or
perhaps Hull and his assistant Francis Sayre never fully understood
just what Canada and Britain were doing. In London, the Board of
Trade was thoroughly disgusted with Hull, who appeared to be
criticizing the new Anglo-Canadian agreement both in public and

through diplomatic channels without knowing what it contained —or, even worse, in full knowledge that he was spreading untruths. J.A. Stirling wrote:

> It seems to me that the sort of answers we have given up to the present have resulted only in a progressively more insolent tone in each of the communications addressed to us by the United States Government.... Mr. Hull has really persuaded himself that the United States Government have alone made a positive contribution towards the liberalisation of international trade and that the United Kingdom is the chief obstacle to further progress.[15]

When he visited Washington early in 1937, the Americans thought that Runciman did not seem to have the terms of the new Anglo-Canadian agreement firmly in mind. It appears that at this point the Americans still did not know just what Canada and Britain had settled between themselves. On 1 February, Sayre set out to remedy that deficiency, asking Marler to provide him with the text of the new agreement before it was signed—an extraordinary request—lest it "present a stone wall which would prevent further progress on our trade agreement program." [16] It must be concluded that Sayre and Hull had not believed the British assurances that the agreement did not threaten the Anglo-American talks.

The British cabinet was not happy to find that Hull was concerning himself with the terms of a trade agreement between Britain and Canada. Although historians might suspect that Hull's acerbity reflected Washington's normal suspicion of British "imperialism,"[17] Chamberlain explained to the cabinet that it "was probably due to his objection to a new manifestation of Imperial preference." Another minister, Lord Swinton, remarked acidly that Cuban and Philippine preferences to American goods were far higher than anything Canada had extended to Britain.[18] There is no evidence that in fixing the final terms of its Canadian trade agreement the United Kingdom had an eye on the fluttering in the dovecotes of Washington. British officials argued that the United States had been able to make its trade agreement with Canada without encroaching on the principle of preferences, thereby proving that the Ottawa Agreements were no absolute bar to Hull's policy. Hull and his officials replied that this American-Canadian agreement had been possible because Canada was an agricultural country which would not buy American farm produce anyway, regardless of the tariff regime. The United States needed an outlet in an industrial country, and the United Kingdom was the only plausible candidate. However, something would have to be done about preferences in that market if American goods were to enter on equal terms.[19]

Although King, an enthusiast for symbolic dates, had hoped to conclude the new Anglo-Canadian trade agreement in time to send a peaceful Christmas message at the end of 1936, last minute problems intervened. Difficulties over meat, dairy products, and the binding of preferential margins had prevented a Yuletide outburst of intra-imperial good fellowship. King did not like the idea of fixed margins of preference, because he thought that such rigidity limited his power to lower mfn rates in negotiations with other countries.[20] The agreement was concluded only in mid-January 1937, and signed on 23 February.[21] King's importunities put London on notice with respect to the probable difficulties of any wider trade talks.

Two weeks later King travelled to Washington at Roosevelt's invitation, and it appeared that all had been forgiven. Roosevelt and Hull had much more on their minds than a trade agreement. The secretary of state talked at King about their mutual liberal passions; president and prime minister concocted a scheme for a permanent conference, worldwide in its scope, aimed at securing social and economic justice.[22] F.D.R. had told King in 1935 that Canada and the United States understood each other better than the Americans and the British. King, the president said, had a high calling as an intermediary between the United States and Great Britain.[23] Roosevelt now urged the Canadian to take their plan to the Imperial Conference which would soon open in London. Hull clearly had similar hopes for his own program. King told them both he would do what he could.[24] Although neither Hull nor Roosevelt had explicitly mentioned the Anglo-American trade talks to the Canadian leader, the Americans were clearly organizing King to manipulate the coming imperial gathering in their interest. Their approach was singularly tactful and indirect, but the prime minister had taken their meaning. It would be very useful, King wrote to Roosevelt a few days later, both to Britain and Canada "to have the North American background so clearly defined in my own mind." King wanted to bring together the British and Americans "in the cause of world peace. If that cause is ever lost nothing else will matter very much."[25]

Hull wrote to King soon afterward, following up on their Washington conversations and echoing the prime minister's letter to Roosevelt. King, said Hull, should help in "the advancement of a broad basic program to remove excessive trade barriers . . . under the leadership, especially, of the two great English-speaking countries."[26] Hull, Norman Robertson of Canada's Department of External Affairs reported, had no objection to "inoperative" preferences which did "not divert imports from foreign to Commonwealth sources of supply." In the revision of the Anglo-Canadian agreement that had just been completed, Canada had already begun to eliminate preferential margins that were "superfluous, hopelessly inadequate," or "on products of which there was no reasonable prospect of the United Kingdom becoming the principal or indeed an important supplier of Canadian requirements," while reducing bound margins of preference "on which there was reason to believe that their height was covering the exploitation of consumers or hindering the completion of trade negotiations with foreign countries." But because such revisions were not designed to erase whatever distortions that the preferential system might originally have created, "this type of revision is exactly contrary to that which, by implication, Mr. Hull would like to see attempted." Britain had not suggested any study of her preferences to Canada, although the dominion might well have "agreed to certain revisions that would have facilitated United Kingdom negotiations with the United States at this stage; because of ignorant public opinion, Canada would have to insist on further concessions by Britain if she were to agree to give up such worthless preferences." Robertson believed that Hull expected Canada to raise the question of preferences at the coming Imperial Conference so as to "try and get the Commonwealth countries, as a whole, to consider as a question of high policy whether or not, on balance, our true interests are really best served in the long run by a system of customs discrimination." The young official agreed that the onus was on Canada: "the problem of preference will not come before the Conference unless the Government of Canada decides to take an initiative in the matter and asks for their consideration."[27]

Neither Canada nor the other dominion governments had yet been told about the American memorandum of March 1937, which we encountered in the last chapter. Some information had been sent to the British high commissioners in Canada, Australia, and South Africa, and to the governor general of New Zealand; as yet there was no high commissioner in New Zealand to whom messages might be directed. "If and when negotiations are begun," a Dominions Office official wrote, "we shall notify the Canadian/Commonwealth/Union government in the usual way, or, if necessary, we shall approach them at an earlier stage; but, in the meantime this account of the preliminary discussions is sent for your own personal information."[28] The word about the March list went out to the high commissioners on 23 April. They were told that, although London was inclined to grant less than the Americans requested, "ministers have not yet decided at what stage an approach to the Dominions is to be made. It is possible, however, that the question may be approached generally with the heads of the Delegations attending the Imperial Conference, although it is desired to avoid any discussion of the subject by the Conference as a whole. . . . The nature of our next move will depend upon whether a reply from the United States is received before the Imperial Conference closes and upon the terms of that reply."[29] No one seems to have been at all concerned by the fact that Ottawa already knew all about the Americans' list of "essential" demands. One wonders why no one in London was wondering whether anyone in Ottawa was wondering.

Lord Tweedsmuir, the Canadian governor-general, thought that Canada and its leadership would "take the long view" with respect to "adjustment of Imperial Preference." Well-known as John Buchan the thriller writer, less successful as a politician, now a public servant, Tweedsmuir had close ties both to King and to Roosevelt, and he shared their vague desire to make a contribution to world peace. Roosevelt had convinced Tweedsmuir that the dominions, and especially Canada, would be the "key point" in any Anglo-American trade talks.[30] Why the governor-general thought Canadians would willingly acquiesce in the sort of tariff cut that Washington had proposed, one cannot discover. Perhaps he did not understand just what had been demanded, perhaps he believed what King liked to say about economic disarmament, or perhaps he was proceeding on the basis of outdated colonial notions about Canada's place in the "imperial" scheme of things.

The Canadian under-secretary of state for external affairs, O.D. Skelton, was not nearly so idealistic or optimistic. Summarizing the situation in unappetizing terms, he wrote that Britain wanted a trade agreement for the sake of markets and to influence American public opinion. Canadian public opinion, however, would never consent to an offering up of major concessions on "the altar of Anglo-American friendship," unless the political payoffs would really be sizeable, or substantial offsetting economic benefits were gained. Skelton did not think that a trade agreement could reverse America's "present policy of isolation," and he thought that other means, such as a resumption of British war debt payments, were available and might well be as efficacious.[31] These were the abstract speculations of a man who was not in close touch with metropolitan ideas. The British would not pay their war debts; the Americans no longer expected them to; neither government was seriously exploring ways by which American isolation could be ended. Skelton's broodings, in any case, did not matter much in this instance. Neither London nor Washington was asking him for his opinion, and King himself was more inclined to listen when the advice better reinforced his biases. He wanted a trade agreement, admittedly on his own and Canada's terms.

By mid-May Ottawa had received a copy of the most recent list of US demands—described by Robertson as a "most secret memorandum outlining those changes which they will seek in negotiations with the United Kingdom and which cannot be secured without the consent of Canada and other Dominions affected"—directly from Washington along with informal suggestions regarding "a declaration of policy which will line up the countries of the Commonwealth in support of the programme of economic appeasement through freer international trade." Robertson thought that such a statement would be "in accord with the Canadian Government's general policy," but that Ottawa could not "move in the matter until it has had an opportunity of examining the implications of such a declaration on Canada's trade relations with the UK and the US." Canada might, he thought, ask the British to waive their right to impose duties on Canadian dairy and poultry produce, or to acquiesce in the "modification of bound margins of preference in favour of Canada" in areas such as iron and steel, glass, and stearic acid. Compensation might be sought from the United States through the automatic extension of mfn treatment on products like whiskey or through the negotiation of a new Canada-US agreement, in which "we should seek, among other things, the maximum reduction on cattle, potatoes, and fish." He also wondered whether the US might be asked to give up some of her guaranteed preferences on such things as potatoes, fish, and lumber in Cuba. With an eye on his political masters, Robertson emphasised that he was thinking of "the possible conditions that would prepare Canadian public opinion for the acceptance of a triangular deal in which Canada would surrender certain preferences in the British market in order to facilitate a trade agreement between the UK and the US."[32]

Neither Robertson nor Skelton was making Canadian trade policy. Nor were the relevant members of the Canadian cabinet. In these matters, as in all others, ultimate authority rested with the prime minister, who was also the minister responsible for the Department of External Affairs and who controlled the direction of policy much more completely than his opposite number in Britain. King was being influenced by three forces—the advice of the Department of External Affairs; pressure from Washington; and, most important of all, his own instincts. All of these forces propelled him in the direction of freer trade. It is hardly surprising that he spoke so warmly in favour of economic appeasement and, more specifically, of an Anglo-American agreement at the Imperial Conference.

The Imperial Conference, which was held in conjunction with coronation ceremonies for George VI, opened on 14 May 1937. As usual, the agenda was almost entirely determined by the host government, and it occasioned the customary heart-burning in the Dominions Office and elsewhere in Whitehall. The conference proved to be of some importance, notably in its reinforcement of Britain's reluctance to become involved in European commitments that might take the entire Empire-Commonwealth into a war in defence of countries that were not thought vital to dominion or imperial interests—countries like Czechoslovakia.[33] Chamberlain, who became prime minister on 28 May, briefed the dominion leaders on the world situation. He was optimistic about the long-run possibility of calming Germany through colonial and economic appeasement. But by May 1937 Italy had invaded and conquered Ethiopia, and Hitler had remilitarized the Rhineland. The Spanish Civil War had broken out, and, in October 1936, the Rome-Berlin Axis had been formed. The short-run prospects, therefore, were anything but cheering, and there was a clamant need to improve Anglo-American relations. These large issues of international politics formed a major part of the conference proceedings, and such developments were surely present in the minds of all participants. Taking this context as given, our discussion concentrates upon the topic of transatlantic trade, the related topic of imperial preferences, and the parallel discussions inside the United Kingdom's official apparatus.

As the conference got under way, the United States responded to the British note of 13 April. Washington was not forthcoming: it was "not possible to make any extensive modifications in requests previously made." New vents for primary products must be found. If Britain could do little for American primary producers, the US would not be able to do much for British goods. "Government of the United States frankly does not believe negotiation of a narrow and limited trade agreement of this type would be worth while in view of opportunities now presented, or constitute adequate leadership in the field of a general liberalization of trade relations.... A satisfactory agreement between United States and United Kingdom would pave the way for similar agreements between the United States and the Dominions, negotiations for which much necessarily remain in abeyance until it be ascertained whether a basis for a comprehensive trade agreement between United States and United Kingdom can be found."[34] Everyone—domestic and dominion producers alike—would gain from a thoroughgoing Anglo-American agreement. Everyone, after all, would be better off in a peaceful, freer-trading world.

Washington had now accepted earlier British proposals on honey and certain dried fruits. With respect to tinned apples, rice, Douglas fir doors, patent leather, and fresh grapefruit, it reduced its original demands. It abandoned its loganberry request. But the American government was making new, more precise, and in some respects more awkward, demands with respect to the treatment of hams, pork, and lard: duties were to be bound, and quantitative controls were to be brought into the agreements.[35] These new counters were difficult because they implied that the United Kingdom would have to denounce or renegotiate a whole series of arrangements with smaller European states. In terms of negotiating time and effort, and of the risk of retaliation in other directions, the cost of an Anglo-American agreement had risen substantially.

Sir Ronald Lindsay was not apparently discouraged. The British ambassador chose this moment to make an appeal for a trade agreement at the National Foreign Trade Week Meeting in New York on 19 May. If the American farmer wanted favourable treatment of his products in the British market in return for "reasonable reductions" in the US tariff, "Barkis is willing." Sir Henry Page Croft, the farmer's champion, called the speech "a shock to all British agriculturalists who, heaven knows, have had a difficult enough time in the past few years." Lindsay was disavowed by the Foreign Office. A trade agreement, as the prime minister had only a few days before made clear, was not by any means "inevitable."[36]

In the Dominions Office the latest American position produced a wave of despair. On 21 May William Bankes-Amery wrote that: "There is of course not the smallest prospect that the Dominions would consent to abandon their existing rights on the scale demanded by Washington, and in my judgement no useful purpose would be served by discussing the United States proposals with them on that basis." It would be "politically impossible for any Dominion, save possibly Canada, to take a step which could be represented as handing over their hard won trade to the United States in pursuit of an ideal, which at the other side of the world would seem to be somewhat shadowy, of European political appeasement through economic means. This would apply especially to Australia who would be called upon to make a far greater sacrifice than any other Dominion, at a time when she is faced with an early election." The solution, the official thought, might be a "duty quota" system under which the tariff would increase when a certain quota had been reached.[37] The duty-quota, one of the many protective gadgets with which the decade abounded, would surface more than once in the course of subsequent talks, but it was not put to the dominions at the Imperial Conference.

The cabinet Committee on Trade and Agriculture had to consider what was to be done about the Americans. And what was to be said to the dominions? The British would have preferred to avoid raising the subject at the Imperial Conference, but knew that the dominions were vital players in any Anglo-American trade negotiation. The Americans were not prepared to involve the dominions directly before the signing of an Anglo-American agreement but were making demands which made that involvement, particularly Canada's, inevitable and necessary.

The trade and agriculture committee met on 26 May. Ministers acquiesced, without comment, in Walter Runciman's announcement that he intended to explain matters to the dominion prime ministers the following morning. Neville Chamberlain, still chancellor of the exchequer but within hours to be prime minister, urged his colleagues to stress the "great political urgency of securing an agreement," and Runciman said that he planned to do so. For the rest, ministers discussed the details of agricultural protectionism, the advantages to British export trade from the probable but still unknown American concessions, the risk that the dominions might demand compensation in the form of a reduction of the preferential margins guaranteed to Britain at Ottawa, and the special problems of tobacco. Sir William Brown, the permanent secretary of the Board of Trade, told the ministers that the Americans were prepared to consider making reductions on some 125 items, that the reductions could well be considerable, and that perhaps the Americans might be less "unbending" when they were seated at a conference table. The committee then talked about apples at some length, and rather more briefly it brooded on the tactics of negotiation. It was suggested that the United States might be willing to join in the regulation of the apple trade through existing intra-imperial machinery. It was also suggested, apparently for the first time, that Britain might have to be prepared to give up some of her preferential margins in the dominions.[38] This suggestion had not yet been put to the Americans.

As arranged, Runciman also addressed the Imperial Conference on 27 May, during its eighth plenary session. He spoke frankly about the prospects for the development of international trade. He reminded the delegates that in his view the Ottawa Agreements had been meant to reduce trade barriers through negotiation, and that the collapse of the 1933 World Economic Conference had demonstrated that multilateral tariff reductions were impossible. Britain had then pursued her goal through bilateral negotiation and by resisting the use of clearing agreements which forced trade into unnatural channels. The United States was doing similar things. Now that Britain and America were themselves negotiating, it was clear that the Ottawa Agreements would have to be adjusted. The dominions would be informed and consulted. Both economic and international political considerations,

Runciman said, urged the importance of success in the American negotiations, and Chamberlain added his own plea for Anglo-American harmony.

The dominion representatives then spoke of the need to expand multilateral trade. C.A. Dunning of Canada, J.A. Lyons of Australia, and N.C. Havenga of South Africa all emphasized the awkwardness of the bound preferential margins that Ottawa contained. These caused trouble in negotiations with foreign states because they limited the possible concessions while reducing their value. Dunning wanted tariff reductions in all directions. Although the British market was of enormous importance to Australia, Lyons pointed out, it was "too limited to allow of the adequate development of our resources." Havenga thought Ottawa had done more for Britain than for South Africa. Sir Zafrullah Khan of India feared that the Ottawa Agreements had encouraged foreign countries to retaliate against the subcontinent. He emphasized India's interest in the restoration of multilateral settlement patterns because of her large debit balance with Britain. Only Walter Nash, the New Zealand minister of finance, sounded a discordant note: advertising his scheme for bilateral balancing and clearing between Britain and New Zealand, he insisted that for his country the British market was absolutely vital; any Anglo-American agreement must allow New Zealand to sell more in Britain.[39]

That evening Runciman sent all the dominion prime ministers the notes that London and Washington had been exchanging since November 1936. These notes revealed to the dominions, both in general and often in very specific terms, what sacrifices the Americans expected of them. Runciman asked each to indicate "how far you think your Government might be prepared to go in meeting the United States' desiderata."[40] The next morning a British interdepartmental committee of officials met to consider "how the Dominions might be approached." The officials decided to begin by talking with their Canadian counterparts, proceeding then to the South Africans and Australians, leaving the other dominions and near-dominions "who were less interested, to be dealt with last." From the Dominions Office, C.W. Dixon advised that "canned and dried fruits were articles on which it would be impossible for Australia to do anything. It was felt that it would be preferable to deal with South Africa before Australia as being, on the whole, likely to be the more reasonable."

The officials discussed the various commodities. They saw no chance of reducing the general tariff on tobacco, but were prepared to consider raising the empire rate, thus reducing the "generous" preferential margin. On timber, they wondered whether American Douglas fir was normally cut in larger sizes than Baltic pine. Could a distinction be made on that basis? As for apples, the officials thought ministers were committed to going as far as Canada would allow; the Canadian officials should be asked to agree to a reduction in the mfn duty from 4/6 to 3/6 per hundredweight or, "if, in the course of the discussions with the United States, it proved to be absolutely necessary, to 3/- per hundredweight." The Americans, it will be recalled, still refused to modify their original demand of 2/3 per hundredweight. As for sugarless tinned apples, the duty should be cut in line with that on fresh apples. South Africa would be asked to let Britain reduce the grapefruit duty to 3 shillings per hundredweight, as Washington had requested, and the various affected dominions should be asked to acquiesce in reductions on dried prunes, apricots, and tinned fruits.[41]

The newspapers had long since begun to take note of the "secret" Anglo-American conversations, and had expected Canada and Australia to favour a movement toward freer trade. Mackenzie King, true to form, noticed what "the papers" were saying.[42] Before leaving Ottawa King had communicated with Charles Dunning about the line to be taken in the finance minister's statement about trade. But King was profoundly suspicious of his minister of finance, who, he feared, "was siding in with those forces in England which want trade as much within the empire as possible" and were "not equally sympathetic with the idea of developing trade more generally." King had instructed Dunning that he must not "use words in expressing Canada's position which would give the British Government the opportunity to say that the Dominions themselves and, in particular, Canada, was unwilling to extend the trade, and give to the Chamberlain crowd just what they wanted for their determination to make an economic unit of the empire."

Neville Chamberlain, King expected, would blame the dominions for Britain's inability to trade with the US, and then produce demands "for naval defence, etc, because of [Dominion] insistence on certain policies of trade." King's reference to the "Chamberlain crowd" indicated his belief, which had its roots in Joseph Chamberlain's turn of the century campaign for an imperial zollverein, that the family represented the quintessential metropolitan manipulators— resolutely against dominion freedom, rabidly for imperial centralization. King also insisted that it was essential to differentiate his trade policy clearly from the hated R.B. Bennett's: "we should be perfectly frank in saying that we were out for lowering tariffs all round, and would join in any movement toward that end." Having swallowed the Cordell Hull rhetorical package whole, King insisted that Canada should consider the "whole question of economic readjustment in a big generous way." This was no time to talk of lumber or apples. [43]

King, however, was soon taking a rather different and less warm and woolly line. Writing formally to Oliver Stanley, the president of the Board of Trade in Prime Minister Neville Chamberlain's new cabinet, King said that Runciman's statement of 27 May was "the first indication we have received of the view of the Government of the United Kingdom on the important questions involved in these discussions." After a short parroting of the Hull line, King laid bare the domestic political realities: "it will be recognized that it is hardly customary or to be taken for granted that when two countries are negotiating a trade agreement for their joint advantage a third country should be called upon to provide a great part of the quid pro quo." The Canadian public, he continued, would not give up advantages in the British market simply for the sake of international economic amity. "It is therefore obvious that it would be necessary to be in a position to make it plain to the people of Canada in general, and to the sections chiefly injured by the relinquishment of preferences in the United Kingdom in particular, first, that the United Kingdom itself was making substantial economic concessions, and second, that either by the United Kingdom or by the United States, or by both, compensatory economic advantages were being offered Canada in return." Canada, he added, would not ask Britain for compensation by the raising of duties on "foreign goods of other classes."[44]

King should have known, as the British knew full well, that almost all Canadian goods already entered Britain duty-free. And the documentation from 27 May should have told King that the Americans would not negotiate with Canada until after they had concluded their pact with Britain. What, then, did King have in mind by way of British concessions? If he was thinking at all, he can only have been referring to the bound preferential margins that had survived in his new Anglo-Canadian agreement.

There was sympathy for King's position from at least one British official. "The Canadians are not very helpful when it comes down to realities," wrote the acting head of the Foreign Office American department. "Of course there is a good deal to be said on their side. A few months ago we were negotiating a new treaty with them and finally reached agreement. Hardly before the ink is dry on the paper, we come along and say we should like to upset some highly important items in it in the interests of world trade and (though this is not said) of our own exports."[45] More generally, the Foreign Office thought the King-Hull vision of a world made more peaceful through economic appeasement showed little understanding of German realities. The problems created by Germany's policies, military and economic, were very complex, calling for a comprehensive response on a wide range of fronts.[46]

King's line of thought can be further understood against the background of a memorandum that Norman Robertson had prepared on 30 May. In response to Runciman's presentation Robertson, who accompanied King to London, recycled materials from earlier memoranda, briefing his prime minister anew. Britain, he wrote, should not ask Canada to concede anything with respect to preferences until Britain itself had made "the initial and heaviest sacrifices herself by a reduction of tariffs imposed under the Import Duties Act of 1932 and under earlier safeguarding of industries acts." Appearing not to have noticed that such concessions would not and could not satisfy the Americans, he went on, "I think we should have some explicit assurance on this point before committing Canada to any relinquishment of preferences now enjoyed." Robertson was already eager to seek compensation from the United States, apparently ignoring the fact that the Americans were not prepared to offer any. He suggested that Washington might reduce its own tariffs on the same items where Canada gave up preferences in Britain, or that Britain might win concessions which would also, under mfn rules, benefit Canada. Timber was to prove a good example of the first, but it is hard to think of any examples of the second. The Americans had already reduced their whiskey duties as much as the law allowed; Canada could not hope to compete with Britain so far as textiles were concerned. Robertson's speculations were ingenious, but somewhat out of touch with the economic and diplomatic facts of life. [47]

Robertson was maintaining close touch with the American Embassy in London. In his conversations there, he was sometimes less than discreet. He told an officer of the Embassy, for example, that Britain's cabinet changes boded ill for the trade negotiations. He also said that Canada's position was difficult because, if Ottawa conceded anything to Washington's demands, they "would in effect be writing the British a blank check," giving up preferences without knowing what they would get. Unaware of Sayre's informal wheat request of March 1937, Robertson expressed some surprise that no concession on that commodity had been proposed.[48] These remarks, needless to say, passed promptly to Washington.

Robertson continued to keep the Americans informed. Following informal Anglo-Canadian talks on 1 June, he again reported to Ambassador Bingham. After telling about the meeting in general terms, he explained that Canada would have to win gains that were politically defensible on their economic merits alone, and that Washington would have to give concessions to Canada as well as to the United Kingdom.[49] The Americans, however, were as yet unwilling to accept such advice; as we have seen, they refused to "pay twice" for Britain's concessions. Robertson was already talking about a "supplementary trade agreement . . . in which Canada could secure direct compensation for further reductions of duty in favour of the United States as well as for foregoing certain margins of preference now enjoyed in the United Kingdom."[50] Some months would pass before the American government could be brought to consider that device.

What would the Americans give the British? The dominions had not been told, but neither had the British government, which still possessed only the general indications that had been proffered earlier in the spring. Hoping that some more definite word from Washington might ease the proceedings in London, Sayre saw Roosevelt on 3 June to get approval for a new and more concrete offer. Sayre explained that on woollens, cottons, blankets, and pottery—the products of greatest interest to the British—the State Department's Trade Agreement Committee proposed to offer "slight or non-existent concessions" in the "coarser or cheaper classes where competition with American production is high," and to offer large cuts "only in the finer or more expensive classes of goods in which the competition with domestic production is less." After a conversation of about fifteen minutes the president approved the schedules and told Sayre to "go ahead."[51]

The next day Sayre and Harry Hawkins gave the schedules to H.O. Chalkley from Britain's Washington Embassy. Whether by accident or by design, these expressed potential concessions in relation to the Smoot-Hawley tariff rates, even though other trade agreements had already reduced some of the effective rates. The submission thus gave a misleading impression of the cuts which the Americans actually proposed, and there is no doubt that Chalkley and the Board of Trade were misled. Only much later was the confusion revealed.

The three officials discussed the situation. Chalkley was not encouraging, explaining that because of Britain's own mfn obligations to the Baltic states it would almost certainly be impossible to make any special concession on Douglas fir timber. He also warned the Americans that Canada would probably not agree to the granting of duty-free entry for American timber. On the lumber front, he said, there would have to be Canadian-American talks. This was advice that the Americans were not willing to take. Washington's three-page memorandum of 4 June identified "the extent and character of the possible concessions which it may be feasible to accord the United Kingdom . . . Of course, the concessions indicated are subject to such revision as may seem necessary." The State Department thought that "the total of items with respect to which concessions appear possible . . . is 246, of which 239 are reductions, and . . . on more than 100 of these it now appears that it would be possible to make reductions ranging from 40 to 50 per cent of the present rates." In addition, there was a good chance of "binding most of these products now on the free list of which the United Kingdom is the chief source of imports." The tabulation revealed the groups—cottons, woollens, chemicals, ceramics, metals, and so on—but not individual products. It covered American imports from Britain in the amount of $43 million (1935), and it suggested an average 34 per cent reduction of existing rates across the 246 items.[52]

In Whitehall it was obvious that the discussions with the dominions would take time. This fact was not obvious to the Americans, who told Sir Ronald Lindsay that they had expected the London talks would reveal in concrete terms "what agreement could be reached with the Dominions." The State Department, he reported later, thought that agreement "in principle" with the dominions represented "no progress at all, and would prevent them proposing negotiations."[53]

Anglo-Canadian discussions had begun on 1 June 1937, when Robertson conferred with British officials. The talks continued on 7 June, when worried British ministers discussed the situation with King, Dunning and other members of Canada's Imperial Conference delegation. King again stressed the importance of the "breaking down of the economic nationalism of European countries" that was such an important part of the Hull formula to lure Germany back into the family of nations.[54] But Canada would require immediate compensation for any concessions it might make as part of an Anglo-American agreement. It would be helpful, but not enough, for Britain to say that she would be sympathetic to any Canadian request to unbind specific preferential margins. If Britain were to adopt the American position that the US could not even be asked to compensate the dominions, there was no point discussing anything at all. Once in negotiation, the Canadians thought, the Americans would be more flexible than they had been on paper: the list of "essentials" need not be taken terribly seriously.

As to compensation, Robertson's suggestions of 30 May were put before the Whitehall officials, and there was some discussion of the American "essentials" in so far as they affected Canada. King explained that his government would be prepared to consider modifications of preferences on fresh apples and pears, tinned apples, honey, and patent leather. Canada was worried about tobacco, but would let Southern Rhodesia make the running; the American proposal on softwoods was not acceptable. And, according to the Canadian minutes (but not the British ones), after stating that the American stand on concessions to Canada was "essentially unfair and impossible," King went on to say that "if it would ease the situation he would be willing to open negotiations with Washington with a view to enlarging the existing Canada-United States agreement."[55]

In Ottawa Dana Wilgress, a high official in the Department of Trade and Commerce, reported that there were many items which both Canada and Britain sold in the United States but of which Britain was the principal supplier. A negotiation of a lower rate for British goods would in these instances help Canadian sales too. British officials were nervous about this idea because they feared the Americans would see it as "direct compensation." It did not bulk large in Canadian ministerial thinking, but in subsequent discussion the idea was not allowed to die.[56]

Although at an earlier stage King had feared that the British would try to blame Canada for a breakdown in the Anglo-Canadian talks, he and his ministers, with the advice and support of their officials, had taken up a stance that would make the charge a true one. King felt that Canada had been placed in a "ridiculous position."[57] By 11 June he was discussing with his ministers the possibility of "our entering at once upon trade negotiations with the United States ... this being the only method of approach to enable us to meet the British Ministers in giving up some things." It should be noted, however, just how small were the "things" that Canada was willing to "give up." What King wanted at this point was a cancellation or reduction in some of the fixed margins he had conceded to Britain earlier in 1937, and lower American duties for some Canadian goods. According to his diary, the British agreed with the prime minister, who instructed Skelton that "from now on we would work on that basis."[58]

Besides the conversations with Canadian officials and politicians, Whitehall arranged parallel talks with the representatives of the other dominions that were present. By 22 June, when Whitehall officials foregathered to devise a long report for Sir Ronald Lindsay in Washington, many things were clear. And the clarity was depressing:

> The Dominion delegates expressed general sympathy with the underlying objects of an Anglo-United States trade agreement.... It became clear, however, that those Governments would find it essential to obtain compensation for any advantages which they might forgo in the United Kingdom market... the only form of compensation which we were in fact able to offer the Dominions was that of being ready to agree to some abatement of our rights in their markets, if these rights should stand in the way of trade negotiations they might wish to conduct... the Canadian ministers seem to be more and more turning in the direction of a simultaneous and linked negotiation between Canada and the United States ....[59]

Because of the discussions with the dominions, no one had had much time to consider the American note of 4 June. As Oliver Stanley observed, in his comments on the draft telegram for Lindsay, nothing could be done for tobacco, and nothing much could be done about softwood, while Australia was still likely to resist any concession on dried prunes, apricots, and raisins. Until the Indian and Burmese delegations had spoken, nothing could be said about rice; until the Australians had had their general elections, they would avoid saying anything definite at all. But on the other items in the American list of essentials, concessions might be possible "subject to compensation" to the relevant dominions. Britain would go some way to meet the American demands on ham, and could approach the dominions regarding the wheat duty. She was also prepared to consider making concessions with respect to her own protective duties on such products as apples.[60] It would apparently also be worth asking the Americans, as Robertson had suggested, if the cancellation of the wheat duty would help at all. "We have not sounded the dominions concerned on this suggestion, but from some remarks by one of the Canadian officials it appears possible that Canada might be ready to consider such a suggestion."[61] The details were not passed on to Lindsay; he was told that "while considerable difficulties still remain, it seems to us that there is ample ground for pursuing the discussions. . . . "[62]

Unless the Americans were to change their entire tactical stance, however, the Anglo-American negotiations were bound to fail. Britain had not abrogated the Ottawa Agreements; the dominions had neither agreed to make unrequited concessions nor to trust the United States and the United Kingdom to recompense them in due course. Furthermore, as the next few weeks were to reveal, Canada's prime minister went back to Ottawa and promptly forgot the most important things that he and his officials had learned in London.

CHAPTER 4

Canadian Complications

June - November 1937

The Imperial Conference had again reminded the British government how complicated could be the management of self-governing, independent-minded and quarrelsome government entities that fell short of being nations in the international sense, and yet were a long way from being colonies. The empire, as Prime Minister Chamberlain said after the conference, made Britain a great power.[1] It was vital to maintain the greatest possible unity of policy and purpose with the dominions, and not to ask too much of them. Whatever the importance of a friendly America, wrote the acting head of the Foreign Office's American department in April 1937, "a friendly Empire is a greater importance still."[2]

The dominion problem was far from solved, and the British had also to decide what next to do about the Americans. On 18 June 1937 the cabinet Trade and Agriculture Committee met to discuss strategy. Oliver Stanley, Chamberlain's president of the Board of Trade, told his colleagues about the state of conversations with the dominions. He was, in particular, only too aware of the obstacle that the Canadian posture had created, and he objected very strongly to the American tactic of defining "essential minimum demands." Anxious nevertheless to proceed by making a "more specific and more substantial offer," he recommended that Britain should propose to remove the wheat duty and reduce the duties on various fruits, patent leather, Douglas fir doors, various tinned fruits, hams, and perhaps lard. He even went so far as to suggest that Britain should offer to explore with

---

Reference notes for Chapter 4 begin on p. 175.

Australia the limitation of the areas of cultivation of raisins and dried fruits, thus setting at rest American fears that preferences might cause uneconomic expansion within the empire and trade diversion to it. Concessions in the industrial sphere would also be needed, Stanley admitted, but he did not suggest what these might be. The dominions would have to be informed about the terms of the new offer, which would necessarily be contingent on their eventual agreement.[3]

There followed a sort of transatlantic dance of officials. J.A. Stirling of the Board of Trade went to Washington; Leo Pasvolsky, a special assistant to Hull, came to London. The result was a parallelism of informal conversation in the two capitals. Sir William Brown, the Board of Trade's chief official, talked at length with Pasvolsky. In his report, the American said that Brown had made an extraordinary claim about the Anglo-Canadian negotiations of the preceding winter. Britain, according to Pasvolsky's version of Brown, had insisted that "in view of the number of bound margins in Canada from which the British had released them they must be prepared to make the concessions needed for an agreement between Great Britain and the United States." In spite of this, the Canadians had taken the position at the Imperial Conference that they would need compensation from the United States. Pasvolsky thought that the British would try to get the Americans to bargain directly with the dominions, a step which he did not think Washington should take. He also believed that the United States should maintain its demand with respect to tobacco, and that she could probably get free entry for wheat.[4]

In Washington, meanwhile, Sir Robert Lindsay was telling Hull that the dominions were "difficult to deal with" in the matter of preferences. Hull replied that the "economic autarchy" of the British empire was a constant matter of complaint among "high officials of other governments in Europe."[5] If so, these high officials were ill-informed. Sixty per cent of Britain's imports came from outside the empire, whose member states likewise imported much more from outside the empire than from within it. Hull, however, was never much interested in detail, or in evidence, and Lindsay was apparently too polite to bring the facts to the secretary of state's attention—even supposing that he knew them.

Stirling, along with Chalkley of the British Embassy, proceeded to discuss the situation with the American officials in early July.[6] A week later the embassy delivered a more detailed statement of position to the secretary of state, explaining that Canada would insist on compensation for any surrender of preferences and that because of the coming election Australia could do nothing much on fruit products.[7] Indeed, Australian and New Zealand ministers had passed through

Washington on their way home from the Imperial Conference; they had conferred informally with American officials, who were thus well aware of Antipodean demands and worries. As yet there was no indication that the Americans would change their ground, or their demands.

After their meeting with Stirling and Chalkley on 21 July, the American officials went away and drafted a paragraph to define their attitude toward the question of Canadian talks. After there was a satisfactory basis for a trade agreement with Britain, they would be glad to start preliminary talks with Canada, presumably the sort of discussions that had been going on with Britain since 1934. However, these would not deal "in any way with the terms of any agreement with the UK or with our trade relations with UK." Hull approved this draft, and it was passed to Chalkley and Stirling.[8] Washington was increasingly unhappy about the British attitude. J. Pierrepont Moffat, taking over as head of the State Department's European Department, recorded in his diary that the British response of late June was no good at all. "Better to go down flags flying than to go down by letting an unsatisfactory agreement gradually disillusion people. However, none of us feel that this is the last British offer but is a final effort to make us pay the Dominions before they start putting [on the] pressure themselves."[9]

Sir Ronald Lindsay got the collective bad news the next day: the State Department would have to tell the secretary of state that the United Kingdom response "did not offer an acceptable basis for negotiations." They would not compensate the dominions in advance; they did not want simultaneous negotiations with Canada, whose leaders were "tending to look at the matter through a microscope." Mackenzie King, it was supposed, would never block an agreement.[10] Lindsay in turn told the Foreign Office that the "London discussions suggest to us that Canada will not believe that United States is not bluffing, until they are brought face to face."[11] He explained the position to his Canadian counterpart, Sir Herbert Marler, who was about to return to Ottawa, and he asked London to explain matters fully and frankly to King, requesting that the Canadian prime minister "send representatives immediately to Washington." He himself would send Stirling, who had been with him in Washington, to Ottawa. There Stirling could explain matters—first, to Sir Francis Floud, the British high commissioner, and then to Prime Minister King himself.[12] Perhaps Canada could be brought to take some initiative.

At first, Lindsay's hope seemed likely to prove vain. Since returning to Ottawa from London King had not discussed the question of a trade agreement with his cabinet. Nor, it seems, had he mentioned it to anyone else. Worse, in the interim, he had been brooding (not, for him, an uncommon pastime) on various slights, real or imagined, that he had received at the hands of the British. Why had Oliver Stanley not sent a written response to his letter of 2 June? Why did certain confidential correspondence contain the statement that Canada would have to be "pilloried" to secure an Anglo-American agreement?[13] Marler saw King on 26 July. The prime minister refused to send any message to the Americans. He would leave the field to Britain and the United States.[14] The next day King discussed the question in cabinet, where he told his ministers that he expected he would soon be getting representations from the United States. Immediately thereafter, Skelton told him that Norman Armour, the American minister in Ottawa, had relayed messages from Hull and the State Department's Dean Acheson. State was wondering what Canada had said to Britain, and whether or not the dominion would give up some preferences.[15] On 28 July Armour called on King. The minister said that because there was no word about what Canada was prepared to do, the Anglo-American discussions were at a standstill, a statement that was manifestly untrue. Britain knew what Canada was prepared to do, and had told the United States, but King was not aware of this. King explained that Canada wanted to help but would need compensation either from Britain or from the United States. Though the Americans would willingly discuss a new trade agreement in due course, they did not want to begin negotiations until after Britain had been dealt with. The prime minister then took the matter to cabinet again, where all were agreed that the next move should not be—could not be—Canada's.

The next day Stirling reached Ottawa and briefed Sir Francis Floud, who also saw King on 28 July. The meeting was an unpleasant one. Australia and New Zealand had become much more co-operative than they had been in London, while South Africa was leaving things to Britain. Canada was the problem, or so King believed he was being told. The prime minister revealed his resentments and flatly refused to do anything. At length Sir Francis asked whether King would send someone to Washington; King responded by asking why he should. He would receive a written request, he said, but London knew his position only too well. Might Canada not begin concurrent negotiations? King replied that the Americans did not want any such thing and that the cabinet had decided "to do nothing at present until there was some very special reason why we should move."[16] The high commissioner reported that an "unaccommodating" King thought a matter of such importance deserved a "definite request in writing from the United Kingdom Government."[17] The Dominions Office concluded that King had not understood British willingness to acquiesce in Canadian manipulation of preferential margins, and it authorized Floud to give the Canadian copies of the British minutes from the Imperial Conference meetings of 1 and 7 June, which it suspected King had misunderstood.[18]

These minutes proved to be important. The Canadian ministers and officials had not previously seen the British version, and had differently (or incorrectly) remembered the events which were recorded. In particular, King had indeed missed the point about the preferential margins. Floud's report also set in motion the wheels that generated, a few days later, a personal appeal from Chamberlain to King. King had changed his view of the British prime minister as a result of the Imperial Conference, where Chamberlain had impressed the Canadians with his grasp and moderation. Chamberlain had stood four-square for Anglo-American solidarity, imperial unity and German pacification—good King causes all.[19] King was also far from immune to the flattery of such an approach. The British prime minister explained that the reason for commercial discussions, and for the trade agreement to which the talks might lead, were as much political as economic. The United Kingdom was most anxious for an agreement with the United States, whose government would not promise Canada anything unless a direct exchange of views should take place. Canada could not allow Britain to sacrifice her interests unless assured beforehand that US concessions would in fact be made, but because Canada already enjoyed almost complete free entry to the British market there was nothing that the United Kingdom herself could offer by way of compensation.[20]

All these arguments had been rehearsed before and in King's hearing. This time he found them persuasive, perhaps because Chamberlain's appeal underlined Canada's central, if occasional, role as a linchpin between Britain and the United States. Here, surely, was a time when the concept of a North Atlantic Triangle—a Canadian conceit that implied a rough equality among the three partners, thus conferring on the smallest a role and importance out of all proportion with reality—could really mean something. At the beginning of August Sir Francis Floud reported that King would send an emissary to Washington.[21] The joint efforts of Lindsay, Stirling, Floud, and Chamberlain had been crowned with success. But who could tell if Canada's envoy would have equal success, or, if so, how speedily?

The whole business about the "unbinding of margins" had been unhappy and puzzling. At the end of July, the minister of finance, Charles Dunning, had told Sir Francis Floud that he had never known of Britain's June offer. King eventually admitted that he "had not caught this clearly while in England, but had since seen that such was

the case from the memo of the discussions"[22] — presumably the copy
that Floud supplied to him on 3 August.[23] Both King and Skelton had
confused the Americans and confounded the British by denying that
Britain had made any such offer.[24] One Foreign Office official wrote
that his "complaints and criticism of the action of His Majesty's
Government are of course a complete travesty of the facts. Unfortu-
nately he [King] has got it into his head that Canada has been kept in
the dark as to the course of the trade negotiations in Washington and is
now being made to pay for an Anglo-American trade agreement."[25]
Skelton had gone so far as to claim that the original suggestion had
been "vague" and that there had been no further reference to the
proposal. Neither statement was true. Floud later explained to Armour that there had been "some misunderstanding,"[26] but it was not
the case of "sharp practice" that the American minister was inclined
to suspect.[27]

King was presumably sincere when he claimed that London had
not said what compensation it could offer. Nevertheless, the Canadian
position reflected confusion, absentmindedness, defective staff work,
or some mixture of the three. Canadian officials, in spring 1937, had
briefed King for the Imperial Conference. Robertson and Skelton had
accompanied the prime minister to London, where, as we saw above,
they took part in discussions and briefing sessions. It does not appear,
however, that Ottawa's senior civil servants played any role in the
discussions of late July and early August. King may have sought their
advice; if so, no record has survived.[28] British officials and ministers
had made their position perfectly clear in June, and the situation is
recorded fully in the minutes of the 1 June meeting of officials and the
7 June meeting of ministers. The British minutes of 1 June say that
A.E. Overton of the Board of Trade remarked that "it seemed to him
that the logical counterpart of any concessions by Canada to facilitate
an agreement with the USA would be for the United Kingdom to give
very sympathetic consideration to any cases arising in Canadian
negotiations with foreign countries where bound margins under the
United Kingdom-Canadian agreement were found to be an obstacle."
The Canadian minutes credit to Overton the following words: "Furthermore, the United Kingdom in return for Canadian co-operation in
the waiving of preferences at this time would undoubtedly adopt a
most sympathetic attitude toward any future Canadian requests to
waive fixed margins of preference if these margins stood in the way of
Canada's trade negotiations with foreign countries." As for the 7 June
meeting, although the British minutes are silent on the issue, the
fuller Canadian minutes record Oliver Stanley as having said that
"this whole question of fixed margins might have to be reconsidered

if it stood in the way of Canada negotiating with foreign countries. He felt sure that sympathetic consideration would be given to any Canadian request for abandoning the principle in the case of specific commodities where it was hindering the Canadian government in trade negotiations."[29] Sad to say, if we are to judge from his diary,[30] King himself apparently did not grasp the point at the time, nor did he later ask for the help of his officials.

Chamberlain's message of 2 August, which reiterated the offer "to consider sympathetically any requests for modification of preferences," seems to have put King's mind fully at rest. London, in addition, did its best to give King what information it had about the industrial concessions Washington sought from Britain and offered to her, and about any more general measures that Britain might have in mind "as a means of satisfying United States public opinion." [31] And, to satisfy the private opinion of the Canadian prime minister, Whitehall shipped to Ottawa a good deal of additional documentation.

Mollified at last, King now proceeded to change the terms of the Canadian-American talks. Whitehall had not really proposed "concurrent negotiations," at least not at this point. What it wanted was an exchange of views at first hand.[32] Norman Armour, meanwhile, was pressing for an informal and tentative probe, one that would just suffice to establish whether there was a "basis for Anglo-American negotiation." Instead King proposed something more concrete and serious to the Americans: talks about "the feasibility of an extension of the present Canada-United States Trade Agreement, concurrently with the discussions between the United Kingdom and the United States."

Armour explained that the United States government had told Britain that it would not engage in concurrent negotiations. Nevertheless, King persevered, suggesting that if and only if the Americans agreed to such a course could there be "exploratory conferences . . . between Canadian and United States officials."[33] Having consulted his cabinet, King was determined that the Canadian-American talks should be as definitive as possible. Believing that the United States position was "indefensible and will have to be abandoned," and more annoyed at Washington than at London (whose suggestions with respect to Canada's own preferential concessions he now understood), King insisted that he would send no one to Washington except "on bona fide negotiation of an extension of our agreement."[34] King had become co-operative, but his desire for concurrent negotiations was causing a new kind of trouble. After discussion in Washington, the State Department authorized in mid-August a much lower order of conversation: "informal and confidential discussions between American and Canadian officials, without prior commitment on the part of either Government."[35]

While awaiting some action from Ottawa, the British diplomats had explained the situation to Washington once again. Nothing could be done for tobacco, except a binding of the preferential margin; not much could be done for timber. Whitehall had also begun to jib at the Americans' form of negotiation. Areas of agreement might be more easily found if the United States requirements in regard to particular commodities were made "negotiable" instead of "essential."[36] It was explained that Canada, Australia, and New Zealand would need something tangible by way of immediate tradeoffs. Britain herself could offer only deferred compensation. Could the United States not examine every possibility of finding something to offer in return for dominion concessions? What about Robertson's suggestion, by which certain American tariffs, though not negotiated with Canada, might be reduced in the Anglo-American bargain so as to benefit the Canadians? Finally, Washington was told that "the United Kingdom government were not now disposed to regard the consequences of unsuccessful negotiations so seriously as they would have done six months ago."[37] The Foreign Office, still regarding an agreement as "essential," would not have agreed.[38]

King had decided to send O.D. Skelton, his under-secretary of state for external affairs, to Washington. Everything now depended on that visit. Skelton saw Hull on the afternoon of 27 August and on the morning of 28 August. He also talked to Hawkins and Hickerson in the State Department. The arrangements having been made on two days' notice, we may presume that Washington had not had time for a great deal of staff work.[39] Skelton explained that Canada was worried not only about the loss of her twenty-one bound preferences in Britain, but about the unbound ones too. The loss might affect not only natural products such as barley but some industrial ones, such as stoves, vacuum cleaners, silk stockings, and cars. Skelton himself did not believe that Canada would lose as much by the surrender of these concessions as was often assumed, but naturally in explaining matters to Hull he stressed "the importance of the concessions sought and the difficulties of any variation." Hull produced his usual platitudes about world peace through economic reform; as for "the details of the situation" he knew little. Talking to Hickerson, Skelton concluded that the "timing factor is the main obstacle in the solution of the present triangular difficulty." Hickerson explained that State saw no point in discussing matters with Canada if in the end nothing would happen, but Skelton took away the view that the Americans had agreed to consider King's idea further. The United States might "be prepared to explore the possibilities of a new agreement without a prior commitment to its being accepted." After Skelton's departure, the officials in the State Department recorded a more pessimistic opinion. An impasse had been reached, they thought, and "we question whether such conversations could serve any useful purpose."[40]

Before leaving Washington, Skelton reported the substance of his talks to J.A. Stirling at the British Embassy, who explained that Anglo-American talks were not likely to start for some weeks. Meanwhile, the Board of Trade was telling Chalkley, Britain would have to bring the Americans to the point by preparing "a maximum composite offer on all their essential requests. . . . Vague promises to consider 'some reduction' were no good."[41]

Ever since Norman Robertson had proposed that Britain should offer to reduce or abolish its wheat duty, Whitehall had hoped that such an offer might bring about a reduction of Washington's "essential" requests. Everyone seems to have forgotten that the United States was, for the moment at least, a wheat importing country, with no interest in the British market. To Canada, the wheat preference was valuable primarily because it generated outbound traffic for the ports of the maritime provinces, and notably for Halifax and Saint John. Ministers also recognized, of course, that it was politically dangerous to upset prairie farmers by removing the duty. Gradually London came to realize that the wheat duty was not central to the Americans. Although the State Department had left wheat off their "essential" list because they wanted to make that list an "absolute minimum," free entry would have a payoff only in political terms. The only "essential" conditions that it could effectively replace would be those on other commodities produced in the wheat-growing districts. Thus a wheat concession would not enable the US to forego its demand on lumber.[42]

As things grew clearer on wheat, they grew muddier on procedure and sequence. By early September Floud reported that Skelton believed the next move was with the United States, while Stirling in Washington thought that Skelton did not think this.[43] There was, understandably, some alarm in Whitehall lest confusion should further delay things. Fortunately, Armour was authorized to tell Skelton that the State Department was "prepared to continue our confidential and informal conversations with Canada at the convenience of the Canadians. It is, of course, understood that these conversations are not only confidential and informal but without prior commitment of any kind on either side." Dana Wilgress of the Department of Trade and Commerce and Hector McKinnon, Ottawa's commissioner of tariffs, Hickerson explained, were well-known "as the ace negotiators of trade agreements for Canada." It would therefore be "preferable," for the sake of safety and secrecy, if the more junior Norman Robertson were to come to Washington alone.[44]

Up to this point, certainly, the secrecy had not been extreme. This was especially true in Ottawa, a small city with a propensity to gossip. Although the Canadian cabinet had originally approved a plan to send Robertson, McKinnon, and Wilgress to Washington, the subsequent decision to send Skelton had been King's alone.[45] In Ottawa only King, Robertson, and Stephen Holmes from the British High Commission staff appear to have known that Skelton was going to Washington at all.[46] After the visit, as before, the Americans were suspicious of Canadian visitors. Returning from the United States Legation in Ottawa on leave, the highly regarded Walton Butterworth visited the State Department during mid-September, "convinced . . . that the Canadians were playing a double game with the British." Butterworth was surprised to be shown "chapter and verse how the British had double-crossed the Canadians."[47] What the State Department officials had in mind is not clear. Had they forgotten that the confusion about British concessions to Canada had resulted from a Canadian failure to read and absorb the documents?

Further confusions were in the offing. In the latter part of September, when nothing particular had happened for several weeks, Sir Frederick Phillips of the UK Treasury visited Washington. The primary purpose of his visit was to discuss the world gold glut with Henry C. Morgenthau, Jr, the American secretary of the Treasury.[48] While he was in Washington, Sir Frederick talked to Cordell Hull about the trade impasse. The British chargé d'affaires, Mallet, was also present. Hull expressed his impatience with the delay, but Phillips reminded him that Britain was waiting for the United States to take the next step with Canada. Observing that Hull was not fully conversant with details, Mallet went to the State Department to see Francis Sayre, who thought that the "next move was up to Canada." The chargé said "that there must be some misunderstanding as we had thought United States was considering question of timing and that they would tell Canada when they may be ready to talk. I asked Sayre whether he was prepared after further consideration to approach Canada and he replied that he was not." It was also pointed out that the United States still had not said what it expected by way of reductions in industrial tariffs, nor had it supplied a list of "non-essential desiderata," or "answers on wheat, barley, and rice." It would not be possible "for His Majesty's Government to sanction announcement of contemplation [of negotiation] until they had some general idea of what would be expected of them."[49] The next day, Hickerson and Hawkins told British Embassy officials that "whatever

Sayre may have said yesterday what he meant was that he could not entertain negotiations with Canada until an agreement had been signed with the United Kingdom."[50] The British took this to mean that Sayre was not simply waiting for Canada to make some move; he would not listen to, or accept, whatever move they might make. "In fact," the Embassy told London, "I am to report that they have reversed everything that we understood Mr. Sayre to say yesterday."[51]

The American documents later published in *Foreign Relations of the United States* do not refer to this volte-face, but they do suggest that the American position was even more rigid than the British visitors realized. Hull said that "the United States had no intention of paying two for one in the matter of an Anglo-American agreement. . . . the countries which made the Ottawa Agreements must themselves be responsible for the relaxing of their provisions."[52] Because Britain "could not go further with the negotiations until Canada had relinquished its preferential rights," the *chargé* responded, it now "remained with the United States to secure the consent of Canada to such a relinquishment." Sayre argued that it would be politically impossible for Washington to "undertake negotiations or even conversations with an agricultural country before we had assurance of a thoroughgoing and satisfactory trade agreement with such an industrial country as Great Britain. . . . All we could discuss with the Canadians was the 'timing problem,' i.e., how to get around the difficulty that we could not enter into negotiations with Canada until after we had positive assurances that the Canadians would relinquish their preferential rights." The "must list" of November 1936, moreover, was precisely that: "each single item was a *sine qua non* for the agreement so that unless this list could be satisfied in its entirety it would be useless to continue further negotiations." The next move was not up to the United States. The problem was "distinctly a British one, i.e. the removal of discriminations and preferences which they themselves created on the very eve of our negotiations, after we had expressed our fears to them on this very point."[53] Sayre also said that Washington's "non-Ottawa list," for which the British were still waiting, should soon be ready. It was in fact provided on 28 September, and a supplementary list arrived on 5 October.

This final point of Sayre's, which had not entered the intergovernmental exchanges since much earlier in the year, was both illinformed and irrational. Sayre certainly had not noticed, or had forgotten, that the Anglo-Canadian trade agreement of 1937 had substantially reduced the number of items on which Britain enjoyed bound margins in Canada, and that it had done nothing to increase or widen the dominion preferences in Britain—the things which must give way if an Anglo-American agreement was to be concluded. These dated in part from the Ottawa Agreements themselves, and in part they followed directly from Britain's strict interpretation of its mfn obligations to Scandinavia. The documents, however, do not seem to record any recognition on the British side that the American objection was based on a completely false reading of the evidence. Instead, Whitehall set to work to provide an explanation of American intransigence that rational persons might accept.

From the British point of view, the problems were numerous and complex, and officials could be forgiven pessimism. Burma and India, with whom trade talks had begun, were reluctant players: India wanted to keep the wheat preference, and Burma was being troublesome on rice. Australia, meanwhile, had not even been asked whether it would object to a wheat concession, and there was fear that British, Australian, and Canadian millers would all react violently to the American suggestion "that wheat would be of no use to her without flour." It seemed unlikely that anything could be done to change Washington's mind about negotiating with Canada. Whitehall now understood the American position to be that, for both political and administrative reasons, they could not begin discussions with Canada. Two important sets of simultaneous discussions would be unwieldy, and would constitute an immense burden for the tiny State Department negotiating team. More important, such a concession might open the door for other dominions, which would clamour for attention, along with such states as Argentina and Uruguay.

There appeared, moreover, to be only a few months of negotiating time before the shadow of the 1938 congressional elections would paralyze the American government. What were the prospects of progress? In the Dominions Office, Bankes-Amery wrote that "I myself feel that, even given earnest good will in all quarters, it would be quite impossible... to reach a final agreement with the United States within 6 months. But there is no sign of any such general good will. ... This criticism applies no less to the United States than to the dominions; for how, assuming effective good will, can one explain the insistence of the United States that we should free ourselves from contractual commitments to 7 self-governing empire countries when she will not herself help us to the extent of negotiating informally with Canada for fear lest she should get into diplomatic difficulty with Argentina."[54]

To make matters worse, Mackenzie King was presenting further problems of his own. At the end of September, the British high commissioner discussed the situation with the prime minister, reporting that he "feels unable himself to take any positive step to facilitate negotiations with the United States for fear of antagonizing one or more of interests represented by different members of his cabinet." Hence three officials, not simply Robertson, had better go to Washington; if the State Department objected, they should send someone to Ottawa instead.[55] The difficulties, Sir Francis Floud later explained, were largely with Charles Dunning, the finance minister, and W.D. Euler, the minister of trade and commerce, both of whom wanted to send officials.[56] King himself much preferred to receive American officials in Ottawa, but he was willing to send a trade negotiating troika — Wilgress, McKinnon and Robertson — to Washington. In this way there would be two officials from Euler's department, Trade and Commerce, and one from King's own Department of External Affairs. The prime minister was prepared to consider giving up the wheat preference, and thought that the minister of agriculture, James Gardiner, might agree, but that other cabinet members would oppose the step. Worried by what Floud had told him, King decided that he would take the question to cabinet. External Affairs was asked to prepare a position paper.[57]

Norman Robertson's memorandum from External Affairs naturally did not report that Skelton and King had failed to understand Britain's willingness to consider unbinding or reducing her own preferential margins in Canada. Indeed, the memorandum did not mention that offer. In other respects, it gave an accurate picture of the events and the alternatives insofar as Ottawa officials understood them. Robertson still believed that the Americans were ready for "informal and exploratory conversations between officials;" neither the British nor the Americans had told him of Sayre's change of front.

As to the "main line of Canadian commercial policy" Robertson had no doubt. It was "a determination to liberalize the system of imperial preference by insisting that freer trade within the empire shall be a stride toward and not a flight from freer trade with the world." There would be payoffs in the broad terms of international politics, and Canada should not let narrow sectional interests stand in the way of negotiations. Hence "it has seemed to us that the Government will wish to examine sympathetically the requests for their collaboration which have been received from the Governments of the United States and the United Kingdom." Robertson also reported on the commodities—wheat, apples, pears, honey, and patent leather— "on which we could forego preferential margins with a minimum dislocation of industry, employment, and prices in Canada and on which the modification of margins would constitute an important contribution to the freeing of international trade." Even on lumber Robertson thought Canada should "go some way to meet" the American demand, and might also "cheerfully drop its contingent

claim to have a preferential duty levied on foreign copper and zinc."
As for the bound preferences that Britain might sacrifice in Canada,
Robertson particularly mentioned window and plate glass, stearic
acid, and diesel engines, as well as West Indian tomatoes. South
Africa might be asked to allow some reduction in the preferential
margin on its maize.[58]

Skelton thought his subordinate's memorandum "admirable,"
although he had some doubts about lumber. The under-secretary's
response focused on economic costs and benefits, not on international
politics. "The first step," Skelton wrote, would be "to show that
reductions in the United Kingdom market can be made on con-
venanted and unconvenanted items helpful to the United States
without seriously injuring Canadian interests." The present
memorandum served that purpose, Skelton said.[59] In fact it did nothing of the sort. It certainly did not show that the reduction of apple and
lumber preferences would be unimportant for Canada, and although
Robertson had uncovered various items on which Canada could surrender preferences without damage, these were not items on which
the United States had asked concessions.

On 8 October the cabinet considered Robertson's memorandum.
Again the focus was economic. Domestic political considerations
were naturally implicit in these, but large international issues do not
seem to have been mentioned at all. Dunning, Euler, and Gardiner
were not very pleased by the prospect that Robertson and King held
out to Canada. However, King got his colleagues to agree that he
might tell the British "how far we were prepared to go."[60] All, however, was to be "contingent on the receipt of assurances that a satisfactory agreement could be negotiated with the United States." South
Africa was to be approached on maize, and External Affairs would
prepare a memorandum for the cabinet on the chances of a Canadian-
American agreement.[61] Wilgress, McKinnon, and Robertson should
go to Washington "as soon as possible."[62]

The British, nevertheless, viewed the Canadian attitude as far
from helpful. Cabinet ministers from lumbering and apple-growing
constituencies seemed "anxious," in the words of one member of the
Foreign Office, "to avoid at all costs any reduction in Canada's preferences." Canada, another official wrote, "is needlessly obstruc-
tionist."[63] But Canada was now committed to the trade agreement
process, and Washington was still insisting that "we must have
signed agreement with Great Britain before agreeing to further
negotiations with Canada."[64] It was far from clear what more Ottawa
could do.

Hume Wrong, on the staff of Canada's minister in Washington,
approached the State Department on 12 October with the news that his

country's "ace negotiators" would arrive in Washington shortly.[65] Francis Sayre spoke of urgency, but also reiterated "that it would be quite impossible for the United States to make any payment to the Canadians for their relinquishment of preferences — that we could not pay twice for the same market opportunities." This note had been sounded before, as we have seen. Presumably Sayre and his colleagues believed it, although what it really meant was far from obvious. Washington was still most reluctant to receive three Canadians, or to send anyone to Ottawa.[66]

Something now happened, however, to change Sayre's mind about simultaneous negotiations. We have not been able to discover how that difficult feat was achieved, what evidence and arguments were applied, or by whom. We can report only that neither British nor Canadian representations seem to have been involved. On 13 October Wrong called on Hull, Sayre and Herbert Feis. Sayre, adamant only the day before, announced that he was reluctantly prepared to allow negotiations with Canada and the United Kingdom at the same time. Wrong telephoned the intelligence at once to Ottawa, where Norman Robertson reported it to King. From Washington, Wrong confirmed by letter that Sayre "was personally ready to waive his objections to simultaneous negotiations."[67]

The Canadians responded at once. The Americans would soon discover why: all by themselves, King and the Department of External Affairs had decided to propose a full-scale renegotiation of the 1935 Canadian-American trade agreement. For the moment, however, King simply said that he would send his three wise men to Washington without delay, and he explained that to prevent the Americans from having to pay twice he "thought it important that the British should be made to agree to give up or revise certain of the margins of preference they now enjoyed in Canada."[68] Britain, of course, had itself made this proposal to King in June. King had forgotten the point, and had then become aware of it, at least for a while, over the summer of 1937. Perhaps he had forgotten again, and thought he was saying something new. Certainly the British had never put the idea to the Americans, so far as we can discover, but perhaps it was a faint glimmering of this possibility that had changed Sayre's mind.

It had become worthwhile for Canada and Britain to discuss the concessions with which they could both live. Until it was certain that the Americans would agree to break the impasse, such conversations would have been a waste of time. Sir Francis Floud reported to Whitehall that the Canadians would concede a reduction in the apple preference to 3/6 so long as there was no reduction until after the close of the current shipping season. Canada would also accept some reduction of the timber duties, and free entry for non-empire wheat so long as the ceiling for Britain's own domestic subsidized output reverted to 6 million quarters per annum from the higher level that had been fixed in 1937. The government was also anxious that the flour preference be retained.[69] These were the concessions that Robertson had proposed and that the Canadian cabinet, hectored by King, had approved. In dealing with the United States, Canada proposed to press for the maximum concessions that were allowed by the Trade Agreements Act.[70] This was hardly a goal that would have caused enthusiasm in Whitehall. The harder Canada might press, the greater the risk that the United States would balk, anxious though its officials were to make some progress before the spring of 1938.

Annoyance in London at Canada's behaviour was growing apace, and it was tentatively decided not to proceed with further Anglo-American talks until it was clear what the Canadian-American discussions would produce.[71] The State Department, however, totally unprepared for the comprehensive proposals that Canada was making, reported that it could not consider doing anything serious about Canada's scheme for at least three weeks. Hull talked to King in Ottawa on 20 October, but nothing of substance was discussed. To make matters worse, Robertson was dreaming of a "reconvened Ottawa conference" which could meet at Washington and quickly resolve all the interlocking difficulties.[72] Robertson, evidently, had forgotten what had really happened at the Ottawa Conference, and what that experience had really been like. Whitehall certainly had not. Nothing would more quickly chill the hearts of the officials in London than the thought of a reconvened Ottawa Conference. Nor would Whitehall accept Canada's condition regarding the abolition of the wheat duty.[73]

Sir William Brown had lunch with R.W. Bingham, the American ambassador, on 27 October. Brown told Bingham that he "deplored" the delay that the scope of the Canadian request would occasion in Washington. He also said that the State Department had suggested to Chalkley that there might be negotiations in Washington with Britain and with all the dominions at once. The idea had perhaps come from Robertson. The prospect, at any rate, filled Brown with "horror," partly because it reminded him of the Ottawa Conference and partly because he thought there was a risk that the dominions might "logroll the United Kingdom into untenable positions."[74] The news of this exchange reached the British high commissioner in Ottawa by the next day, at which time he transmitted it to King.[75] Washington's conference proposal is hard to credit. The Americans, after all, had fought against simultaneous negotiations with two countries; a conference would represent an even more drastic shift in position.

Whitehall immediately asked Washington not to embark on any complex structure of negotiation:

> in normal circumstances we should have welcomed simultaneous negotiations by the United States also with Australia, New Zealand, and South Africa, but in view of the limited time now available for finding a basis of negotiation of a United States-United Kingdom agreement such a course would introduce complications which would be likely to make the conclusion of negotiations impossible within the time available. . . . Our anxiety in this regard arises solely from the time factor but on that score it is very serious.[76]

While pleased that the United States seemed to have changed its mind regarding the impossibility of simultaneous negotiations, Whitehall was more than a little put out that Canada had failed to consult Britain before approaching the State Department with its very long shopping list. Because of that, there was even less reason for the British to consult Canada before acting to move the Anglo-American conversations a step further.[77] The dominions would be informed: that would be all.

British officials had been examining the concessions that the United States seemed to be offering. The closer these were studied, the less their value. As R.M. Nowell of the Board of Trade noted, "while the duty reductions offered in the US memorandum of [4 June] are not a great advance ... on the reductions offered in the schedule of late 1936 ... it is appreciated that they represent a considerable proportion of total dutiable imports from the United Kingdom." They did not, however, cover all the items of which Britain was a principal supplier. The Americans' June 1937 list seemed to have added goods to the value of a mere $1.2 million, taking the total to $43.1 million[78] — 23 per cent of Britain's 1936 exports to the USA.

Nevertheless, British ministers wanted to proceed. Britain would have to develop a more concrete and attractive response to America's list of "essentials." No one suggested that such a response would necessarily resolve the impasse; the idea seems to have been that if the Americans knew exactly what Britain would do, they might get on faster in their discussions with the Canadians. The chancellor of the exchequer, Sir John Simon, argued that some dramatic action on Britain's part was necessary: "the difficulties in the way of discussions between Canada and the United States have been overcome. . . . It seems, however, most improbable that any solution of the difficulties will emerge from these USA-Canada discussions. Our future policy should now be settled on this assumption ... if the present deadlock is to be removed some positive step by the United Kingdom government will be required."[79]

When the cabinet discussed the situation in the afternoon of 27 October, the minutiae quickly came to dominate the discussion, as indeed they had in the Canadian cabinet. Such a tendency, inevitable in parliamentary government, would be bound to plague any attempt to pursue "appeasement," whether economic or political, by means of tariff-bargaining. From the agriculture minister there was much opposition to the suggestion that the apple duty should be cut.[80] He was not pleased, either, about the prospect of free flour, or about a reduction in the tinned loganberry duty, which sheltered a British canning industry (presumably he meant a factory). The other suggested improvements from Britain's earlier offer[81] occasioned little discussion. Neither the Board of Trade nor the Trade and Agriculture Committee was yet prepared to concede anything on dried prunes, apricots, raisins, tobacco, or softwood, but they would offer to remove the wheat duty. The question of the flour duty was still under discussion. The president of the Board of Trade suggested that, in view of the latest news from Washington, Britain should not wait for the Canadian-American talks to end but should simply inform empire governments before transmitting its new offer to Washington. It was everyone's wish that the "warning" should be short, lest the dominions make trouble. No one liked the Americans' method of proceeding, but Oliver Stanley noted that Britain had tried to alter it in the preceding spring without success, and "it was therefore barren to discuss it further."

The British decided to transmit their latest ideas to the United States on the explicit understanding that there would have to be adequate compensation by the US and that the dominions would have to agree where necessary. If American offers were attractive, it was hoped that the dominions would agree in the end.[82] The word went to the dominions on 29 October;[83] the United States would hear a week later.

The Canadian government at once became agitated. If the apple preference fell to the level the UK proposed, Floud reported from Ottawa, the minister from Nova Scotia, J.L. Ilsley, would probably leave the cabinet. Canada asked if the offer might hang fire until after its cabinet had considered it, but Whitehall refused.[84] The next day Floud transmitted King's request for an American-apple duty that was 8 per cent higher than what Whitehall had suggested, and stated that Ian Mackenzie, British Columbia's leading minister, was unsettled about concessions on Douglas fir doors.[85] There was still potential, King cabled Neville Chamberlain, for Anglo-Canadian discussions regarding pears and lumber. Canada still wanted Britain to reduce its domestic "wheat quota" by 25 per cent as a condition of acquiescence in abolition of the foreign wheat duty, but it was willing to lose the UK preferences on copper, lead, and zinc. Canada was, as well, still unhappy about the British "Schedule 1 reservation" affecting free entry of dairy and poultry products.[86] Chamberlain refused to consider a change in the wheat quota, but he agreed that, for the time being and subject to the need for modification if the Americans were not forthcoming, the suggested apple duty should be what Canada had proposed.[87] Britain agreed because "it is understood that in the informal conversations between the United States and Canadian officials" the Canadians had already said as much.[88]

Sir Ronald Lindsay conveyed the British proposals to the Americans in Washington on 5 November 1937. Stanley gave a copy to Bingham in London.[89] Sir William Brown, continuing his informal talks with the American ambassador, explained some days later that Britain had gone as far as she could go for the time being. Canada, Brown explained, had responded encouragingly, but Australia had not, and he was still afraid that joint Australian-Canadian demands would put Britain "in an impossible position." Britain was prepared to apply pressure to the other dominions, but not to Canada. The senior dominion's special relationship to the US dictated that any Canadian-American talks would have to be "closely geared" to the Anglo-American negotiations. As for the other dominions, "we will, of course, bear the responsibility of exerting the pressure."[90]

Cordell Hull told John Hickerson that he felt like telling the British "to go to hell." Perhaps the United States should lay down some more battleships and withdraw into "our own shell."[91] This, however, was the heat of the moment. The Americans had come too far and Hull wanted an agreement too much. Bingham simply expressed to Brown the American disappointment at the small advance over previous offers.[92]

The latest British proposals were considered not only in the State Department but in the Department of Agriculture, which appears not to have been consulted heretofore. President Roosevelt waited until Henry Wallace, the secretary of agriculture, had recommended that formal negotiations should begin before giving his own approval. Wallace explained that, if the trade agreements program was to be satisfactory from an agricultural point of view, there would have to be an Anglo-American understanding that would produce "real and substantial" gains in the British market. Although Wallace thought the most recent British offers an improvement over those of April and July, they still seemed "in some degree disappointing." Something more would certainly have to be done about empire tobacco and about lard, and it was reasonable to hope that an agreement would represent "a definite retreat on the part of the British away from the preferential system."[93] Hull and Wallace, it seemed, were as one on the nefarious influence of the imperial preference. The agriculture secretary, furthermore, was concentrating singlemindedly on the possible economic payoffs for American farmers. No large international visions for Henry Wallace.

The Americans, then, were still far from happy with the British position. Substantial improvement was "essential." They had nevertheless come to the point that they were willing to say that they "contemplated" negotiations with Britain, and also with Canada.[94] A formal public announcement to this effect was made on 18 November 1937.[95] Privately, however, the Americans still said they assumed that Britain would obtain the "concurrence" of other empire governments, and the UK government was obliged to explain that she could not commit the rest of the Commonwealth in this way.[96]

The leading protagonists were all convinced that their actions had enormous potential in the realm of international politics. British prime minister Neville Chamberlain wrote to his sister that the "reason why I have been prepared . . . to go a long way to get this treaty is precisely because I reckoned it would help to educate American opinion to act more and more with us, and because I felt sure it would frighten the totalitarians. Coming at this moment, it looks just like an answer to the Berlin-Rome-Tokyo axis."[97] Mackenzie King hoped that the process might "lead to further freeing of trade barriers between Northern European countries;" it was "certain to affect trade relations with France, and may be the means of bringing about the economic appeasement of Europe which alone can save another world war." Forgetting the Ottawa Conference, in which he had not taken part, King told his diary that "the negotiation means the beginning of the largest international trade transaction which the world has thus far witnessed."[98] Cordell Hull was less sanguine. The world was "on fire" with international unrest in both Europe and the far east. He told Lindsay that "unless those who share common desires to protect the precious things of our civilization stand together in some practical program, such as the trade agreements program, we may be too late."[99]

It had taken almost five months to bring three willing parties to the stage where the public preliminaries to negotiation could be commenced. If such tortoise-like pace was meant to avert world war, one could only hope that the Axis powers would mount their offensives not with tanks and aircraft, but with oxen and three-toed sloths. The lengthy talks about talks do not reflect credit on any of the participants. In Washington there was a regrettable pertinacity in the face of an impossible negotiating situation, and there was also a noticeable tendency to ignore the information which flowed from

London. In Ottawa there was a remarkable ability to misunderstand what London was saying, and a not very attractive eagerness to seize the economic advantage—an eagerness which went against the grain of King's rhetoric, perceptibly increased the delays, and certainly added to the risks of failure. In London one detects a certain reticence, and perhaps suspicion, especially in dealing with the Americans on economic matters: if Whitehall had told Washington that it was willing to let the dominions reduce some of their "bound preferential margins," perhaps the United States would have come more speedily to the realization that it not only could but must negotiate with Canada and Britain simultaneously.

In their own internal processes of decision-making, furthermore, none of the governments had been exactly quick off the mark. We must remember, however, that all three were contemplating something quite new—a trilateral co-ordination not only of negotiation but of concession. Even at the Ottawa Conference nothing of the sort had occurred. To some extent the dominions had negotiated collectively with the United Kingdom, but in devising their several bilateral agreements among themselves they made no serious effort at "linkage." Britain, the United States and Canada had not only to work out a goal, but also to find a path to that goal. Mutual suspicions and confusions made the task more difficult than it need have been, but the problem itself was inherently complex.

The international situation, meanwhile, had not improved since the Imperial Conference so far as Britain was concerned. France still reeled from one domestic crisis to another, the Spanish Civil War continued, and Japan had renewed its attempt to conquer China. But Hitler's aggressive words had not yet been translated into really worrisome action. Thus the putative negotiators in London, Washington, and Ottawa might well have hoped that there was still time for "economic appeasement." Sad to say, that was not so.

CHAPTER 5

From "Contemplation" to "Negotiation"

November 1937 - April 1938

One might suppose that after so long a period of preparation, formal negotiations could now begin almost at once. Not at all. American law required a series of steps which consumed almost five more months. Furthermore, with the benefit of hindsight, the historian can see that Britain and the dominions had reason to be glad of this law-imposed delay. Before Britain or Canada could safely approach Hull and his officials, there were many problems which they themselves would have to sort out. It was thought that things would not really get moving in Washington until after the end of December 1937. In the event, nothing of any significance happened before mid-April 1938 — just when things were becoming really unpleasant in central Europe. Long before that time the British delegation was in Washington, while Norman Robertson regularly journeyed between the Canadian and American capitals by overnight train. As week followed week with no progress, both British and Canadian tempers became perceptibly shorter. Officials and ministers in Ottawa intermittently considered possible demands and concessions, while in Washington and also in London there were much more elaborate consultations among government departments, and also between government and industry.

Meanwhile, the international crisis accelerated, creating no perceptible increase in the sense of urgency that anyone seemed to attach

Reference notes for Chapter 5 begin on p. 179.

to the prospective trade talks. Perhaps it was hoped that, for the time being, Berlin would be pacified by the mere knowledge that talks were soon to begin. If so, the hope was a vain one. The Sudeten problem was pressing itself ever more forcefully on London's attention, and so was the question of Austria, which Germany would annex on 11 March 1938.

One element in the negotiating situation was the American government's timetable, determined as this was not by the international political situation but by the Reciprocal Trade Agreements Act. Before the United States could begin formal negotiations either with Britain or with Canada, it had to go through the lengthy procedure which that Act laid down. In the ritual and terminological dance that the legislation prescribed, "intention" followed "contemplation" but only after a certain delay. First came the compiling of lists of commodities on which concessions were contemplated. On 6 January 1938, Francis Sayre sent President Roosevelt a copy of the forty-seven-page draft press release that named these contemplatives. He explained, "I need hardly add that we will not make concessions with respect to every item appearing in the list. ... I do not think it is necessary for you to pass upon this list, for no commitments are being made with regard to it."[1] A formal announcement was made the next day of the American "intention to negotiate." The officials continued to argue about a "supplementary list," and this was published only on 24 January 1938.

These lists in turn formed the basis of representations to the Committee for Reciprocity Information, the interdepartmental body of officials that held hearings and received briefs before actual negotiation could commence. Briefs from interested parties could be received up to 19 February; the committee also arranged, at its own initiative, for conversations with importers and exporters. Before the various negotiating lists were even established, the two governments had to match up, so far as possible, their tariff-classifications, definitions, and important export statistics. This was no small task. In the autumn of 1937 Washington had sent a senior Customs official, W.T.M. Beale, to work closely with the Board of Trade in coordinating tariff schedules, nomenclatures, and requests. The problems were severe indeed, and Beale worked on them into 1938. One example may suffice to show just how difficult the task was. To match terminology and satisfy the Nottingham trade without alarming the American lace interests, the original US tariff item 1529(a), "machine made laces and lace articles," became "laces, lace fabrics, and lace articles made on Levers or go-through machines, coarser than 12 points, wholly or in chief value of cotton, whether or not embroidered and however described and provided for in Paragraph 1529(a)."[2]

Working inside the Board of Trade, Beale acquired an intimate knowledge not merely of the procedures by which Britain was formulating its requests but also of the actual concessions that the country's trades were proposing. He wrote that the board "bases its requests for concessions almost entirely on trade representations." Where there was any question, "procedure in each case has been to give me their file on the item in doubt." This included the representations received by the board "and in most cases the recommendations of the trades as to the concessions to be sought." "In those cases," he added, "where the eventual requests of the British Delegation differ from the requests of the trade the information may be of use in negotiations."[3] Beale told the State Department that it was the Lancashire trade and Nottingham that were responsible for the board's very sweeping requests on cottons and laces.[4] One wonders whether the British knew just how much they were giving away.

The hearings before the Committee on Reciprocity Information began on 14 March, giving (in the words of a contemporary) "ample opportunity for the expression of opinion by sections of the community who were alarmed at the prospect of competition from British imports." Around 650 sworn statements were submitted; more than 400 witnesses testified. Some of the petitioners aimed at concessions in the British market, but the majority had in mind the threat of increased British imports.[5] Although, as we have already observed, the United States did not allow any negotiation unless Britain was a "principal supplier" of a given commodity, the final lists did not include all or even most of such goods.

With respect to the demands the Americans would put forth, information had been accumulating in Washington at a sustained pace. Late in 1937 and early in 1938, there were vigorous representations regarding plywood doors, milled rice, apples, pears, ham, bacon, and lard. It is noticeable that the requests from these trade associations, especially from the American Institute of Meat Packers, passed directly into the demands that the American negotiators would make later in 1938. The meat packers, for instance, wanted a 50 per cent increase in quota, reduction or abolition of duties on lard and canned meat, free entry for ham and bacon, and "greater flexibility" in the administration of Britain's ham and bacon quota.[6]

The lumber interests were another potent example of the work of American lobbyists. In February 1938, the National Lumber Manufacturers' Association asked for "tariff parity" as between American and imperial timber in the United Kingdom, or, if that could not be attained, strong punitive measures against Canadian timber in the US market.[7] A few days later, Francis Sayre having asked the Department of Agriculture to comment on the "wisdom of including forest products" in the negotiating package, that department recommended some concessions which might be proposed. A steady stream of representations from governors, mayors, and other political functionaries in lumbering states followed.[8] All asked for "absolute parity" in lumber duties; none mentioned the measures of tariff, quota, and country-of-origin discrimination with respect to the marking of individual deals and planks that the United States applied against Canadian lumber. Indeed, at this very time the lumber interests were pressing the Congress to impose new and more stringent measures, especially with respect to marking, measurement, and taxation. In March 1938, Sayre tried to explain the problems to Wilson Compton of the National Lumber Manufacturers' Association. The new measures, he said, would make it "much more difficult for us to secure proper outlets for American lumber in the United Kingdom." Sayre returned to the fray the next month, but the lumber interests continued to argue that every piece of lumber should be marked with its country of origin, and they criticized him for bringing the inconsistency to Congressional attention.[9] Sayre may have been anxious to achieve moderation with respect to new protectionist measures on the American side, but he and his negotiating team certainly pressed the substance of the lumbermen's case, without significant deviation, in their negotiations with the British. And, lest there be any wavering, the demand from the lumber lobby for "tariff parity" continued through 1938.[10]

American consulates both in Britain and in Canada provided a torrent of information—some requested, much not, some well-digested and to the point, and most not. The consulates in Birmingham and Manchester reported that there was a good deal of domestic annoyance that the Board of Trade was not publishing a list of its possible concessions as the United States had to do. The Federation of British Industries was mobilizing the protectionist cause. Manchester, however, remained resolutely free trade, and strongly in favour of a trade agreement, having seen its textile exports to the United States fall from 174 million square yards in 1923 to 13 million in 1936, at a time when the American market absorbed 7,000 million overall.[11] Birmingham suggested a bargain on car tariffs. The Americans should reduce the duty on low-powered cars, while the British should do the same for high-powered ones. But, the consul observed, any cuts would be "violently resisted by the powerful British automotive and allied industries."[12] Washington's negotiators certainly saw the Birmingham consulate reports.[13]

The American consul in London sent a memorandum that kept its gaze firmly fixed on what had gradually come to be the real purpose of the trade negotiations from the American viewpoint. There might, he admitted, "appear at first glance to be some embarrassment from the fact that the British trade figures for 1937 reveal an increase in the United Kingdom's imports from the United States of 22.5%, while British exports to the USA increased by only 15.2%." Thus British commodity imports from the United States cost 114 million pounds, while Britain earned only 31 million pounds by selling goods to the United States. Fortunately the consul, an earnest disciple of Cordell Hull, was able to find a "however" that would satisfy the secretary of state. Britain's imports of tobacco, fruits, and other important agricultural products, and of miscellaneous manufactured products other than oils, metals, and machinery, showed no marked increase in 1937 while many of these actually declined in value. It was clear that the increase in British imports must be regarded as temporary and abnormal, caused by extraordinary demands for certain products required for rearmament work and for the accumulation of stocks for defence purposes, not by "any lessening in the hindrances to our own export trade to the United Kingdom which lie in the tariff duties and especially in the Ottawa preferences." The consul went on to remark that the Americans had a smaller share of British imports of canned fruit, apples, pears, grapefruit, leather, timber, tobacco and doors — apart altogether from the stimulation of Britain's own production that protection was causing.[14] In the course of 1938, all of these products figured largely in US demands.

The British were less highly organized. The pre-negotiation phase began in November 1937 as campaigners against the agreement continued their battle. Sir Henry Page Croft, L.S. Amery, who had been secretary of state for dominions affairs in the Baldwin government of the middle and late 1920s, and a substantial parcel of MPs in the parliamentary committee of the Empire Industries Association, were in the forefront of the opposition.

Neither home nor empire protection, they argued, must be sacrificed for the sake of "some illusory project for the revival of economic internationalism." The president of the National Union of Manufacturers urged the government not to be in too much of a hurry, while the Federation of British Industries, worrying about the instability of the dollar, urged that no agreement be made which could not be modified or quickly ended. Doubtless sensitive about the idea that they were engaging in an exercise for entirely the wrong reasons, the government felt it necessary to state publicly that it was seeking a trading bargain and not a political agreement.[15]

On 14 December 1937 the British Embassy gave the State Department a "provisional list of the items in the United States tariff on which the United Kingdom government will probably request duty reduction." It was explained, however, that the Board of Trade had not yet completed its consultations with trade interests. The British would probably wish to make certain additions to the list. Then, at a later stage, requests would be deliberately limited so as to confine concessions as much as possible to those "which are likely to yield the maximum benefit to United Kingdom exporters."[16] Later that month the British asked for conventionalization of the existing duties on whiskey and gin and on many items then duty-free; more than four dozen items were also added to the mid-December list.[17]

Most of the records of British industrial representations seem not to have survived. The commodity files for American industrial requests do still exist, however, and these illustrate the way in which the Board of Trade proceeded. Wherever appropriate, it asked for the advice of the Customs Department and of the Import Duties Advisory Committee. The former generally restricted its report to questions of revenue and the complexities of administration, while the latter worried about such matters as protective requests from industry, problems of defence-related activities, and the implications for domestic economic activity. Trade interests were not always approached.[18] Often the officials themselves gathered the basic data, the aim sometimes being simply to establish whether or not the United States was the "principal supplier." There was also a good deal of concern about the question of empire versus foreign supply, and a remarkable willingness to explore subdivision of customs classifications so as to avoid the extension of benefit, through mfn arrangements, to third parties.

When the trades were consulted, there was no standard pattern for doing so. Thus, for instance, the industry was not asked to comment on the question of wireless sets, but the British Electrical Manufacturers' Association provided a detailed report on vacuum cleaners, and the Society of Motor Manufacturers and Trades reported at length on the question of the car duties. The automobile manufacturers were very worried about competition from the subsidized German firm of Opel. This firm was American-owned, but that fact was never mentioned, and one suspects it may not have been realized. Officials and manufacturers alike noted that the "high-class" automobile firms, which might face more vigorous American competition if duties were lowered, were important ingredients in the defence build-up which was by then underway.[19]

An amusing though insignificant puzzle arose over peanut butter. The officials did not know what this was. Authorities thought "it would be difficult for a Customs officer to be satisfied as to its nature," and Unilever, approached on the question, said that it was almost

Plate 1
John W. Dafoe's *Winnipeg Free Press* and its famous cartoonist,
Arch Dale, were among the campaigners for lower tariffs
Winnipeg Free Press, 13 November 1936

Plate 2

Seated left to right, Cordell Hull, Mackenzie King and Franklin D. Roosevelt sign the 1935 Canada-United States Trade Agreement in Washington

National Archives of Canada C31017

Plate 3
"My old friend." Prime Minister King (left) and President Roosevelt
at Quebec City, 1936
National Archives of Canada C16768

Plate 4
Preparing to ward off the imperialist dragon, a dapper Mackenzie King
arrives at St. James's Palace, London, England, 1937
National Archives of Canada C117665

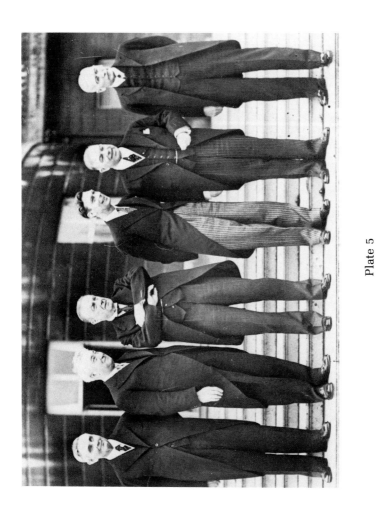

Plate 5

The prime ministers of the Commonwealth at the Imperial Conference of 1937. From left to right, Savage of New Zealand, Lyons of Australia, Baldwin of Great Britain, King George VI, Mackenzie King of Canada, Hertzog of South Africa

National Archives of Canada C13193

Plate 6
The dominion high commissioners and other high-spirited well-wishers see
the British prime minister, Neville Chamberlain (hat raised) off to his conference with Adolph Hitler in Munich, September 1938. First to the right
in the first row, the Australian representative in London, Stanley Bruce;
fourth to the right is the Canadian high commissioner, Vincent Massey;
Lord Halifax, British foreign secretary, is fifth to the right
Canadian Forces PMR 74-937

Plate 7

The dignitaries arrive for the signing of the Canada-United States trade agreement, Washington, 1938. From left to right: Mackenzie King, Cordell Hull, O.D. Skelton

National Archives of Canada C38741

Plate 8

The American president and Canadian prime minister in President Roosevelt's office, just after the signing of the 1938 Canada-United States trade agreement.
Dr. Skelton is standing third from the left
National Archives of Canada C62098

unknown in Britain, being "rather unpalatable to the ordinary taste, and manufactured solely for retail sale in the Vegetarian Restaurants." Unilever thought that "no objection would be raised to allowing this stuff to be put on the free or reduced list." Movies, however, were another matter. The Americans wanted the British to reduce, or perhaps abolish, the "quota" regulations that for more than a decade had provided protection for British films. This response was handled wholly inside the Board of Trade, where officials were fond of quoting from Imperial Conference resolutions, when empire politicians had talked about the cultural importance and impact of the cinema.[20]

In addition to the Anglo-American preliminaries, and besides the elaboration of lists and demands in the two major participants, the empire countries themselves had a great deal of work to do before anything serious could happen. Neither Canada nor Southern Rhodesia had formally agreed to Britain's "composite offer" of 5 November 1937. Australia had attached two conditions to its consent. Britain, first of all, should help Australia to negotiate with the Americans. Secondly, in order to provide protection during the months when Australian apples arrived in Britain, American apples should not pay a lower duty in the period from 15 March to 15 August. Canada did not like the Australian suggestion because it would expose Canadian apples to competition from the US; Britain thought the Americans would not agree unless the cheap rate ran on at least to 15 April. The Americans agreed to hold informal discussions with Australian officials.[21] Australia had also asked if Canada would like to exchange cables on questions of mutual interest rising out of the trade negotiations. The Canadian cabinet replied that it would be glad to do so.[22]

As a sop to the dominions, and in accord with Canada's suggestion, Britain quickly proceeded to waive her "Schedule I reservation" which allowed her to impose duties on empire dairy products. This "reservation" had been in the original set of Ottawa Agreements, and the United Kingdom had preserved it through later negotiations with the several dominions.[23] The waiver would apply until 20 August 1940, and it did not extend to quotas. British officials argued, however, that there was little point for the time being in offering America free entry for copper, lead, and zinc, in that none of these metals figured on the American lists of "essential" and "non-essential" (or industrial) goods. As for softwood timber, the question was still under study, a position which it would occupy for many months to come.[24]

So far as the co-ordination of empire offers and tactics was concerned, there matters rested. It was obvious that nothing important had been settled among the several realms of His Majesty in this curious, complicated, easily-misunderstood empire, where dominion autonomy made common imperial policies or actions next to impossible. Furthermore, by this time Canada had passed its list of requests—the list which had been put to the Americans in the autumn of 1937—to London. There was amazement and consternation at the package the senior dominion had prepared: Ottawa wanted concessions on 226 separate items, which together seem to have covered well over $43 million worth of Canadian sales to the United States in 1936—some 13 per cent of Canada-US export trade in that year. Canada, in other words, was seeking concessions on a volume of trade as large as that on which Washington thought concessions to Britain might be possible.[25] Whether Ottawa realized this fact is not clear.

At the beginning of February 1938, the United States had yet to tell Ottawa what concessions she might desire from Canada.[26] The Canadians themselves were becoming alarmed because domestic pressures would probably force the King government to make unilateral tariff reductions at the time when it brought down its budget. Among the affected items would probably be such things as cotton, cream separators, and automobiles, goods on which Canada had hoped to offer concessions to the United States. Officials feared that they would not be able to get quick release from Australia on raisins if the United States raised the question of Canada's preferential duty only at the last minute. An informal list of American demands did reach Ottawa in February. Only then did Canada learn that the United States would demand concessions on raisins, currants, and anthracite—the first two commodities of immense importance to Australia, and the third to the United Kingdom herself.[27]

There were already signs that the elaborate American tariff-planning machine had seized up. On 27 January, the State Department reported that "because of the very large number of new commodities included in our published lists ... we suggested that the British delegation might prefer to defer its sailing for two weeks."[28] Even this, however, would not nearly be enough time for the Americans. The Committee on Reciprocity Information would need many weeks to do its work, first on British requests and then on Canadian. There had been some sense, after all, in the American reluctance to undertake parallel negotiations both with Britain and with Canada. When the British delegation did arrive in Washington late in February 1938, it was met, according to a contemporary account, by an intensive State Department "broadcasting and lecturing campaign to educate the American public on the value of the impending agreement."[29] Despite such apparent good will, the British delegation found little to do. For many weeks it was forced to restrict its attention to the "general clauses"—that decorative fringe of non-tariff matters which trade agreements and commercial treaties so often contain.

What could really be achieved, indeed, remained uncertain. In 1935 Britain provided only 7 per cent of America's imports, and 60 per cent of those goods paid no duty, although on the dutiable group the average *ad valorem* rate of duty was 43 per cent. The negotiators could not have known, although they may have suspected, what sorts of commitments to domestic interests the American side was making, or soon would make. In February a State Department memorandum spoke of making efforts "to obtain concessions which will increase our apple exports."[30] Early in March, Sayre told a lace-making senator that "there was no intention of granting any concession which would seriously injure American industry"—and this at a time when the domestic lace industry, sheltered behind a duty of 60 per cent *ad valorem*, supplied 99 per cent of US consumption.[31] Sir Ronald Lindsay's early optimism that narrow national interests might be set aside in the cause of international harmony—and Cordell Hull's reasoning along similar lines—seemed far from the minds of the people actually doing the detailed planning. And, in the absence of contrary instructions from higher authority, it is not surprising that the larger issues of economic appeasement and international politics had vanished from the American view.

It was agreed that the British and Canadian delegations would keep in touch and be frank with one another. Norman Robertson and the British officials then proceeded to air their joint perplexities regarding flour, timber, apples, and hams. A.E. Overton, leading the British negotiating team, explained that his government's customs and excise authorities were anxious to limit the scope of specific duties on timber because in order to levy such duties they would have to set up and train an entire corps of timber surveyors, but it was agreed that any discussion would be deferred until the full Canadian delegation had arrived. Overton gave Robertson a list of the items of interest to Canada where Britain was thinking of concessions, and Robertson explained what was known of American demands on Canada. The Canadian was inclined to favour suspension, but not abolition, of certain margins of preference, such as those on lumber and "possibly wheat." Britain, said Overton, was prepared to consider a wide range of concessions.[32] Whitehall did not propose, however, to give free entry to any of these goods.

The American "must list," and later submissions, had not explicitly treated Britain's dependent empire, although Whitehall had long known that in due course Washington would have proposals to make affecting these territories. On 23 February, just as he and his

British colleagues reached Washington, Overton learned for the first time just what the United States was demanding. There were to be no new preferences, or any enlarging of existing preferences, anywhere in the colonial empire. Preferences on eighteen important commodities[33] were to be wiped out. All surviving preferences were to be cut by 50 per cent.[34] As Overton remarked, Robertson was rather shocked by these "pretty sweeping" demands "aimed directly and principally at the preferences enjoyed by Canada in the British West Indies." Any substantial modification of the present preferences, Robertson noted, would compel his government to give notice of the termination of the Canada-British West Indies Trade Agreement. How could progress be made on this basis? Robertson and his government would examine proposals for modifying particular colonial preferences, but "would not give any general waiver."

Robertson immediately approached John Hickerson of the State Department. "I explained," he reported, "that we were worried by the continuous postponement of the opening of negotiations.... We would have to talk in terms of specific rates and could only do this when we have received the United States requests in definite form." Hickerson thought that he could do no more than pass on, in ten days or two weeks, a confidential copy of recommendations that his team was submitting to their Trade Agreements Committee for approval. The Canadian team would soon come back to Washington to consult with the British, but Hickerson said that the Americans would not be ready for any sort of "continuous negotiation" until the end of March.[35]

By mid-March Robertson knew that public hearings on the Canada-United States proposals would begin on 4 April. He asked his prime minister to let the Canadian delegation go down in the week beginning 21 March in order to advance preparations for the negotiations themselves. The addition of the colonial empire to American demands seemed to Robertson to be an afterthought, and he warned the prime minister that it would give great trouble in the negotiations.[36] By this time Ottawa knew that the Americans wanted Canada to modify her bound preferences to the West Indies, South Africa, Australia, and Britain, but "we do not know what concessions the United States is asking," and so serious preparations or intra-imperial discussions had not been possible.

Canadian prime minister Mackenzie King was inclined to overlook the difficulties. After all, the whole tripartite development had been his handiwork: not only had he commenced to talk to the Americans in August 1937, but the example of the Canada-United States trade agreement of 1935 had "led to this wider effort at reciprocal trade between the United Kingdom and the United States." His own part in the business, he wrote, "has been indispensable. I have . . . been able to bring matters to the stage they have now reached."[37] We do not know what Washington thought of King's role. In Whitehall, the Foreign Office had recently taken uncomplimentary note—a "minor, & less effective, Roosevelt"—of King's endeavours on the world stage.[38] To British official observers the behaviour of the little round man with pretensions to statesmanship very often seemed difficult, ignorant, dilatory, confused, selfish and emotional— anything but indispensable.

After almost four years of talks about talks, the trilateral trade negotiations had not yet begun. Furthermore, the negotiating partners were still in a good deal of disarray. Canada did not yet know definitively what the United States would ask of her; Britain was better informed, but understood that new demands would be forthcoming. The British negotiations did not yet know just how unhelpful their American counterparts would be, but they were aware that they could not possibly give America what was on its "must list." Canada had been drawn in because, given the nature of the American proposals to Britain, there appeared to be no alternative. It had seized the opportunity with a vigour which seems to have annoyed both Britain and the United States. Within the empire, it was already perfectly clear that the several dominions would not meet the American requests at all readily. Parallel difficulties existed with Britain's trading partners in northern Europe. And the demands with respect to Britain's colonial empire, in which Canada had an important stake, must have generated a chill wind in the corridors of power. To the outside world, the trilateral trade talks might have seemed a symbol of democratic amity. To the participants, the discussions were proving to be as unpleasant as they were prolonged.

CHAPTER 6

Discussions to Some Purpose

April - September 1938

In the spring of 1938, three delegations began to negotiate two trade agreements—one more than the original sponsor of the project, the United States, had wanted or intended. In November 1938, exhausted and irritable, the negotiators finished their task. The real problems arose over particular commodities, especially softwood timber, apples, wheat and flour, lard, and anthracite coal. The system of imperial preference proved not to be a special irritant. It was simply one element in the net of circumstances and commitments within which trade agreements would have to be devised; commitments to other parties and domestic imperatives were more productive of difficulty than the "imperial" dimension. The trilateral nature of the process added further perplexities.

The negotiations proceeded in parallel with two outside developments—one economic and one political. The year 1938 saw a renewal of slump, as the economy of the western world slipped from the not very impressive peak it had reached in 1937. Prices, production, and employment all turned downward. Partly because the statistical data were better in North America, the renewal of slump was more noticeable in the United States than in the United Kingdom, where, indeed, politicians' attention was directed primarily toward the political developments in central Europe. On March 11, 1938, Germany occupied and annexed Austria. At once the Sudeten Germans began to agitate anew for an *anschluss* of their own. When British and French leaders met in London on April 28 and 29, 1938,

---

Reference notes for Chapter 6 begin on p. 180.

they agreed to press the Czechoslovak government to make suitable concessions. Late in May came rumours of German troop movements, and a partial Czechoslovak mobilization. Through the summer of 1938 the Czechoslovak government negotiated with the Sudeten German Party, and the Nazi menace increased. On September 15, Neville Chamberlain would meet Hitler.

The Washington negotiations were run on the American side by two State Department officials, John Hickerson and Harry Hawkins, chief of the Division of Trade Agreements. Both had been involved since the beginning of the talks in 1934. On some technical issues they received assistance from other officials, but to a remarkable extent they carried on the conversations by themselves, and were apparently obliged by lack of time to carry the record of proceedings in their heads. It should be remembered that they had to produce two inter-related agreements, vastly increasing the complexity of the negotiating task. Furthermore, they were at home, directly exposed to pressure from all directions, and endowed with no independent power to take decisions or make commitments. Everything had to be referred to an interdepartmental committee, and all important points had to go to Hull or to Roosevelt himself. The secretary of state, who knew remarkably little about the details of the negotiations, might fix his theoretical gaze on the large questions of international politics to which his trade agreement program was related. By the nature of their mandate, his officials had to set their sights much lower, on the horsepowers of various cars, the exporting seasons of apple orchards, and the dimensions of timbers, deals, and scantlings.

British negotiators often remarked on the frustrations and delays caused by the American machinery of negotiation. They had been given very precise initial instructions,[1] probably because (unlike Ottawa in 1932) no cabinet ministers would be present. The inter-departmental delegation, under A.E. Overton of the Board of Trade, conducted its business in an orderly and organized manner. Although major policy questions and shifts in position were referred to Whitehall, which was kept informed by cable, the delegation proceeded from principles which were clearly understood and not subject to day-to-day alteration.

The British found particular difficulty in coping with the American tendency to change the terms of the negotiations. America's demands tended to increase, often in unexpected ways, as concessions were swallowed without trace and new demands were generated, while old imperatives were pursued with fundamentalist vigour. The Americans were loath to understand that negotiations involved concessions by both sides, or that there were some things which the United Kingdom, with the best will in the world, could not do. They seemed remarkably uninterested in the possibility that there were domestic political realities in the United Kingdom as well as in the United States, or that the British had treaty obligations with other countries, obligations which could not be casually cast aside.

The British delegation consisted of representatives of the Dominions Office, Agriculture Ministry, and the Customs, as well as Overton and J.A. Stirling of the Board of Trade. The Foreign Office was of course already on the spot in the British Embassy. The delegation was housed at the luxurious Shoreham Hotel, where it occupied spacious quarters for a much longer time than anyone could have imagined. In the delegation's instructions there was no reference to larger considerations of international politics. Everything was couched in terms of trade. The delegation was told to seek the "greatest possible concessions," especially for woollens, cottons, linens, and other textiles. Cuts in these areas, the Board of Trade judged, might genuinely help the export market. Something should also be got for Britain's own agriculture; for the rest, the delegation was told to concentrate mainly "on those items for which it appears that the greatest expansion of trade is likely to follow...." The British delegation might also be asked to negotiate with the Canadians "on the reciprocal modification of margins of preference." The closest contact, at any rate, should be maintained with the dominion delegation.[2]

The British delegation met with Secretary of State Cordell Hull on 23 February, shortly after its arrival in Washington.[3] Various general matters were settled with Hawkins and Hickerson the next day. British officers also saw Norman Robertson, visiting from Ottawa, and a negotiating structure began to take shape. Pointing out that Britain's "essential list" could really be reduced to the textile items, Overton wanted to start on these as soon as possible, but he was not to be allowed to do so. The Americans would not be able to discuss matters of substance until after the Committee on Reciprocity Information had finished its hearings late in March. Hawkins wanted to begin at once on the general clauses, but that was all that could be done for the time being.

There were various bilateral negotiating committees, at which the lists of desiderata were considered. The documentation is often scanty, and no full set of minutes appears to have survived.[4] There was a general tendency for each meeting to be nastier than the last; the last meeting, which took place on 25 August, at the height of the Sudeten crisis and almost three months before the signature of the agreement, was very stormy indeed.[5] On 26 April, at the second of these "main" meetings, the American officials handed the United Kingdom delegation the draft of an agreement, giving for the first time a definite idea of the offers they would make to Britain, Newfoundland, and colonial empire. British officials found the proposals alarmingly slight.[6] The Americans were now proposing less on some items than in June 1937, and on some others, nothing at all.[7] American tariffs would be very much higher even after concessions than the duties the US was demanding. Little—not nearly enough—had been done for cottons, woollens, laces, and earthenware.[8] Certainly there was a disjunction between the American proposals and the Hull rhetoric. On cotton yard goods, for instance, the Americans offered to reduce the duty from 43 per cent to 38 per cent, but they would concede nothing on cotton clothing or on lace curtains. On woollens the average duty would fall from 88 per cent to 75 per cent, and on woollen apparel from 58 per cent to 48 per cent. Nothing was offered on blankets. The duty on plain bone china would fall from 65 per cent to 61 per cent, but there was no offer on silver plate or linen towels.[9] And so it went.

The Americans were retaining very substantial protective tariffs, and not giving as much as they could under the trade agreements act. The British delegation believed that the tariff cuts were not enough to generate any significant additional trade. Hickerson and Hawkins, however, insisted that these were "really substantial" offers; they were not meant as bargaining counters, and the Americans "could hold out no hope of any substantial improvement." Without consulting London, Overton at once told the Americans that their offers were "altogether inadequate," especially on textiles and tableware. The Board of Trade official added that "an offer of this character could not justify us in confirming the offer we had put forward last November subject to a satisfactory agreement." He was "at a loss to understand their outlook. . . . They must understand that the resulting position reached was really difficult."[10] The Americans went away to lay the matter before their Trade Agreements Committee, although they did not think the offer could be much improved.[11]

With respect to the concessions on industrial products that the Americans demanded of the British, things were equally difficult, and the Americans were equally demanding. Their original list had been submitted to Whitehall in October 1937, but after reaching Washington the British delegation was presented with three additional lists. Some items had been dropped after discussion, but on 26 April 1938 the Americans had repeated the original requests on a large number of industrial products where the British had already indicated that no concession was possible. This included some instances where the United States was a negligible supplier and on which, therefore, the benefit of any tariff concession would accrue to other countries. The new schedule also included certain items which had not previously been mentioned. Among the most worrying demands were those on typewriters, machine tools (which were thought vital for defence), tractors, and cars.[12]

What had gone wrong? Overton had three explanations. First of all, the administration was nervous about its domestic political position. Relations with Congress were bad; conservatives in the Democratic party were critical of Roosevelt; farmers, their surpluses mounting, were restive.[13] And the 1938 mid-term elections were rapidly approaching. Secondly, these considerations, and the possibility that further criticism would result from a trade agreement that was not a clear victory, were made all the more important because of a recent economic slump. Thirdly, Overton suggested, there was "no doubt an element of bargaining . . . particularly for example on items such as cotton goods where offers are described as tentative."[14]

After talking to Hull, Sir Ronald Lindsay also guessed that the change in the American domestic political climate had frightened the administration, which "has made up its mind to put up with a trade agreement with us of such modest dimensions that it will not seriously perturb their own electoral prospects. To secure that I take it that our delegation will have to do some hard bargaining." None of this, however, dampened Lindsay's customary optimism, and he did not foresee any breakdown.[15] The Foreign Office was afraid that the Board of Trade might bring negotiations to an end because it thought the American offer so extremely disappointing. This course Foreign Office officials thought "shortsighted;" they preferred a small agreement to none at all. But the Board of Trade, too, remained hopeful. Although the agreement would not be wide, Sir William Brown was reported as saying that it would be "quite useful nonetheless."[16] He was certainly thinking of economic benefits.

On 19 May the Americans said that they could not do anything to improve their offer unless they knew "more definitely what the United Kingdom was prepared to offer." The British, making an "act of faith,"[17] duly provided such a statement, but the Americans dismissed it as "very disappointing," especially on flour, lard and hams, lumber, and tobacco. The first three items had not been included in the original list of "essentials" or in the second list, although Britain had long known that it would face demands regarding pork products. The position on the last two—lumber and tobacco—had been explained many times to the Americans since the spring of 1937. Even so, the State Department's negotiators told the British that they would rather have no agreement at all than accept the offer as it stood.[18] Overton, presumably because he was so annoyed at the American offer, told the Canadian delegation that nothing could be done about their requests for abatement of Britain's preferences in the dominion. For the present, he said, "this question would largely depend on what inducements they themselves were able to offer Canada." It was also learned that Australia would make no further concessions on bound margins in Canada unless and until Australia herself could consider an agreement with the United States.

Meanwhile, American and British officials were busy making out lists of items on which they did find each other's offers acceptable. These lists were compared on 25 May, at which time the officials decided to meet twice daily so as to discuss the unacceptable offers. During these talks some headway was made by the end of June, but the advance could be described, from both viewpoints, as glacial.[19]

Then, suddenly, there was marked progress—perhaps because of the worsening international situation, more probably because of hard bargaining on the British side.[20] The Americans had improved their offers, especially on textiles, to the point that for a whole range of trades there would be gains for British exporters. The dispensations that might have to be made regarding Britain's preferential margins in Canada did not seem disproportionate to the sacrifices in the British market that the dominion would have to make on such products as apples, and London's concessions would be offset by American ones on British manufactures. Some British industries might suffer slight losses, but overall there would be relatively little disruption.

On 16 July, however, Hawkins called Overton to his Washington office. The Czech crisis had become still more acute and threatening, but nobody mentioned this fact. Cordell Hull, Hawkins explained, did not think that the trade negotiation was proceeding well. The British position was still unsatisfactory. The Americans thought Britain's offers so inadequate, Overton surmised, that they "intended to go pegging away indefinitely. . . ." The chief British negotiator told Hawkins "with some warmth" that if the Americans wanted to create an impasse this was the way to do so. The discussions could not go on forever and there were genuine limits to what Britain could do about lumber and flour. Overton told London that "the only way of meeting these tactics is to decide definitely how far we are prepared to go and then to be absolutely firm even at the risk of a breakdown." The British, in the American view, were "stalling interminably . . . they won't budge an inch from their present position until they hear from Chamberlain."[21] There is no suggestion in the American documents that anyone thought the international situation might make the British more forthcoming. But it is difficult to believe that the idea had not occurred to the men of Washington. Hawkins reported his conversation with Overton to Hull, who cabled Joseph Kennedy, the American ambassador in London. Kennedy called in turn on Stanley, and "conveyed a somewhat gloomy message." This visit convinced Stanley that "no Agreement could be reached unless we were prepared to go a little further on certain items."[22]

Members of the Foreign Office, under Lord Halifax since Anthony Eden's resignation in February, continued to believe that a trade agreement was extremely desirable. Like Eden, Halifax attached great importance to transatlantic co-operation, and most of his officials were of the same view.[23] In the summer of 1938 such views can only have been reinforced. The conclusion, wrote one Foreign Office official, "of a satisfactory agreement—which is now within sight—at the earliest possible date would be a definite factor in favour of peace (and maintenance of British prestige) during the very anxious period ahead of us." Germany, particularly in this Czechoslovakian summer, was likely to be watching closely.[24] As time wore on, indeed, German and Italian commentators took note of the many delays in the trade talks. The Nazi organ, *Völkischer Beobachter*, drew the moral that Hitler's way was "the proper one, the method of simplifying the vast problem which has developed in the field of world economics so that a sound national economy is built up on simple principles." Virginio Gayda, editor of *Giornale d'Italia*, added that the economic interests of the great English-speaking nations, whatever their pretence of commercial freedom, simply did not harmonize. Great Britain and the United States were both major industrial powers, and they would defend their interests come what may.[25]

The British government was by no means placing all its hopes on the United States. Channels must be kept open to Berlin. In July the Foreign Office's Frank Ashton Gwatkin wrote of his desire for an economic settlement with Germany that would lead to a "further extension of mutual trade" and thus "a practical advance towards economic appeasement." Even as the United States condemned bilateralism and repeated its pleas for an open world economy, the Chamberlain government extended the Anglo-German payments agreement to cover the new situation created by the *anschluss* of Germany and Austria.[26] As David Reynolds has explained, the hope and intent of British foreign policy was that no other country—not Germany, not the United States—would become too dominant, "that Britain could maintain her independence, and that of her Empire, against *all* the powers."[27]

The British cabinet's Trade and Agriculture Committee, which had last scrutinized the Anglo-American negotiations in October 1937, considered them once more on 21 July 1938. It did so without explicit reference to the international scene, or to the crisis in central Europe. Oliver Stanley wanted power to sign a trade agreement without having to summon his cabinet colleagues from their August holidays. The situation in the Washington negotiations was changing from day to day. In mid-July an agreement was in sight, although real problems remained, but almost immediately the Americans had increased their demands once again. Stanley recognized that there were still substantial problems and that most of the new American demands, including the industrial ones, could not be entertained. He did think that something could be done for lard, to which Washington attached great political importance in spite of its quantitative insignificance in Anglo-American trade, and Stanley urged his colleagues to co-operate. Sir Frederick Leith-Ross, the Treasury official who held the title of chief economic advisor to the government, emphasized the importance of the agreement from a political viewpoint, given the parlous international situation. But W.S. Morrison, the secretary of agriculture, would not agree to a reduction on lard. Morrison naturally objected to a substantial cut on the order of one half, arguing that this would eliminate the profit on offals and thus destroy all profit in the trade. An agreement, he maintained, was being bought at the expense of Britain's farmers.[28]

Even as the British considered and reconsidered their position, the Americans decided to heap on the pressure through Joseph Kennedy in London. Kennedy, however, was of two minds about the trade talks. He wanted to be involved and he was anxious to prove his usefulness to the secretary of state. Up until now his main role had been the more public one of salesman, urging the message of economic disarmament upon British and American audiences alike. But Kennedy was sympathetic to the British and not inclined to bully them, especially when the American bargaining position "was an intrinsically weak one for British imports." American concessions were paltry. "What leverage we possessed was less from the economics of the situation than from such political advantages as might accrue to the British from an Anglo-American accord."[29]

Kennedy impressed upon Hull that the British were negotiating in good faith. Surely the "soft" rational approach was to be preferred to the hectoring one. Hull did not agree, and instructed the ambassador to preach forcefully to the British about the opportunity that was being missed. Again Hull sounded the note of economic appeasement. He may even have been reminding the British authorities, however indirectly, of the link between the trade talks and the European crisis.

> I wish you would say to the Prime Minister that we seek this agreement, and we hope that the British seek this agreement, not primarily for the dollars and cents immediately involved, valuable as that is and without in the slightest degree minimizing that side of the trade agreement. We seek it primarily as a powerful initiative to

help rectify the present unstable political and economic situation everywhere. In our judgment, no single act would contribute so much to quieting the threats to world political and economical stability, not only in Europe but in other parts of the world, as the announcement that these two great countries have come together with a broad, basic trade arrangement which might well be regarded as a foundation for a restored structure of world order. That is the big objective as we see it, and unless we can get Mr Chamberlain and the British Government to accept this view and to approach this problem on a broader front, it might well be charged in Germany, Italy, Japan, and other countries that our two countries are utterly incapable of sitting down and making simple, mutually profitable trade arrangements with each other. I have not the slightest doubt that these negotiations are being watched by those countries to see whether we are capable of working out an agreement that is really worth-while, and I think that it would greatly harm not only our two countries but also the whole outlook for peace and economic improvement if we, after months of haggling, should turn out a little, narrow, picayunish trade agreement.[30]

Kennedy accordingly met with Oliver Stanley, the president of the Board of Trade, and then with Chamberlain. Stanley told Kennedy that he was "surprised and grieved" at Hull's point of view with respect to commercial concessions. The British thought they had moved considerably to accommodate Washington. Chamberlain said there would be more concessions but held out little hope on lumber or tobacco. The same message was conveyed by Overton to Hawkins in Washington. Why did the Americans think that, in order to achieve a fair agreement, the British must give in on every single US request? J.P. Moffat, returning to his State Department desk after a vacation, characteristically noted that Great Britain had still not "receded from her position that the United States should play Santa Claus."[31]

The whole question went to the British cabinet on 28 July.[32] At that meeting no one suggested that Hull might be blackmailing the United Kingdom, using the international political situation to extract commercial concessions. But it is difficult to believe that no ministerial mind harboured the idea. Stanley was still not sure that an agreement would be possible at all, but he was certain that without a lard concession nothing could be done; Morrison continued his passionate advocacy of the pig-farmers; everyone agreed that there would have to be an agreement of some sort for political reasons both at home and abroad. At length Sir John Simon, the chancellor of the exchequer, dissolved the agricultural difficulty by suggesting that, if the lard duty had to be cut to satisfy the Americans, Britain's bacon-curers should be given a three-year price guarantee with a subsidy if required. "The Treasury would lose doubly," he admitted. "In view, however, of the great political importance of reaching agreement with the United States, he felt justified in facing that."

The cabinet agreed to give Stanley authority to sign an agreement during the parliamentary recess. He could reduce the lard duty.[33] If the terms of any draft agreement were such that Stanley would not want to sign it without consultation, he should try for delay until the cabinet could meet. It was also agreed to record formally the importance the government attached, from the point of view of both domestic and international politics, to an agreement with the USA. In Washington Overton interpreted this to mean that failure could not be entertained.[34]

During the months of August and September, however, slight progress was made. Whenever an explosion in Europe seemed imminent, the Foreign Office attached great importance to an Anglo-American accord; at one point it went so far as to suggest a direct appeal through the American ambassador to Roosevelt. In calmer moments the department worried somewhat less about the political question, and was more inclined to acquiesce in the Board of Trade's attempt to hammer out a satisfactory commercial deal.[35] The British were aware that the Americans were likely to have a shrewd appreciation of their predicament.[36] On 19 September Francis Sayre promised the British ambassador, Sir Ronald Lindsay, that Washington would not use the Czech crisis to force an unfair agreement on the British.[37] Late in the month, as Chamberlain met Hitler in Munich, Hull told Lindsay that the US would not take advantage of a war in Europe to capture Britain's trade. These assurances simply served to underline the atmosphere of competitive co-operation that characterized Anglo-American relations in these years.[38] America's trading demands did not moderate.

The Canadians showed little comprehension of Britain's difficulties, whether commercial or political, whether domestic or international. Norman Robertson, Canada's chief negotiator, was losing his patience with his British colleagues and urged Prime Minister King to communicate directly to Chamberlain. King did so at the end of September, but to no effect.[39] The three delegations, at least, were continuing to meet and negotiate. With respect to the British sacrifice of bound and unbound preference in Canada, some adjustments were made, but on anthracite the Americans made no yards at all, and the British were not eager to accommodate the other US demands.[40] Nor were the Canadians by any means sure that they could meet the American demand on apples. Canada's acquiescence, it will be recalled, was needed because Britain's preferential margin on apples was "bound" to Canada. In Nova Scotia the Annapolis Valley apple producers depended almost wholly on the British market; a reduction in the preferential margin would directly reduce their returns from apple growing.[41]

Dissatisfied on lumber, as we shall see in the next chapter, the Americans had begun to demand free entry for plywood in August. This was much to the annoyance of the British, who observed that other states sent much more plywood to Britain and that mfn rules would require an extension of the concession in other directions.[42] On 13 September the Americans devised the new lumber formula which, after consulting their national capitals, both the British and the Canadians accepted. This, however, did not cause the Americans to discontinue their plywood demands, which were now "essentials."

Nor had the paths of the negotiators been lubricated significantly by Britain's offer on lard, in that the United Kingdom cabinet had refused to countenance American demands regarding anthracite, wheat flour, planed softwood, plywood, or motor cars.[43] The Americans were also now injecting the question of the exchange rate into the discussions, a question with which we will deal in some detail in Chapter 8. The pound had been trading at just under $5, but as the negotiations ambled along, it was tending to decline in value. On 9 September Sayre had suggested that if sterling were to fall further, as his Treasury expected, the concessions made to United Kingdom trade might have to be revised. Lindsay answered tersely: "That would be the end of the whole negotiation immediately."[44] The American attitude appeared to the Board of Trade to be one of "blackmail and obstruction."[45] Since mid-August the American attitude had worsened, so that Hawkins and Hickerson demanded "more and more concessions and [wished to reopen] matters on which it was thought agreement had already been reached in principle."[46]

What the Americans were up to is not completely clear. American documentation is far scantier than the British, and much more ill-organized—a commentary on American methods, and inefficiency, as a tiny staff struggled to keep up with two sets of negotiations. The fall in the exchange rate of sterling was certainly upsetting some officials in Washington. It is also reasonable to suppose that Washington had realized just how much Britain wanted a trade agreement for reasons of international politics. And, doubtless most important of all, there were the representations from members of Congress and interest groups of all sorts, some of whom had important political connections. Consider motor cars. The United States did not produce many cars in the 20-25 horsepower range, and two of the big three American firms had large factories in Britain, while others could supply the British and imperial markets from their Canadian factories. Some small independent American firms, however, such as

Nash and Willys, produced light cars and had little or no productive capacity within the British empire. Such firms certainly made representations, and it is reasonable to suppose they were listened to. Among other interests to consider, New England opposition to tariff cuts on textiles could be offset by support from agriculture. But this did not take account of lumber, where concessions were essential, or rice and lard, where a deal was important. Sayre worried that the United States and Great Britain "were descending too much into a horse trade" with "the whole future of the world at stake."[47] But the Americans were after a big agreement—big in spirit, impact and commercial benefits. Only then would domestic political necessity be satisfied. Only then would the imperatives of the international situation be met.

The British delegation in Washington had firm instructions that in light of the international situation "on no account must the negotiation break down."[48] Whitehall, of course, was anxious to appear no more flexible than absolutely necessary. Believing that the American negotiators had been told to squeeze hard, and that some officials were knowingly acting in the interest of particular industries, the Board of Trade told Overton in late August to refuse to make any further concessions.[49] The board, however, recognized that "if it proves impossible to move the Americans any further . . . we shall have to give way on political grounds."[50]

Overton himself thought that the two governments were negotiating from different theoretical perspectives. Britain thought each government should give what it could. The "American case, however, is that under a fair agreement they should receive concessions of which the value is X (a constant). X apparently consists of what we have offered already plus free entry for plywood and lard and an undertaking to halve the existing preference . . . on tobacco . . . in 1942. Failing this reduction . . . they . . . add that if we cannot meet them in full . . . they are entitled to alternative concessions (unspecified) of equivalent value." The balance of advantage, Overton thought, was hopelessly adverse to the United Kingdom, and the United States negotiators paid no attention to the remaining disparity between the two tariff structures or the fiscal and domestic political costs of their demands. He concluded, "The Americans made a great point of the value from their point of view of window-dressing. How do they suggest that we should 'sell' our public what is perhaps the most valuable concession they have to offer us? The effect of this concession is that the incidence of the duty on a woollen cloth valued at 75 cents per lb will be reduced from 116% to 98%, and, on a cloth valued at $1.00 per lb. from 100% to 92.5%."[51]

By the end of the month of September, there was a Canadian-American agreement in principle. The Dominions Office, furthermore, thought the Americans had given up demanding impossible concessions with respect to tobacco, and it observed with pleasure that Britain had just offered a new concession on motor cars. On rice, ham, and lard, however, the Americans were still pressing and the UK delegation was still resisting.[52] There was "little evidence," said Norman Robertson, "of disposition in either camp to settle things quickly. They blame each other for the delay and each is waiting for the other to give ground."[53] The Munich Agreement of late September had settled the Czech question in a fashion that Herr Hitler found satisfactory. The immediate risk of war had receded. The Anglo-American agreement, if there was to be one, still had a long way to go.

CHAPTER 7

The Dominions in the Later Stages of the Negotiations

April - September 1938

The interlocking of two sets of negotiations increased the risks and added to the troubles the officials faced in reaching a satisfactory outcome. The task was particularly complex and difficult for the tiny American team, which had to carry the burden of negotiating both with the British and with the Canadians. The presence of a fourth party, Australia, made things more difficult still. With respect to some products these complicated negotiations, furthermore, acquired a momentum of their own. The sheer complexity of the subject matter almost guaranteed an isolation from the larger movements of world politics and economics. This was especially true of the "Baltic pine perplex."[1]

The Canadians arrived in Washington in late March 1938, just before the Committee for Reciprocity Information hearings on the Canadian-American talks were to open. The Canadian negotiators were the familiar threesome of Hector McKinnon, Dana Wilgress and Norman Robertson. Robertson was the most junior but clearly the most important: he had an aptitude for the work, great force of intellect, and a solid connection with the prime minister, who was also his department's political master. Robertson was to oversee the whole range of negotiations; Wilgress and McKinnon were given the task of working out the specifics of offers and counter-offers.[2]

Reference notes for Chapter 7 begin on p. 182.

There was little system to the Canadian negotiating process. The key documents were memoranda from Robertson, discussed and approved by cabinet in October 1937 and March 1938. Robertson carried on a correspondence from Washington with his superior in the Department of External Affairs, O.D. Skelton; Skelton corresponded with the prime minister. Even so, Robertson and his colleagues were unable to extract clear and concrete instructions. Professor J.L. Granatstein's biography of Robertson draws a vivid portrait of negotiators left very much to their own devices.[3] After a draft agreement was reached in September, Robertson returned to Ottawa, where with some sense of relief he "managed to get retroactive sanction for the instructions I've had to invent all summer."[4] At this point, the cabinet was brought back into the process, having been ignored, in Robertson's words, "until a balanced whole could be presented. If Cabinet Ministers once get their hands on a first list of demands each one automatically vetoes concessions where he is interested and the result is invariably no agreement."[5]

The contrast between the Canadian-American and Anglo-American discussions is striking. Except where they were interlocked with the Anglo-American talks, as with timber and anthracite, the Canadian-American negotiations proceeded quite smoothly, although naturally the participants did not always think so. This is not to say that there were no irritations, but these stemmed largely from the actions of the US Congress, which took several protective measures against Canadian timber while the negotiations were in course. For example, the Congress required that for certain purposes every piece of Canadian sawn timber should carry a mark of national origin. The effect of such actions was to make the eventual timber settlement even more complicated than it would have been, but they did not diminish the good feelings that developed between the Canadians and Americans.

The two empire delegations, on the other hand, spent many hours of often difficult and acrimonious private discussions. American demands often required an Anglo-Canadian understanding, and Robertson and his friends more than once found themselves sympathizing with the US position: regarding British intransigence on coal, for example, and especially on timber. Robertson wrote that he could cope with the United States and its negotiators, "but not with God's Englishmen and the inescapable moral ascendancy over us lesser breeds."[6] As the Munich Crisis came and went, Robertson could not understand why the British "should feel that their self-respect compels them to take so much firmer a line in negotiating with the United States than they ever have shown in their discussions with Germany or Italy, or even with Poland or Hungary."[7]

Such outbursts, coming as they did from a self-styled British "imperialist,"[8] are in some measure explained by differences in philosophies of negotiation. If we compare the Canadian negotiating stance with the British, there is an obvious difference. The Canadians wanted to get as much out of Washington's Reciprocal Trade Agreements Act as they could; they were prepared to make "such purely bargaining concessions as might be required," if possible at British expense, to make that happen.[9] This was an approach the Americans could understand and even appreciate. In mid-September 1938 Francis Sayre wrote that the Canadians "have been playing the game very fairly . . . [they] have given us all kinds of things. The Canadian trade agreement is bully. The trouble we're having is with UK."[10] The British, however, believed that they neither could nor should concede very much beyond their original proposals. That is to say, they thought that, since they had made real concessions, it was up to the Americans to reciprocate. Furthermore, Britain took her contractual commitments to the dominions and the smaller European states very seriously, while Canada was anxious to take whatever room for manoeuvre the "mother country" would give her.

With Canada, as with Britain, the Americans first presented a list of requests, only later supplying a list of possible concessions. American requests at first took the form of proposals for reduction in preferential margins. That was one of the assumptions that underlay United States participation in the whole trilateral exercise. Britain would allow Canada to reduce some of the margins that were fixed by the Anglo-Canadian trade agreement of 1937, if Canada would allow Britain to do the same. A reduction of the preferential margin, of course, was the same thing as a reduction in Canada's mfn tariff rates.

The Americans had been quite remarkably coy about the reductions in bound margins that they expected Canada to make. Not until 15 April did the Americans present Norman Robertson with their list of proposed changes, and this said nothing about the actual reductions for which the United States would press. America sought concessions on such products as chemicals and drugs, acids, aluminum shapes, iron and steel sheets, tinned and galvanized plate, stainless steel, railway equipment, diesel engines, motorcycles, aircraft and dental instruments.[11] Altogether, some seventeen items were involved. It was Robertson's impression that the State Department's negotiators, Harry Hawkins and Jack Hickerson, "would probably be ready to accept the substitution, for anything but anthracite, of other items from that list covering more or less comparable volumes of trade."[12] The British authorities were very sensitive on the subject of anthracite, the Canadians much less so. As one British official observed in July 1938, "I am not at present prepared to agree to any concession, as it appears to me that this would involve serious loss of trade in a market of vital importance to South Wales without the possibility of any compensatory advantage."[13]

The Canadians were also at first disappointed to see how little the Americans were willing to concede. Receiving a list of proposed American concessions late in May 1938—the first one to be supplied—Robertson wrote:

> while it contains additional concessions of substantial value ... it falls a long way short of the objective, set out for us in our instructions, of a comprehensive and definitive trade agreement that would exhaust the president's powers under the Trade Agreements Act ... it is not big enough as it stands to swing the modification of our overseas preferences that we will be forced to face ... neither does it represent the trading counterpart of the tariff concessions the United States will seek and that for reasons of general policy we assume the Government would be inclined to grant.[14]

Fifteen items of this "May list" were referred to the United Kingdom Board of Trade, which deferred one item, agreed to one wholly and three partially, but put aside the remaining ten, while offering to "select parts of three items for relaxation." Robertson thought this response niggardly and "disastrous," but it did no lasting harm. Anglo-American and Canadian-American conversations continued, and on 1 July the Americans submitted a revised list. Lo and behold, some of the American proposals had been modified, although anthracite still figured largely on the new list. If nothing was done for coal, the Americans kept saying, John L. Lewis, president of both the United Mine Workers of America and the new Congress of Industrial Organizations, would come out against the trade agreement policy. The Board of Trade, however, was still not prepared to give in on anthracite. It also wanted to resist on tin plate and diesel engines.[15]

On the Canadian side, the negotiations were entangled with the Liberal government's desire to cut tariffs unilaterally. There were several goods on which Canada might reduce tariffs in any event, where the United States would gain, but where Washington was not pressing for concessions. Among these were farm implements and cream separators.[16] Should these be inserted into the Canada-US agreement? Ottawa characteristically failed to answer the question directly.[17] Robertson was prepared to contemplate reductions in tariffs and margins that were not bound to the United Kingdom, and he made some effort to keep A.E. Overton, head of the British team, informed about such items, of which the most important was cotton textiles.[18] The Americans, it seemed, would be disappointed with the concessions on ball bearings and diesel engines that Britain could tolerate, but Overton was willing to ask his government to authorize further concessions on margins.[19]

Thus on the matter of margins the British and Canadian delegations were keeping in reasonably close touch, and what Canada was offering was, in general, what Britain was willing to accept. The British negotiators were inclined to think that, with the exception of anthracite, "what we are being asked to give up in Canada is not disproportionate to what we have asked Canada to give up in the United Kingdom."[20] Both on Canada's unbound preferences in Britain (cars, for example), and on the UK's unbound Canadian preferences, the two delegations tidied up matters with relative ease, although not always without misunderstandings. Regrettably, these offerings were rather less than the Americans were hoping to swallow. Robertson found the administrative arrangements confining. On 24 July he told Overton that "except in a few items, Canada had no protective interest to watch. Over the remainder the Canadian Delegation were, therefore, only a channel for the communication to the United States of decisions taken by the United Kingdom . . . it might be better either to have tripartite discussions or . . . for the United Kingdom Delegation to negotiate direct with the United States on these requests."[21]

In mid-August Robertson wrote that he and the Americans were "still quite a distance apart on some pretty important questions, but our differences are primarily of degree and technical in character."[22] In Ottawa, however, O.D. Skelton was growing nervous:

> the necessity for a quick decision in the end may involve us in a 'squeeze play' between London and Washington. There is a possibility that we may be 'pilloried' if we do not make wide last-minute concessions. My own feeling is that the time is coming when we will have to tell the United States that we must have some substantial concessions. . . . It is time that somebody else besides ourselves should show a little readiness to make concessions for the good of the world.[23]

Three weeks later both Skelton and Prime Minister King were making the same point: Canada would not be "stampeded into making unwarranted concessions or into deciding in undue haste."[24]

They need not have worried. By the end of September 1938, King's negotiators were able to present him with a draft agreement that represented a considerable triumph. Canada received many new concessions in the American market, and in Britain had not surrendered much of importance. Its own concessions had been in accord with government policy, and as politicians and officials understand such matters, Canada had won a great deal. She had certainly not been "pilloried." The prime minister was delighted: "I confess the agreement is even better than I thought it would be possible to have it."[25]

But what of that other concerned British dominion, Australia? As it turned out, the southern dominion proved to be an intractable problem, both for Britain and for Canada. First of all, some background beyond that already provided is necessary. Immediately after passage of the Reciprocal Trade Agreements Act in 1934, Australia had begun to seek a trading accord with the United States. The Americans showed little interest, making Australians all the more likely to regard US economic policies as restrictive, selfish, damaging. The Americans, Sir Henry Gullett told the ubiquitous J.P. Moffat, consul general in Canberra at the time, "had enormous sales for which you never so much as said thanks. You excluded our goods by tariff; you drove out our shipping by subsidies; you threw our fruit overboard; you surrounded yourself by a tariff wall that could not be surmounted." Gullett's remarks were in defence of the Australian government's 1936 decision to embark on a deliberate policy of diverting her trade from the US to other, mainly empire, countries. The Americans retaliated by placing Australia on a black list of countries to which the mfn tariff did not apply.

At the Imperial Conference of 1937, as we have seen, the British approached Australian Prime Minister Joseph Lyons with a request that the Ottawa Agreements be modified as part of an Anglo-American bargain. Lyons, an election coming up, refused even to be seen near the Board of Trade. The election having been won, however, and in the hope of an American agreement of their own, the Australian government agreed in late 1937 to end trade diversion and to give up some of her preferences in the British market. Lyons did so unilaterally, without any promises from either London or Washington. A Canadian minister correctly—but rather tactlessly—told the head of the Australian commerce department that Canada had been "too wise" to relinquish bargaining chips before it had assurances of good behaviour from the US and UK governments.[26]

The Australians hoped, nevertheless, for advantages from both the Americans and British. From the United States Australia wanted concessions on apples, pears, tallow, mutton, lamb and especially wool, on which the existing American duty was 72 per cent. Australia insisted that nothing could be done to retard national development or materially to hinder her trade with Britain. The preferential formula of the Anglo-Australian Agreement, negotiated in Ottawa six years before, should be "replaced by specifications of margins in scheduled lists ... this is important from the point of view of bargaining with foreign countries." Australia was entitled to seek an expanding share of Britain's import flow, with new restrictions on foreign suppliers if necessary; "essential under any circumstances" would be Britain's preferences on meat, sugar, wine, dried and canned fruits. So far as wool and wheat were concerned, neither Britain nor America was likely to absorb Australia's prospective exportation. Hence the importance of Europe and Asia, and the need to modify the preferential formula to which Australia had committed herself in 1932.[27]

Moves were now made towards a formal Australian-American trade negotiation. Lists were exchanged in early 1938, but the United States government postponed the talks in March, telling the Australians that "the political situation" made it impossible to even consider opening negotiations until the end of May. Australian indignation almost led Canberra to withdraw its promise that it would surrender preferences in the British market. Canada, after all, had secured a separate negotiation with the US. To make matters worse, Ottawa was asking Canberra "to reduce preferences in Canada on Australian produce in order to facilitate Canadian dealings with the USA."[28]

Earle Page, Australia's minister of commerce, arrived in London in May 1938 to discuss re-negotiation of the Ottawa Agreements. After several weeks in the British capital he proceeded to Ottawa and then Washington. In London, Page pressed Britain to introduce general quantitative restrictions so as to give Australia a guaranteed and rising share of the British market.[29] He and his colleagues disagreed profoundly with British ministers, and their talks could only be "preliminary and exploratory," as the dominions secretary termed them some weeks later.[30] The official *communiqué*[31] said nothing about primary products or about the Anglo-American negotiations.[32] Oliver Stanley, president of the Board of Trade, was completely unsympathetic, threatening Page with the end of free entry into the British market for certain goods. Certainly there could be no real trade talks with the Australians until the end of the Anglo-American negotiation.

Neither in Washington nor in Ottawa did Page advance matters much. On 12 August, in Washington, he had no more than an hour to talk about Canada-Australian trade. He "absolutely refused," Robertson later wrote, "to discuss any aspect of the modification of preference. He . . . said that by consenting to modification of our preferential margins in the United Kingdom, particularly in respect of lumber, we had surrendered the hope of maintaining preferential margins in Australia." Page then asked, in vain, whether Canada could postpone its negotiations with Washington until Australia and the United States were in negotiation, or at least for four to six months; he made the same request of the British through Overton. After meeting with Page in Ottawa, O.D. Skelton concluded that, without "hard and fast counter commitments on a much bigger scale," Australia would not unbind the preferential margins about which Canada had asked. Fortunately, Skelton thought, the commodities were "trifling," and doubtless the United States would in the end agree to overlook them.[33]

Understandable Australian awkwardness about making concessions without any *quid pro quo* whatsoever was met by an apparent American willingness to talk about an agreement. After leading the Australians to believe in June 1938 that direct negotiation would still be possible, however, the Americans decided that nothing useful could be done in the scanty time available. There would be no point in an Australian-American trade agreement that did not cut the wool duty, and any such agreement would have to be hastily concluded over the summer, while Congress was out of session. The Americans offered to reduce the wool duty only by 26 per cent, not by the full 50 per cent that the Trade Agreements Act allowed. Australia was thus thrown back into the position of having to defend her own interest in the British market without any hope of offsetting compensations on the American scene. The Australian historian Ruth Megaw concludes:

> To sum up, Australia did play the part of the sacrificial lamb in relation to the American trade agreements with Britain and Canada. As she had feared she had surrendered preferences in the British market, ended trade diversion and made concessions to Canada and in return received nothing except faint praise for aiding the cause of a world peace that was scarcely evident in 1939. The State Department had read Canberra sanctimonious lectures on the virtues of the American system of trade, while remaining wilfully blind to the very real difficulties Australia faced. The British had intervened to protect Australian interests only sporadically and when, as in November 1937 or March 1938, it seemed that Australian intransigence might hinder the Anglo-American agreement.[34]

Although Great Britain could no longer act for the Canadians or even the Australians, it could and did negotiate on behalf of Newfoundland and the dependent empire. It is hard to understand the American obsession with the colonial empire, except on the basis of principle or habit: ever since the Revolutionary War, American politicians and officials had seethed with indignation when they thought of Britain's "mercantilist" leanings, especially with respect to the West Indies. In the 1930s, however, colonial preferences and mercantilism surely did not count for much. Britain could not exact preferences from A and B class League of Nations mandates, and much of her African empire was still covered by the network of nineteenth-century treaties that enforced an open door; with respect to these arrangements, French action had cleared the way for the introduction of imperial preferences in Nigeria, but the opportunity had not been taken. By 1937 there were African imperial preferences only in Somaliland, Gambia, Sierra Leone, and the larger part of Northern Rhodesia; these territories were annually importing less than 5 million pounds worth of goods.[35] Admittedly, in these and other colonies there were quotas that controlled textile imports, but the quotas, aimed at Japan, were of no concern to the United States. And India, for these purposes, was certainly not defined as part of the colonial empire. American demands on this front continued to grow, however, even though Britain had already ruled out the suggestions of November 1937.[36] Both British and Canadian officials must have been surprised by the vigour of the American attack, an onslaught that had nothing to do with any large conception of international economic disarmament.

The Anglo-American talks about the dependent empire had indirect implications for Canadian trade. Canadian trade with the dependent African empire was insignificant, but not with Newfoundland and the West Indies. Canada's negotiators, therefore, watched the empire component of the talks with interest; British negotiators did their best to keep the Canadians informed. If Britain could get the Americans to cut their tariffs on Newfoundland goods, the tariff-cut would extend to Canadian goods through mfn provisions. If, moreover, Newfoundland tariffs against American goods were to be cut, Canadian goods would pay less duty, because at the Newfoundland frontier Canadian goods paid the general tariff, not a preferential rate. Thus Robertson's elation when, on 26 April, Washington offered Newfoundland substantial reductions on frozen blueberries, fresh lingonberries, salt cod, pickled or salted herrings, fluorspar, seal oil, and sealskin.[37] In that salt cod was Newfoundland's only important export, these concessions were of real value.

American concern about colonial preferences in the West Indies, where Canada had long enjoyed a preferential access, did not diminish. There was, admittedly, already some pressure from Canada's maritime ports for denunciation of the Canada-West Indies Trade Agreement—a necessary step if Britain was to accede to America's demands on the issue. Sir Francis Floud, the British high commissioner in Ottawa, reported that the agreement was unpopular because it was thought that trade had been diverted from Canadian ports, and that the costs in terms of freight subsidies and duty remissions was excessive. Therefore the Canadian government might well give notice of denunciation.[38] In the event, this action proved not to be necessary.

More directly linked with Hull's idea of economic disarmament— and more directly relevant to the American export trade—was the

American attack on dominion preferences in the British market. Several commodities were involved, and it would be tedious to examine them all. We will treat apples, wheat, and softwood timber in some depth. Among the dominions, only Canada worried about timber; both Canada and Australia cared about apples, wheat, and flour. American apples were a real problem not simply because of competition but because it was suspected that, when crops were good, American apple-growers would simply dump their surplus on Britain regardless of duty. Thus, in arguing for stringent anti-dumping provisions, the British had apples (among other commodities) in mind. However, such arcane provisions would not satisfy Britain's own applegrowers, whose interests were defended by the agriculture minister, W.S. Morrison, or the dominion orchardists, whose interests were defended by their national governments.

When Stanley Bruce, the Australian high commissioner in London, discussed the matter in November 1937 he thought that apples would be the only difficult problem for Australia. Mackenzie King, too, had made it very clear that apples worried him as well. Early in 1938 there was direct consultation between the two dominion governments. The problem was twofold. Because trees bear fruit at different times in the northern and southern hemispheres, and because Canadian apples matured a little later than American, with respect to their desires for protection in the British market the two dominions had different concerns and hopes. Australia would accept a seasonal reduction in duty, but both Canadian and British interests were unhappy with that idea, because to spare Australian grief the cut would concentrate American supplies within the period when their own apples were coming on to Britain's market.[39] Only on 6 August did the Americans accept Britain's final offer on apples, although they "felt it was inadequate."[40]

Britain's wheat and flour duties, a very important issue because before 1932 American wheat and flour had entered Britain duty-free, also became contentious. The Americans had assimilated Britain's offer of free entry for wheat, dropped nothing from their essential list by way of recompense, and proceeded to demand free entry for flour as well. Britain would not concede this, nor would Australia, and Canada was most reluctant to consider it at all. Ottawa insisted that its acquiescence in the loss of the wheat preference was contingent: the Americans would have to make the maximum possible cuts in their own wheat and flour duties, even though everyone recognized that the United States would normally be exporting these products. What Ottawa needed, Robertson wrote, was a "political make weight." The Americans were prepared to offer cuts in milling offals, and with great ingenuity they re-discovered the Corn Laws sliding scale from the years before 1846, by which British duties varied in accordance with the price level. But these concessions did not add up to much. Robertson argued that instead Canada should "try to get in return for the waiver of the wheat preference in the United Kingdom an undertaking that the United States should not subsidize the export of wheat to world markets."[41] As for Britain, Overton told the Americans in late May that "we could do nothing on flour, both on account of Australia and because of our home industry."[42]

Lumber was another major difficulty both for the British and for the Canadians. Canada was prepared to admit more American lumber to Britain, but only if the United States would take more Canadian lumber. However, Canada was not prepared to make changes that would simply bring more Baltic softwood to Britain, largely because those countries already supplied more than 90 per cent of British softwood needs. So far as the British imports were concerned, therefore, it would be necessary to devise some arrangement that differentiated by value, type, size, species, or some combination thereof. The timber duties produced a good deal of revenue for the British exchequer, which at first was reluctant to sacrifice any more than it could help. Gradually, however, Whitehall became anxious to concede as much as Canada would allow, so long as it could find some way to do so without infuriating the twelve interested Baltic countries, at least two of which—Sweden and Finland—had requested and received assurances that Britain would do nothing inconsistent with her mfn obligations.[43]

The problem was that Baltic pine was a perfect substitute for North American Douglas fir. As a delegation from the British Timber Trades Federation explained to the Board of Trade, the trade used one or the other, depending solely on cost and price. Fortunately, although the Federation did not want lower duties on fir plywood and doors, it had no objection to a cut in the timber duty.[44] The Treasury and the Board of Trade thereupon proceeded to elaborate a plan[45] for an "alternative specific duty" instead of the existing *ad valorem* system. A rate of 28/- per standard was suggested. In January 1938, well before transmitting the plan to the Americans, Whitehall asked for Ottawa's opinion.[46] The Canadians accepted the idea, but asked Britain to keep the *ad valorem* rate out of the negotiations. Canada also proposed a higher mfn rate[47] than Britain had envisaged, lest its preferential margin be reduced.[48] Given the dominion's own eagerness to erode Britain's margins of preference in the Canadian market, this was a quite remarkable request. The Americans, however, rejected it because it would do nothing for low-priced American lumber.[49]

On 4 April the Canadian cabinet decided that it would let Britain admit all Douglas fir and southern pine free, and would acquiesce in a duty of 7.5 per cent on other softwood. In return, the Americans would reduce their duty on Canadian timber by 75 per cent (from the equivalent of 16/- per standard to 4/-), abstain from enacting further anti-Canadian timber proposals then before Congress, and eliminate the awkward and costly arrangements regarding the marking of Canadian timber. The Canadians suggested that London should not consult the smaller Baltic countries, but rather tell them what was happening and what compensation Britain would offer. Having consulted the American negotiators, Overton advised the Board of Trade to consider these proposals.[50] But Whitehall did not think well of the idea, responding to Overton:

> it is incompatible with an honourable interpretation of our treaty obligations to contemplate free entry for Douglas fir and mainte- nance of present duty on other softwoods. We think it would be useless to approach European timber supplying countries with a proposal to give free entry to Douglas fir and to reduce the duty on competing European softwoods to 7 1/2 and we are not accordingly prepared to approach them at least at this stage. If we were to consult them it would be necessary to consult every country having most-favoured-nation rights which sends us any softwood. . . . We could not take a strong line with any country. . . . You will no doubt consider whether it is possible to bring to the notice of Mr Hull the question of principle involved.[51]

Learning of this response, Robertson asked Overton to propose that his government should "reconsider their position," and he agreed with the Americans that they would consider the question of dif- ferentiation by size, not type or value. The American negotiators, meanwhile, held out some slight hope for useful Congressional action with respect to the discriminatory measures being taken against Canadian lumber. Once the Americans had gone, Robertson em- phasized "a little more plainly than was possible in a three-cornered discussion, what I thought would be the reaction in Ottawa upon receipt of information about the United Kingdom's attitude."[52]

The situation was especially difficult because the Americans had already rejected the original British proposal for an alternative specific duty on the ground that they must get some concession for cheap lumber too. In London, the Dominions Office worried about the chance of a breakdown in the talks over the issue.[53] From Washington, Overton reported that the American officials sympathized but dis- agreed, arguing that "it is common practice in many countries to differentiate between plants, etc., by species." The Americans, he thought, "would probably be willing to support our representations" to the European supplier countries.[54]

At the end of April 1938 the Americans made a new proposal.[55] Canadian timber, it seemed, would still have free entry to Britain, but with a reduced preferential margin against the Americans and no immediate concessions at the US frontier, while the Baltic softwoods would still pay 10 per cent. In the Dominions Office Norman Archer wrote:

> The last proposal of the United States seems to get us nowhere. . . . In any case, even if the United States offer had been wholly favourable to Canada the Board of Trade are still apparently adamant on the mfn point. The fact that the United States offer is not what Canada wants may, however, save the BT from the inconvenience of having to reconsider the question.[56]

And William Bankes-Amery minuted angrily: "The latest request of the US is preposterous . . . the US idea of bargain is that we should infringe on our mfn promises, that Canada should suffer penal taxation in the US, and that the US should have an immediate reduction of duty from 10% to 5% in the UK. This does not strike me as being business."[57]

The Americans continued to press for differentiation by species, and the Board of Trade continued to resist:

> it is clear that what matters for purposes of commercial agreements is not whether goods can be distinguished by some scientific or other means but whether goods can be distinguished for commercial purposes in the market of the importing country. For example, white cows can be distinguished from brown cows with ease and certainty, but a customs differentiation on this basis would be indefensible unless in some country—perhaps in connection with religious ceremonies—brown cows and white cows were used for different purposes. This case seems to border almost exactly on the case of lumber.[58]

Naturally the Americans and the Canadians were still unhappy, and the UK delegation in Washington asked whether the Board of Trade would not consider approaching one or more of the concerned third parties.[59] The Canadians believed that "if Baltic countries fully appreciate position they will consent."[60]

But they would not. Sweden, sounded out informally, said she would not consider the American plan.[61] By mid-July Overton was urging Robertson to accept 7.5 per cent plus free entry for Southern pine.[62] And thus matters remained deadlocked for some weeks. The Americans, mightily aggrieved that anyone would suggest they wanted to produce a breach of mfn obligations, produced elaborate arguments to the effect that it was chemistry and botany that mattered. The British responded by insisting that what mattered were morality and substitutability. The Canadians wrung their hands.

At last, on 13 September, the Americans produced a proposal that formed the basis for agreement. Because Baltic trees were shorter and smaller, one could differentiate by the length and width of the planed timber. Robertson found the idea acceptable, but Overton did not want planed lumber to receive the benefits, as the Americans proposed, because the United States sent such a tiny proportion of it into the British market: the benefit would accrue almost wholly to the Baltic states, at enormous cost to the UK exchequer, which would lose the revenue.[63] The British Customs was horrified, as well, by the administrative implications. Because lumber was not sorted in the appropriate fashion, presumably the officials ought to measure every piece and tax it separately. This obviously could not be done, and there were bound to be many problems about valuation and evasion. However, both Customs and the Treasury agreed that the greater good would have to prevail.[64] There was no trouble in devising a Byzantine phrase by which the United States would not get the benefit of these concessions until Congress had removed its special discrimination against Canadian lumber. It was not until much later in the day that the American negotiators finally acquiesced in London's insistence that planed lumber should not be included.[65] Doubtless everyone remembered the epic American phraseology of the summer, when Hawkins and Hickerson had explained that they were anxious to "satisfy their lumber interests of whose log-rolling activities they were much afraid."[66]

It was softwood timber that forced the British to depart from the principles with which they had begun. The reader will recall that, in early 1938, the Board of Trade had argued that all softwood timber was the same. There could be no fair basis on which one could discriminate among Canadian, American, or Baltic pine and fir lumber. Yet the American "solution" of September 1938 involved a non-commercial discrimination. To argue that tariff rates should differentiate on the basis of size was not consistent with a commonsense interpretation of mfn rules. The documents do not tell us just why Whitehall and the British delegation gave in. One can only suppose that they were convinced there could be no agreement without some compromise on this principle. In all likelihood, when Prime Minister Chamberlain was shuttling to and from Hitler's realm during September 1938, and when war appeared to be imminent, no one in London was willing to accept the idea of a breakdown.

CHAPTER 8

The End at Last

October - November 1938

Early in October 1938 Cordell Hull went off to Atlantic City laden with documents. He wanted to consider the latest British proposals and decide whether to withdraw or modify any of the remaining American demands. By this time the Munich agreement had been signed and the Czech crisis seemed to be resolved. There was almost complete agreement on unplaned lumber, and Britain had got the Danes and the other pig producers to agree on the separation of Britain's ham and bacon quotas, and on the American share of each. President Roosevelt had also approved the "final list" of industrial concessions to the United Kingdom and to Canada.[1]

Hull, however, decided to persevere in his demands, and to make more. He was still unimpressed with the British offers, and he was not prepared, he told Ambassador Sir Ronald Lindsay, to sign an agreement "which does not contain more comprehensive concessions on the part of your government."[2] Hull and Sayre continued to press on the tobacco front and for free Canadian entry, from December to April, for American anthracite coal.[3] A draft agreement with an explanatory memorandum was presented to Lindsay that Sayre described as "governed by American political requirements" and that the British negotiators—and Joseph Kennedy in London —were inclined to regard as an ultimatum.[4] There was no such thing, Sayre replied, as an ultimatum among friends.[5]

Kennedy was anxious to be helpful but, as before, he urged moderation. "I think we need," Kennedy wrote on 7 October, "to

Reference notes for Chapter 8 begin on p. 184.

move reasonably quickly. . . . If you can give me some inside advice as
to what you will take to settle, I will go to work on it." But the
desperate mood of Munich had passed, and the hard bargaining was
obviously taking its toll. Oliver Stanley, Kennedy reported, was now
"definitely against the trade agreement as is all of the British Cabinet
with the exception of Chamberlain." The last demands had just arrived, and Stanley felt wrung out. "He feels that he has got concessions from everybody in order to make this deal and he feels that not
only will Parliament regard it as a complete sell out but he believes
that it will accentuate the already bad balance of trade. . . . " To add to
the difficulties, J.M. Keynes, the respected economist, had only that
day warned of precisely these kinds of problems in a letter to the
London *Times*.[6]

The outlook, said Lindsay, was so gloomy that it might be as well
if he went home for consultations. Explaining the position to London,
he said:

> concessions demanded of us represent the absolute limit of Ameri-
> can requests and would if granted lead immediately to signature.
> The protracted negotiations which have led to this have brought me
> personally to that state of bitterness and exasperation which usually
> results from dealings with United States Government. Their delays
> and tergiversations have been intolerable, they can see no point but
> their own and their demands cause His Majesty's Government loss
> of revenue and administrative difficulties out of all proportion to
> the benefits likely to accrue from American trade. We are being put
> through the mangle of American politics.

But Lindsay's patience somehow held despite it all. Though he
thought the Hull trade policy had no deep roots, and putting aside his
own deep dislike of American tactics, Lindsay was still sufficiently
impressed by the economic benefits, by the implications for Canada,
and by the risk of alienating the Americans to conclude: "I myself . . .
should prefer to accept the draft as it stands rather than break."[7]

The Foreign Office brooded on the possibility of a breakdown,
and began to blame the empire. One official wrote of the "extent to
which our hands are tied . . . it is not too much to say that a point has
been reached at which the interests of some forty million people in the
UK are to some extent jeopardized by our endeavour at every point to
meet the Dominions, India and the Colonies. . . . I think myself that the
day is rapidly approaching when a more independent attitude will be
necessary." Another official wrote that "the existing guaranteed preference on tobacco is a stumbling block not only in the American
negotiations but also in our efforts to save the Balkans from German
domination. If we want to use economics as a political weapon, we
shall either have to free our hands to a large extent from the self-

imposed restrictions of Ottawa or else persuade the Dominions and Colonies (and a large section of public opinion at home) that a rigid preferential system is for the present at least incompatible with the needs of foreign policy, and, in the last resort, with their own ultimate interests."[8] These thoughts were sparked by reflection on the impasse over lard that had nothing to do with the empire, and the tobacco perplex, which did.

Although the Foreign Office still wanted an agreement no matter what, Oliver Stanley at the Board of Trade no longer did. On 10 October he made his first report to the cabinet's Trade and Agriculture Committee since 16 July.[9] An agreement on a timber scheme had now been reached, and Britain had offered to reduce the duty on non-empire rice by 33 1/3 per cent—thereby infuriating India, Burma, Australia, and the home rice milling industry. Britain had also offered a much larger ham quota, which had involved difficult discussions with Denmark and Poland; further, she had reduced the duty on tracklaying tractors from 33.3 to 25 per cent. Now Hull wanted large new concessions.[10]

Stanley, hitherto a forceful champion of a trade agreement, was willing to give way on maize and lard, but he feared European competition in lighter-weight cars, small portable typewriters and wheat flour, where new concessions were now demanded. Because the Americans had so little of the trade in plywood and planed softwood, he observed that the cost to the UK Treasury could easily exceed the total value of US exports. He objected to the rigidity that a binding of the silk stocking preference would introduce into the tariff system. Stanley had also already promised larger concessions on electric appliances that used small motors, and he wished to maintain the three-year limit on the guaranteed ham quota because that term was worked into the scheme for the Exchequer's subsidy of the bacon industry. Naturally nothing could be done about anthracite. As for the tobacco proposal, this struck him as "fantastic." It would mean nothing as a legal commitment, and it would be "impossible" to take on the moral obligation "to do our best to obtain parliamentary authority" for a reduction in preferential margin four years hence.

The Trade and Agriculture Committee decided to reserve the main policy question—"whether we should now give the Americans our final offer and be prepared to break off negotiations for a trade agreement if that offer is not accepted"—for cabinet decision. Over Foreign Office objections, the committee endorsed Stanley's recommendation that the only new concessions should be on maize, lard, and tobacco: conventionalization of free entry for the first commodity, free entry for the second, and a new formula for the third. All the other

US demands it thought should be rejected. American concessions would be valuable, but they were already much outweighed by those made by London. The British had "now come to the point where the possibility of a breakdown must be faced, as the alternative was an indefinite prolongation of the negotiations and the continued raising by the Americans of new and intolerable demands."[11]

The cabinet discussed the problem on 19 October.[12] Stanley argued for a firm stand, although he was prepared to consider a concession on ham, "notwithstanding the difficulties involved." The foreign secretary, Lord Halifax, had argued the week before that "the political reasons for getting a treaty through must outweigh trade and economic considerations."[13] But even he thought "it was impossible to make concessions in regard to some of the requests." The prime minister asserted that he "had never hoped that we should obtain any great economic or political support from the United States as a result of making this agreement"—a statement that would have surprised the dominion premiers who had been urged in 1937 to offer concessions to that end. "The advantages to be derived," Neville Chamberlain explained, "were of a somewhat negative kind. It was clear that if after months of negotiations no Agreement was reached, hard things would be said."[14] To bypass the perverse and myopic American officials, Britain's last offer should go directly to Hull through Kennedy. Room should be left for a final appeal to the president, and "some final concession" should be reserved for use if such an appeal was needed. Kennedy accurately reported the British mood: "to grant any further concessions would make this agreement a farce as far as Great Britain is concerned." Stanley wanted an agreement, but not at any price. The British government, like its negotiators in Washington, regarded the last Hull démarche as an ultimatum.[15]

Britain's "final offer," including free entry for lard but rejecting almost all of the other American demands, reached Hull on 25 October.[16] Whitehall had already transmitted a tobacco formula that simply observed that Britain would "examine afresh the possibility of making some reduction in the margin of preference" after August 1942 if there was a fall in purchases of American tobacco.[17] Thereafter things moved fast. On 1 November, following many modifications, the British delegation reported that "agreement on lumber was virtually reached this morning with Americans and Canadians."[18] What was involved was a complex interlocking of dimensions, values, and rate of duty. A week later, Chamberlain was able to tell his cabinet colleagues that the "United States Government had agreed to the latest proposals which we had submitted"—apparently those of 19 October and the special arrangements regarding lumber and tobacco.[19]

Hull sent an elaborate report to Ambassador Kennedy explaining his rationale. He had decided, and Roosevelt had agreed, to

> accept the pending British offers (slightly modified in several respects) . . . the present offers represent the ultimate limit to which the British are prepared to go without reopening our proposed concessions to the United Kingdom. . . . We have had various indications from the British delegation here that they are dissatisfied with our concessions, and yesterday a specific request for improvement was made on an important item. This request was immediately rejected. While it might be possible to obtain improvements in the British concessions, I am certain that this would result in increased demands upon us, and such additional concessions as might be obtained from the British would not warrant subjecting American industries to the risk of additional concessions on our side.

In addition, delay was causing doubt and trouble in business circles, and note had been taken of Kennedy's own comments regarding "growing doubt in British official circles as to the desirability of an agreement. . . . In these circumstances I do not feel that such improvement in the British offer as might conceivably be obtained would warrant the delay and inevitable risk in these negotiations."[20] Despite all of Hull's rhetoric, this is what it all came down to: the British had been pushed to the limit. So much for economic appeasement. So much for a spirit of transatlantic solidarity in the face of the dictators.

There was one final snag over exchange rates. In a general way it was recognized by all governments that these rates might vary in such a way as to offset, nullify, or re-inforce the impact of any tariff concessions that might be negotiated. The issue had surfaced in the early 1930s, when many countries imposed special levies to offset the effect of exchange-depreciation. Britain herself, in 1931-32, had suffered greatly from such levies. Doubtless one reason why Whitehall and Threadneedle Street hoped and worked for stability of exchange rates, both inside the empire and outside it, was to stabilize the competitive situation. At the World Economic Conference of 1933, several governments, most notably the Canadian and the French, pressed for stabilization of exchange rates as a necessary preliminary to tariff reductions. By floating and devaluing the dollar in 1933-34, and by refusing to consider the renunciation of the presidential power to devalue it further, the American government inspired international distrust, not least in Whitehall, for the rest of the decade.

In 1935, the UK Treasury had learned that the United States wanted to include in its trade accords a provision that allowed parties to re-open or denounce an agreement if exchange rates should vary widely. British officials had recognized that such a clause might well be demanded in any Anglo-American bargain. Britain, after all, could hardly object, since she had used such a clause herself in the Anglo-French agreement of 1934.[21] However, in the preliminary Anglo-American discussions of 1935-37 the question of the exchange rate does not appear to have been discussed, perhaps because the rate itself was being held steady, by the British government's Exchange Equalisation Account, at a level the Americans found satisfactory. When a member of parliament inquired whether "questions of currency stability and the level of world commodity prices will be taken into consideration" during the trade talks, the Foreign Office and the Board of Trade agreed that the answer should be, "No, sir."[22]

The first British draft of the trade agreement's general clauses had therefore contained no provision respecting exchange rates, and there is no sign that any Whitehall department wished to include any.[23] However, on 21 February 1938, the State Department gave the British ambassador copies of draft general clauses, and these did include the following words: if the rate of exchange were to vary "considerably from the rate obtaining on the day of the signature of this Agreement, the Government of either country, if it considers the change in rate so substantial as to prejudice the industry or commerce of the country, shall be free to propose negotiations for the modification of this Agreement or to terminate this Agreement in its entirety on thirty days' notice."[24] Harry Hawkins explained that this had become standard American practice, and it would disarm criticism; A.E. Overton predicted that the UK Treasury would dislike it, but agreed to transmit it to London for scrutiny.[25]

The Treasury noted that "substantial" was undefined. Sir Frederick Phillips was worried, in addition, by the fact that the reference point was the date of signature, when the rate "for all we know [may] be $5.05 or something of that sort." Phillips suggested that Britain might ask the Americans to name some figures—for instance, plus or minus ten per cent around the old par of $4.86—so as to deny to the US "the power to tear it [the agreement] up whenever the exchange rate varies a few points." Other senior Treasury officials thought that numbers should not appear in the agreement. It was agreed by everyone, including the chancellor of the exchequer, that the Treasury's representative in Washington, T.K. Bewley, ought to ask American Treasury secretary Henry C. Morgenthau, Jr, what he thought would be "substantial."[26]

Although Morgenthau was away, Bewley shortly reported that American officials were promising the prospective article "would not be used unreasonably." Bewley was told that "the essential question was whether or not depreciation was or was not deliberate to obtain trade advantage." Apparently feeling that the "American attitude is reasonable,"[27] he suggested that Overton might assume responsibility for the matter, as part of the general negotiations. The Board of Trade, indeed, had already decided to accept the clause, so long as an understanding satisfactory to the Treasury could be devised.[28]

The British Treasury still wanted a definition of "substantial," and on 8 June it proposed that a range of 10 per cent on each side of the $4.86 figure should be agreed upon.[29] In the United States Treasury Harry Dexter White, always mistrustful of British intentions, suspected that London was trying to learn how low an exchange rate Washington would tolerate. This was not, as we have shown, London's intention. Another official believed it would be best to trust to the principles of the Tripartite Currency Agreement of 1936—in other words, "no competitive devaluation."[30] This was in fact the line that the State Department negotiators were taking. Hawkins had already told Overton that it would be better to "avoid precise definition . . . as it was the degree of injury rather than the amount of the change that mattered."[31] By early July Washington still wanted no definition while UK Treasury official Sigismund Waley wondered what all the fuss was about. Surely the idea of a 10 per cent margin would present no problem. It was, after all, unlikely that sterling could move outside the implied range, roughly $4.50 to $5.50, in the term of the agreement. Waley found force in the argument that to specify a range was to commit both parties too precisely and publicly, and he accepted American logic that it made no sense to specify the old "gold par of exchange" as base because $4.86 no longer had any legal standing in either country. Finally, he observed that the Board of Trade wanted some such clause to silence parliamentary criticism.[32]

Because there had been speculation that there were monetary negotiations in relation to the trade talks, the Americans wanted an exchange rate clause that was exactly the same as in other US trade agreements. It was hoped in this way to prevent any suspicion that something special was implied. Assured by the British negotiators that there was "no difference of substance," and believing that "the agreement will be signed at a time when the rate is sufficiently close to the old par to give us no anxiety," the British Treasury had no trouble in giving its assent, which was transmitted to Sir Ronald Lindsay in Washington on 23 July 1938.[33]

Thus it appeared that the question of the exchange rate had been solved. The Americans would be tactful in their interpretation of any depreciation. The British would not press for more precise definition. Treasury Secretary Morgenthau, however, had been too fatigued to consider the matter fully in June and July, and he took the view that the apparent decision to retain only the ordinary "hedge clause" had not really been a deliberate one.[34] When sterling fell more, and continued to fall, Morgenthau felt justified in raising the matter once again. Between April and September 1938, as the crisis proceeded in central Europe, sterling had gone down about 3 per cent—no great amount, but enough to excite H.D. White, and any other Anglophobes in the American Treasury. White argued that the Treasury could not tell Britain "how much of a change in exchange rates may be regarded as prejudicial . . . obviously small changes would not be so interpreted." Besides, the State Department, not the Treasury, had to interpret the provisions of a trade agreement.[35]

Morgenthau discussed the decline of sterling with his officials in early September.[36] He wondered aloud whether he should send a letter to Hull calling attention to "the relationship between the fall of sterling in recent months and the trade agreement now being negotiated." The pressure for a Treasury initiative seems to have come from the obviously agitated White, who wanted Morgenthau to write the president, and who reported that the Concessions Committee in the State Department "are worried too, because . . . many of the concessions that have been granted have already been neutralized by this drop."

Morgenthau himself was not anxious to appear to be torpedoing the trade negotiations, "especially when you get all through and done sterling is not fluctuating so terribly much." A warning, however, was issued from the Treasury in the form of a memorandum to Herbert Feis at the State Department. Feis discussed it with Hull, Sayre, and Hawkins. "There was common agreement," Feis reported, "that this movement of the pound—especially if it went substantially further—might give rise to new difficulties both in regard to the trade agreement and in the monetary field. It was judged that it might serve a useful purpose if the British Government could be made cognizant of the fact that the movement of the pound was under close observation." Sayre told Lindsay that there might have to be revisions in American concessions. The movement of the rate "was a matter of some moment," agreed Lindsay. But the ambassador also pointed out that the British simply could not allow the terms of the negotiation to be changed in this way.[37]

Although we cannot be sure how seriously the State Department's negotiators took Morgenthau's representations, it is plausible to argue that they had something to do with the American intransigence, and with the new American demands, of September and October 1938. Life would have been simpler for everyone, however, if the American negotiators had outlined their concerns more clearly.

Worse was in store. Sterling fell yet further, and Morgenthau intervened again. On 21 October he convened a conference of officials and academics. Should the United States insert a definite exchange rate floor into the draft treaty? The agreement had been figured at $4.90. Sterling was now roughly at $4.75. Morgenthau, remaining a moderate on the issue, was not at all inclined to accept the prompting of White, who believed that the British could have supported the pound simply by selling more gold. Morgenthau said that London had done "everything humanly possible to maintain sterling." He wondered, however, if Britain might "do what they are doing up to the minute the trade treaty is signed, and then the bottom drops out."

After a long and confused interchange Herbert Feis entered a note of good sense. "This whole discussion," he said, "is taking place against a background in which our chief difficulty in making our commercial relations an effective weight in our general international relations is our very marked excess of exports.... Second ... this negotiation with Great Britain is connected with the one with Canada." A trade agreement formula, Feis reminded the Treasury secretary, could not deal with the effect of sterling's depreciation in the Canadian and in other third markets, "so to summarize I am led to the conclusion that you're going to find it difficult to do anything practical that is much of an improvement over that general formula." White wanted negotiations for rejigging the treaty to begin when sterling touched $4.72, and the trade treaty to be automatically terminated by a secret protocol, known in advance to the British, when sterling touched $4.52. Feis said that the United States did not do such things, and it was finally decided to pursue the question of the exchange rate not through the trade negotiations but through the provisions for consultation that were part of the Tripartite Agreement of 1936.[38]

Morgenthau was not quite done yet. The Bank of England and the Federal Reserve Bank of New York co-operated in the management of the sterling-dollar rate. Each day after control passed westward with the shutting down of the exchanges in the Eastern Hemisphere, London told New York the rate at which to work. The New York bank routinely told the Treasury secretary what instructions it had received. It was through this mechanism that Morgenthau learned, when the trade agreement was on the point of signature in mid-November, that London had decided sterling would have to fall a little more. He went at once to Roosevelt, telling the president that the trade agreement had been "worked out on the basis of around 4.93 and it was now 4.70." What did the president think? Roosevelt asked how low sterling might go before the United States would suffer, and Morgenthau said that studies in the Treasury suggested the figure was $4.60 or even $4.50. It should be noted that Morgenthau did not wish to raise the question of sterling with the British until after the agreement had been signed. He was not advising Roosevelt actually to do anything, but the matter had been put before the president, and in a way that might well have been disastrous. Roosevelt asked about the relation between the Canadian dollar and sterling. Morgenthau explained that the fall of sterling did not affect the rate between the two North American currencies. Roosevelt said that he wanted a treaty with Canada very much, and could not get one unless he could get one with Britain as well, so "if you'll tell me that the Canadian dollar is all right let's let this thing go. . . . We'll sign the British trade treaty, but when we sign it—and at the time of signing it we'll put the British on notice."[39]

After Morgenthau's departure Roosevelt seems to have changed his mind. Almost at once he telephoned Francis Sayre at the State Department, telling him to put the British on notice at once. Sayre went to see the British ambassador, asking him if something could not be done to "sustain the pound, particularly during the coming few days." He also suggested, and Lindsay agreed, that there should be a public statement denying the rumour that the agreement "contains a provision stabilizing the rate of the pound at 4.50."[40] Lindsay reported to London that Roosevelt was "gravely alarmed at the fall in sterling today and . . . urged him [Lindsay] to consider carefully what should be done if . . . fall were to be further accentuated." According to the ambassador, Sayre had said that the United States would sign the trade agreement even if there were a severe fall in the pound, but he asked Britain to support sterling to a reasonable extent in the meantime.[41]

In April no one had expected sterling to fall at all. By early November no one expected it to do anything else. The British Treasury was informed of Roosevelt's worries, and it is possible that some extra support was applied to sterling in mid-November, although we have found no documentary evidence to that effect. But why had Roosevelt become so agitated? It seems likely the president had realized that he might be criticized if he signed an Anglo-American trade agreement when the pound was sliding downward. It should be remembered that in earlier years he had been inclined to make a scene whenever sterling stood below the $5.00 mark. He was also aware that some influential American export interests, knowing that cheaper sterling meant lower dollar prices for their exports, watched the course of the exchange rate with extreme attention.

It is perplexing to learn that President Roosevelt regarded the Anglo-American agreement merely as a necessary bridge toward a new agreement with Canada. This was not the view of the American government in 1937. In that year the State Department began to talk with Canada only when it became clear that there could be no agreement with Britain—indeed, no Anglo-American talks—without a Canadian-American agreement. Had the president really agreed with, or accepted, these priorities? Certainly, as we have seen, he allowed the Anglo-American talks to begin formally only when Henry Wallace had assured him that there would be worthwhile concessions for American farmers.

Roosevelt's autumn enthusiasm for a Canadian agreement must remain one of those intriguing historical mysteries. The president's papers are irritatingly silent on this topic, as on so many others. It should be remembered that Canada was the largest single trading partner of the United States. Perhaps someone had reminded the president of this fact. Furthermore, the floating Canadian dollar had been hovering around par with the American for almost four years. Unlike the pound, it had shown no tendency to fall during the international political crisis of summer 1938. Fluctuations in the Canadian-dollar exchange rate, therefore, might be thought improbable, so that the Canadian-American agreement was not likely to be disrupted by exchange-rate movements. Moreover, solid Canadian-American relations were on the presidential agenda. Roosevelt had worked hard on his relationship with Mackenzie King, and he had reason to hope for North American (and hemispheric) solidarity against the coming storm in Europe. The president, indeed, had only recently visited Canada, giving his assurance "that the people of the United States will not stand idly by if domination of Canadian soil is threatened. . . ."[42]

The British government and the American president thus saw the treaty in very different terms. Whitehall and Westminster now looked for the payoff not in terms of economic benefits but on the highest plane of international politics. The British sought an Anglo-American trade agreement in order to improve their political relations with the United States, and to help construct a united front against the Rome-Berlin-Tokyo alliance. The Foreign Office could wax embarrassingly lyrical on the subject. But the president of the United States now apparently wanted an Anglo-American bargain just so he could have a trade agreement with Canada.

To the Canadians who had taken part in the negotiations it appeared that things had gone very well. Britain had acquiesced in a considerable derogation from her preferential privileges in the Canadian market, even though substantial privileges still remained. From the Americans the dominion had won many concessions, even enticing Hull to breach his own mfn doctrine for the sake of Canadian cattle exports. Canadian officials believed, in addition, that they had conceded less than the Americans.

Neither the British nor the American negotiators, however, could possibly have viewed their own labours so positively. As the British had foreseen since 1934, they had been unable to meet American demands with respect to such products as tobacco. As for timber, it is reasonable to suppose that the final agreed provision would have proved unworkable in peacetime practice. Nor did the Americans concede as much as British officials had at first hoped. American duties on cotton textiles remained very high indeed, often well over 50 per cent *ad valorem*—quite high enough to constitute a prohibitive barrier against British textile exports. Thus the Anglo-American agreement was a "balanced" one in the rather negative sense that neither side won significant concessions of real substance. The provisions of the agreement could not possibly have made a real difference to the prosperity of the American primary producers whose interests the administration was so anxious to advance. It could not have done anything much to remedy the massive bilateral imbalance in Anglo-American trade that was already so worrying to the officials in Whitehall. For Britain the United States was an insignificant market. The trade agreement did not alter that fact.

In terms of *realpolitik*, perhaps, the term "balance" could also be applied, but in a different sense. Chamberlain could say that he was co-operating with Hull's Grand Design, while hoping for the more limited end of Anglo-Saxon unity as the international clouds gathered. Mackenzie King could with more justice proclaim himself a genuine Hullite, while at the same time he could boast to his electorate that he had honoured his pledges to reduce tariffs and to avoid any elaboration of the preferential system. The Roosevelt administration could claim that it had won Britain's co-operation in the Hull plan for the reconstruction of the world economy. It could tell supporters that it had breached the walls of the Ottawa system, although the extent of the breach was not really very great. And it could make the case that gains had been made for America's farmers and lumbermen, although the claim would not have much substance. The result, in short, was a set of agreements that dispensed a very mixed assortment of gains and advantages, some real and some apparent.

The agreements themselves were complicated documents — monuments to the twentieth-century commitment to tariff differentiation.[43] There were actually only two agreements, one between Britain and the United States, and another between the United States and Canada. It had not been thought necessary formally to renegotiate the Anglo-Canadian agreement of 1937, although both Britain and Canada had agreed to many derogations from that agreement. The Americans made new commitments on some four hundred items, and the British on almost as many; some of these commitments involved no more than promises not to increase rates, while others involved an actual reduction in the rates of duty charged. The Canadian-American agreement also involved both sorts of commitment, and made these on many hundreds of items. The Americans promised not to impose marking regulations on Canadian lumber, and to tax such lumber at a rate of $1.50 per thousand board feet. The British said that if the Americans were to reduce the rate to fifty cents per thousand board feet they would charge no duty on American softwood, so long as the pieces were at least nine inches wide and at least fifteen feet long; meantime, a complicated scheme that differentiated by size and by value would apply. Britain also agreed to admit unmilled wheat free, to charge no duty on ham and to fix a minimum US ham quota of 500,000 cwt per year, to charge 25 per cent on tracklaying tractors and to charge 33 1/3 per cent on motor cars of 25 HP or more, thus effectively denying Germany the benefit of the conventionalized tariff. American apples would pay only 3/- per hundredweight from 16 August to 15 April. Sad to say, there was no British commitment respecting peanut butter.

On the American side, rates remained considerably higher than on the British, and tariff differentiation on cotton textiles still ran rampant. The Americans had not modified their scheme for taxing textiles, in particular, by simultaneously levying specific and *ad valorem* tariffs on the same good; in addition, they still applied extra *ad valorem* levies as the count of the textile increased, thus penalizing the higher-quality goods. On Nottingham lace the scheme was simpler, but the rate—50 per cent *ad valorem* —remained penal. The Anglo-American agreement contained an exchange-rate proviso. "Wide variation" in the exchange rate would allow either party to re-open the negotiations, and, if not satisfied by the result, to denounce the agreement. Although in earlier conversations the Americans had maintained that this arrangement appeared in all their trade agreements, there was no such proviso in the Canadian-American agreement. One must suppose either that the Americans trusted the Canadians to keep the exchange rate near "par," or that they still distrusted the British. The Americans granted free entry to agricultural implements. The Canadians did not.

If "economic appeasement" was to mean anything, the bilateral concessions would have to be generalized and extended to other countries through the mfn provisions of other trade agreements, not only British but also American and Canadian. The concessions, however, were so compartmentalized and subdivided that, although no doubt Germany could extract some industrial benefit in the American and British markets, there was no chance of anything large—certainly nothing sufficiently dramatic to affect the course of German foreign policy. Indeed, as we saw above, the British concession on automobiles was cunningly devised so as to do the Germans no good at all. Furthermore, insofar as the British and the Americans had simply promised not to increase many rates of duty, there were no new gains for the Germans to seize. Nor was the United States eager to contemplate uncovenanted extension of benefit to third parties. On cattle, for instance, she had conceded lower rates on cows that weighed less than 200 pounds, and 700 pounds or more, so as to avoid extending any benefit to Mexico, where cows typically weighed somewhere in between. And on lumber she had fought for a British tariff that would extend no benefits to the Scandinavian states—small democracies that depended on the British market. On hams, she had extracted a larger quota at the expense of the Baltic states and Holland. No doubt Cordell Hull was sincere in his advocacy of "economic disarmament." But when his officials seated themselves around the bargaining table, other considerations came into play.

What did it all mean? What was the larger political and economic effect of the negotiation? As we shall see in the next chapter, the agreements almost certainly could not have had any very interesting economic effect. But perhaps that does not matter. Perhaps politics—whether domestic or international—were all.

CHAPTER 9

Conclusion: The Trials of Trilateralism

As we meditated on the gloomy story that we have recounted above, we were led to reflect on motivations and tactics, and to ask questions about the machinery both of government and of tripartite negotiation. Did the delays arise through ill-will or through inefficiency? What part was played by the system itself, with its inherent complexities? Were the trade negotiations worthwhile, and if so, in what sense, and to whom? Who gained and who lost, or is it even sensible to look for winners or losers? Do the agreements have any wider significance? In this final chapter we turn to these larger issues.

Trade negotiations are often viewed as a kind of game, in which the object of the exercise is to concede as little as possible while winning as much as possible. In this approach, "little" and "much" are defined on the basis of the number of concessions given and received, the amounts of the various concessions, and the presence or absence of benefits to third parties. From any single country's viewpoint, it is also possible to ask how closely the final bargain approximates to the initial set of demands: the country that does best is the country that manages, measuring from the starting positions of the negotiating parties, to force the biggest concessions from the other country. The winner is thus the country whose negotiators best defended their initial position, conceded a little, but won major concessions from trading partners, while preventing any unconvenanted extension of benefits to third parties. These are the terms in which

---

Reference notes for Chapter 9 begin on p. 186.

both officials and politicians congratulate themselves, in private and in public, once trade talks are over. Indeed, one Canadian participant in the 1938 talks recently rejoiced because Canada had got the Americans to cut their cattle tariffs while introducing a rate-differentiation that prevented the Mexicans from benefiting, through mfn provisions, from the new and lower rate.[1] Economists certainly do not discuss trade negotiations in these terms, and historians ought not to. Trade concessions can have important effects on the allocation of resources and on consumer welfare, not only in the signatory countries but elsewhere as well. Surely it is with reference to these effects that a trade negotiation ought to be judged an economic success or a failure, whether for any one signatory or for all.

Both President Roosevelt and Prime Minister King hoped that the trilateral trade agreements would do something for economic appeasement, with its expected benefits for international politics. In the last chapter we argued that under this heading the negotiations, and the agreements, seem to have achieved nothing. But what of more narrowly-defined economic effects? Naturally the negotiators and the politicians of the three countries did not employ the precise microeconomic calculations which the present-day analyst of trade agreements would use. They deployed much cruder techniques. "Gain," "loss," or "equality of concession" were often measured simply by the volume or value of traded goods on which concessions were offered. The negotiators wanted to raise prices, win sales, produce profits for domestic producers, and avoid extra unemployment. They had no interest in the efficient allocation of resources, either within their own countries or internationally. Present-day scholars, we believe, ought not to be so cavalier.

The American negotiating strategy seems to have had little connection with American economic reality. It will be remembered that the main thrust of that strategy related to meat products, animal fats, tobacco, and sawmill products; in dealing with Canada, there was also much concern about anthracite. But the British would not or could not do anything for American tobacco, and with respect to coal the British and the Canadians were equally adamant. Sad to say, the Americans were obsessed with commodities whose weight in the domestic economy was extremely small. In 1936, American exports of meat products were 0.04 per cent of US national income; of animal fats and oils, 0.02 per cent; of sawmill products, 0.07 per cent. Canada's imports of British anthracite were 0.01 per cent of American national income. Britain's total import of tobacco was 0.1 per cent of American national income. But most of that tobacco already came from the United States, so that the gain from a reduction in the tobacco duty would be very small indeed. Britain's total imports of ham amounted to only 0.02 per cent of American national income. British imports of softwood, which totalled 0.2 per cent of American national income, may seem to represent a prize more worth seeking. Yet it is reasonable to suppose that if Britain were to reduce the duty, the main beneficiary would be the Baltic states.

All these calculations, admittedly, understate the benefits in terms of extra sales or higher prices that a tariff cut would have dispensed to American producers, because they do not allow for the stimulating effect of a lower British price or a larger British vent. But among all the primary products with which the American negotiators were obsessed, it is only those which consumers buy and eat where one might expect any pronounced stimulation under that heading. And in 1936 Britain's total imports of such goods — ham, apples, and dried fruit — summed to only twelve million pounds, or less than 0.01 per cent of American national income: even if a tariff cut were to double Britain's imports — a most implausible outcome — the US gain would be insignificantly small. In these calculations we have deliberately employed the American "national income," as published in the 1930s, not the more sophisticated measures of gross national product that are available today, because we want to emphasize that any American official or politician could have made exactly the same calculations at any time during the 1930s. Our numerical results must make us wonder what the Americans thought they were up to. Perhaps they never thought to do the calculations.

Because war broke out less than ten months after the agreements were signed, we cannot hope to detect their impact on trade flows. We also have to be careful to remember the longer-term trends in trade patterns. In 1938, 63 per cent of Canada's imports came from the United States, and 18 per cent from the United Kingdom; in 1939 the figures were 66 and 15 per cent. Should we give credit (or blame) to the Canadian-American trade agreement, which narrowed preferential margins and lowered Canadian duties on many American goods? Probably not. Ever since 1933 Britain's share of Canada's imports had been falling, and America's share had been rising. As for Britain's import trade, one might have expected some diversion from empire outlets, whose preferential margins were reduced in many instances, to American sources, which often faced lower duties once the agreements had come into effect. In fact, both in 1938 and in 1939 Britain imported precisely the same proportion, 40.4 per cent, from empire sources. Even though Britain's total imports were lower in 1939 than in 1938 she bought slightly more from Canada, so that 8.6 per cent of her imports came from that source in 1938 and 9 per cent in

1939. Obviously there had been no diversion of trade from the senior dominion. As for the United States, 13.2 per cent of Britain's imports came from there in 1939 as against 12.8 per cent in 1938, even though total imports from that source went down by 700,000 pounds, which was 0.6 per cent of Britain's 1938 purchases from the USA.

As we have seen, the most obvious targets—and potential victims—of the American negotiating strategy were the countries which supplied Britain with meat and timber. Here the picture is a mixed one, but it does not suggest very much trade diversion. Argentina's sales to Britain went up, both in percentage terms and in absolute amount. So did those of Australia, Holland, Sweden, and South Africa. Finland and the Soviet Union sold much less, so that their shares went down. The apparent explanation of the Russo-Finnish experience, however, is the outbreak of war, with its disruption of Baltic shipping. Much the same thing happened to Germany. If we exclude Germany, the Soviet Union, and France, we find that the remaining countries of northern Europe, a group which includes all the relevant European producers of timber and livestock, won an increased share of the British market: from 20.6 per cent of all imports in 1938, their share rose to 21.1 per cent in 1939.[2]

Thus the relevant European states had a greater share of the British market after than before. So did the United States. Nor were the losers empire countries. Rather it was the states of Central and Eastern Europe, with which the threat of war was already inhibiting trade by the summer of 1939. At first sight it would seem that the United States had not succeeded in its aim of substantially diverting trade from low-cost European suppliers to higher-cost American ones. However, it should be remembered that from mid-1938 until September 1939 the pound depreciated considerably in comparison with the American and Canadian dollars—since 1933 the pound had hovered around the five-dollar mark, but in 1938 it slipped to about $4.68—while some of the Northern European currencies floated downward with the pound. The British government supported the pound at 1938 levels until the summer of 1939, but it then allowed a slide to $4.03, at which level the pound was pegged until 1949. In the absence of any other changes, so sharp a movement of exchange rates ought to have worsened the competitive position of American suppliers in the British market. America's relatively favourable showing, therefore, may be to some small extent a tribute to the trade-diverting effects of the Anglo-American agreement.

The Canadian data, however, give one pause. Because the Canadian dollar also appreciated in relation to sterling, from nearly $5 in 1937 to $4.43 in 1939,[3] one would have supposed that Canadian goods, like American, ought to have lost position and market share in Britain. As we have just seen, however, both purchases and shares increased between 1938 and 1939. Perhaps we have to conclude that, although the movement in the two sterling-dollar rates looks very large, it was not sufficient to alter established trading patterns. If that is so, we must in turn surmise that the Anglo-American trade agreement had little effect on the trade in the "North Atlantic triangle." Nor should this conclusion surprise us. After all, Britain's main purchases from the United States were tobacco, raw cotton, petroleum, and wheat, none of which were affected by the new arrangements. It is true that Britain had agreed to abolish her duty on non-empire wheat, but the duty was believed to have had no effect on trade patterns. As for tobacco, Britain had conceded nothing, and the UK never taxed raw cotton or crude oil at all, while the retail taxation of petroleum products was not protective in intention or in effect. It was because they recognized these facts of economic life that British officials had argued for such a long time that they had nothing to offer the Americans in a trade agreement.

Besides the economic issues, in these as in all trade negotiations there are many non-economic issues as well. Both domestic and international politics were involved in the tripartite talks of the late 1930s. At certain points it was awareness of the international ramifications that kept the talks going; in fact, it was this awareness that finally led the United Kingdom to sign a trade agreement with the United States. Although both the Canadian and the American negotiators seem to have lost sight of these larger issues in the course of the negotiations, neither government would have begun the talks if their leaders had not been concerned with very large issues — peace, war, transatlantic solidarity, economic appeasement, international amity.

These large issues centre upon the Anglo-American negotiations, and on their result. Obstruction by Canada could have prevented success in the Anglo-American talks, but a new Canadian-American agreement, in and of itself, could do little for world peace, despite the hopes of the Canadian prime minister. Nevertheless, in the process of negotiation both Canadian and American officials, as well as the political leaders in the two North American states, were drawn much closer together. Mutual accommodation and common understanding would be important during the Second World War. The trade talks of 1937-38 undoubtedly made some contribution to their growth, although other developments and imperatives in Canadian-American relations were undoubtedly more important. Something similar probably happened between Britain and the United States. British distrust of the Americans was certainly not lessened. Whitehall's decision to sign the agreement, in the final analysis, was in some large measure a negative one, in the sense it was felt that failure to reach an agreement would have damaged the relationship even more. But it was not the British who required to be conciliated. It was the American government whose good will would be so badly needed if war were to break out, and it is reasonable to suppose that some of that intangible commodity was purchased by the success of the talks.

Sweetness and light, however, did not extend to the Axis powers. During the trade talks themselves the Czech crisis occurred; soon after the agreements were signed, Germany polished off the rest of Czechoslovakia. There is no sign that the demonstration of transatlantic solidarity had the slightest impact on Hitler's plans. Nor did it do anything much for "economic appeasement," even if we assume that Hitler could have been induced to follow that particular will-o'-the-wisp. Cordell Hull believed that if countries would trade more freely, and if discriminatory measures could be reduced or eliminated, peace and prosperity would break out in all directions. It is easy to make fun of this idea, but it was passionately shared by a great many prominent men of the time, Prime Minister Mackenzie King not the least. No one now believes that Nazi Germany rearmed because of the Ottawa Agreements, or that free and open trade could have solved Germany's balance-of-payments problems in a world where its economy was running full-blast and few other economies were running at more than half-throttle. Even if Hull and King had been right, the 1938 agreements would not have been a good test of their ideas, because both were carefully arranged to have the least possible value to third countries, such as Germany, Scandinavia, or Mexico. German cars would not gain from British tariff cuts, which were carefully designed to exclude them. As for Baltic pine, the agreements contained scandalous provisions whose form was determined almost wholly by American pressure. To the Germans and the Japanese, and to the smaller democracies of western and northern Europe, it must have looked as if the Anglo-Saxon democracies were doing a deal among themselves—a deal from which the Axis powers were carefully shut out.

So much for economic appeasement, which was of course aimed at political results. What did the American government really expect of the British? A clue might be provided by Hull's remark: the British empire had made the Ottawa Agreements; it was up to them to unmake them. Perhaps Hull hoped that the British could be induced to denounce the agreements so as to free their hands for dealing with the Americans. Perhaps the vague American proposals of 1934, and the somewhat more concrete proposals of 1937, were meant to induce some such response. In these terms, the substantially less attractive offers of spring 1938 make some sense, since by that time the Americans would have realized that the British had no intention of denouncing the agreements, and that London had never realized Washington wanted it to do so or hoped that it might.

If the Americans had really been hoping for denunciation, their hopes were certainly in vain. The British authorities never considered such action, and never recorded any suspicion that the United States might want or expect them to take it. Certainly they would have been mad to do so. For British exports, the several empire markets were far more important than the American one, and the concessions that the Americans might make would be far more than counterbalanced if the dominions and India retaliated by reducing or eliminating the trading preferences they gave to Britain. There would be every reason to expect that all the southern dominions, plus India and probably Canada, would do precisely that. The other empire countries could and probably would maintain their own preferential trade agreements, many of these antedating Ottawa and most involving mutual gains that would continue to be valuable even if Britain withdrew, or was forced to withdraw, from the preferential system. British denunciation, furthermore, would still leave many preferences intact because it would not remove them from British goods in the dependent empire, these deriving from executive actions not from trade agreements. Nor would it dispose of all Britain's own preferences. Many of these dated not from Ottawa but from a variety of preferential concessions under Finance Acts and Safeguarding of Industry Acts, going all the way back to 1919.[4] Further unilateral preferential concessions had been offered in the course of the 1920s. Of course, once freed from the network of the Ottawa Agreements, the British government would be free to bargain about the dependent empire and about its own preferences. It might or might not be induced to withdraw these.

In the course of the negotiations, the Americans actually did not make much of a dent in the preferential system. The wheat preference was abolished because no one attached any value to it. For flour, where serious interests were involved, no headway was made. With respect to anthracite coal, the same thing could be said. On ham, lard, and bacon, American "progress" was largely at the expense of the Baltic states, which did not belong to the preferential system, and at the expense of the British Exchequer, which had to find more subsidies for pig-breeders. In their negotiations with Canada, United States officials did convince both the dominion and the mother country that some preferential margins should be reduced. They were able to do this because Ottawa itself favoured a more flexible approach to such margins. However, Canada did not want to abolish the preferential system, either at its own frontier or at other frontiers, such as the British, the West Indian, and the Australian, where such advantages helped Canada's trade. Prime Minister King was theoretically convinced by Hull's general preachments on the topic of economic appeasement and world peace, but in the actual conduct of negotiations, he and his officials were far more hard-headed.

Thus when war broke out the system of imperial preferences was still more or less intact. It is hardly surprising, therefore, that during the war itself the American government renewed its commercial offensive of 1934-38, employing new weapons that London's dire financial needs placed ready to Washington's hand.

It has been suggested that the trilateral trade talks of 1938 should be seen as an incident on America's Grand March of tariff reduction. No one doubts the progress from the Smoot-Hawley heights, when the average rate of duty on America's actual imports was 49.1 per cent and when rates of 100 per cent or more were common, to 1978, when the average was 8 per cent.[5] Even though non-tariff barriers had increased during the later 1970s, the United States economy had certainly become much more open. Furthermore, non-tariff barriers were anything but unknown during the 1930s, and the Americans were as prone to employ them as anyone else. Canadian negotiators and politicians have been known to claim credit for moving the Americans along the route. The landmarks are familiar—the Trade Agreements Act of 1934, then the 1938 agreements, then various renewals and extensions of the President's tariff-cutting power, the creation of the General Agreement on Tariffs and Trade (GATT) and the negotiations thereunder, and the Kennedy and Tokyo Rounds in the 1960s and 1970s. With the benefit of historical hindsight it is certainly possible to tell the tale in this way. Indeed, before we completed our research we were inclined to do so. But such an approach leaves almost all the interesting questions unanswered.

The story, we now believe, is a more complicated one, not only in the commercial sphere but also in the financial. Rather than believing that the great English-speaking nations "came to their senses" following the experience of the depression, we now think that they had learned little from that experience, so that if the uneasy peace of the 1930s had continued, there would have been little chance of fruitful innovation either in international financial affairs or in commercial matters. There is a great gap between the texture of the negotiations we describe, and the later evolution of international economic institutions. The tale we tell is, in fact, a tale not of unity but of disharmony—a tale of vision not clear but clouded. Our skepticism is increased when we survey some of the economic developments that followed the agreements.

In the winter of 1938-39, and indeed until the final dismemberment of Czechoslovakia in March 1939, the British cabinet was desperately anxious to conciliate and appease the Hitler government. Until the outbreak of war, the cabinet appeared to be grasping at straws in its search for accommodation. For example, ministers still pondered the possibility of a deal by which some of the former German colonies might be returned.[6] But nothing more was said about conciliating Germany through trade: by the end of 1938 economic appeasement, in the minds of the British cabinet ministers, was almost a dead letter. On the other hand, American support came to seem ever more important.

Late in 1938 it was decided[7] to keep President Roosevelt appraised of European developments, and of British attitudes toward these. This was systematically done. Also, the Chiefs of Staff told the cabinet that "if war were to break out, the ultimate outcome might well depend upon the intervention of other powers, in particular the United States,"[8] while in July 1939 Sir Richard Hopkins, permanent undersecretary of the Treasury, reminded the cabinet that Britain's war effort would depend crucially on American support. The national "war chest," he explained, contained only two hundred million pounds' worth of easily saleable securities, and only five hundred million pounds' worth of gold, an amount that was rapidly being drained by the effort to support the pound at $4.68. It was known that the Americans attached great importance to this figure, and Hopkins did not suggest a devaluation. But at the current rate of depletion, which Hopkins said would certainly be quickly surpassed in wartime, the war chest would not last three years. The position, he said, was worse than in 1914, unless the United States was prepared to extend support. And that could not be assumed. Furthermore, even devaluation could probably be attempted only after discussion with the United States, because Roosevelt could easily defeat the British intent simply by raising the dollar price of gold.[9]

Roosevelt himself was known to be sympathetic to the democracies, and he disliked the Neutrality Act, which had the effect of requiring belligerents to pay cash, and which forbade Americans from exporting war materiel. But he was not much concerned about the Johnson Act, which forbade credits to such international defaulters as Britain, because he thought that "money seeps through barriers." At best, he thought, Congress might be induced to extend the cash-and-

carry provisions of the existing Neutrality Act to cover war materiel
and munitions. As a British official reported, "the President thought
that ought to be enough for us . . . we had ample funds in the United
States." He also thought that any new war would be shorter than the
war of 1914-18.[10] Thus it was increasingly necessary not only to change
President Roosevelt's mind but to massage American opinion, where,
though there was plenty of good will, there was also much suspicion
and little understanding of Britain's plight. Nor were the Americans
forthcoming in other directions. When Britain tried to arrange for a
joint Anglo-American credit that would help finance the Chinese war
effort by supporting the national currency, Washington responded
only after a long delay, and eventually opted only for "parallel and
simultaneous but not identical action."[11]

When a senior American senator invented a barter proposal by
which Britain and the USA would co-operate to acquire commodity
reserves, it proved impossible to make the Americans understand just
why the proposal was so awkward. The scheme sprang full-blown
from the mind of Senator James Byrnes, and it was soon adopted by
the president, although it seems that Cordell Hull may not have been
enamoured of it. Byrnes' idea was as follows: America would barter
cotton, whose price the American government was with difficulty
supporting, and perhaps wheat, in exchange for rubber, and perhaps
tin, which the British government would supply.

The proposal was unattractive in London for several reasons.
Britain held no stocks of rubber or tin, and the international commodity cartels that controlled production would not allow an increase in
supply from empire territories alone, so that Britain could clinch the
deal only by buying commodities in the open market, perhaps at
considerable cost to the foreign exchange reserves. By supplying the
USA with wartime stockpiles in exchange for cotton, Britain would be
depriving herself of the chance to earn dollars by selling empire
rubber and tin in the usual way. And the price at which the barter
would consummate itself was a matter of some importance, given that
the cotton price was an entirely artificial one.[12] Britain, on the other
hand, could buy cotton from many non-American sources, and did
not really know how much cotton she ought to hold as a "wartime
reserve." If the scheme were to go through, the only real gainer would
be the US government, which would be able to unload much of the
cotton stocks that the ordinary channels of trade would not absorb.

Yet it was recognized from the beginning that London would
have to meet the American proposal "to some extent:" the scheme had
Roosevelt's backing.[13] Sir Ronald Lindsay, still in Washington, was
asked to enquire whether, if the deal were to go through, the Senate

might see fit to modify the neutrality law. Lindsay reported that the scheme would not significantly affect Congress but that the United Kingdom should adopt "a forthcoming attitude."[14] Certainly the Foreign Office officials, true to form, were anxious to do just this, even though it was reported that Hull was lukewarm and even though the British Board of Trade found the scheme distasteful. The permanent undersecretary at the Board of Trade, Sir William Brown, indeed described it as a "political stunt." However, the foreign secretary thought that "for political reasons it is necessary that the deal should go through."[15]

The barter negotiations took place in London. The American side was managed personally by the ambassador, Joseph Kennedy, whose enthusiasm was such that some British officials suspected he might have a pecuniary interest in the outcome. Kennedy wanted Britain to buy more cotton than the Whitehall officials thought they needed, and at the very last minute he demanded a higher price for the cotton. He explained that the Americans "might be prepared to break off negotiations" if they did not get their way. The President of the Board of Trade felt obliged to bring both matters to the full cabinet, "in view of the importance of our relations with the United States at the present time." And as Chamberlain said, it would be very unfortunate if there were to be a "breakdown of negotiations, or negotiations in a grudging spirit, particularly at the present time"—June 1939.[16]

These barter discussions echoed the trade negotiations of the preceding year. Once again we see America's special interest in farm products, her extreme selfishness, her unwillingness to recognize the difficulties of others, and her tendency to raise the stakes at the last minute. On the other hand, the rubber-for-cotton agreement reveals yet again the British willingness to make unsatisfactory economic arrangements for the sake of international politics. These similarities are not surprising. The participants were all the same, while the international conjuncture had grown worse.

Why, then, was the wartime and postwar evolution so much happier than than this pre-war experience might have suggested? There is already a considerable literature on the development of the GATT and the IMF, and that literature, we believe, is consistent with the conclusion to which we incline: that it was the War that made the difference.

Our conclusion is, we readily admit, a speculative one. But surely it is reasonable. Why should a peace-time United States have moved in such a direction? Why would the position of the United Kingdom have changed in a fashion that would cause her to acquiesce in the sorts of demand that the United States certainly made in

1937-38? Had anything happened that would have made Commonwealth preferences less valuable to those former British colonies,
such as Canada and Australia, which had defended the system in the
late 1930s? What was there in the nature of events that would have
provoked the United States Congress to grant successive presidents
more and more sweeping tariff-cutting powers?

    After all, neither in domestic political terms nor in the economic
terms that were then employed did the 1938 agreements produce
much, either for the United States or for Britain. Nor did the United
States, during the war, show signs of magnanimity or change of
heart. The anti-preferential crusade was pursued anew in the wartime
Lend-Lease Agreement, and when the Reciprocal Trade Agreements
Act was renewed in 1944, it did not expand the presidential power to
cut tariffs. Britain and Canada, also, remained attached to the preferential system, and the British remained skeptical about the real
worth of the American market, in circumstances where they expected
that they would continue to face insuperable barriers when sending
manufactures to that market.

    The main gainer from the 1938 talks had been Canada. Far from
being the scapegoat, or the subject of a pillorying as it had feared, the
dominion was first the gravel in the works, and then a free (if essential) rider. King's government won many concessions from the Americans, while conceding tariff cuts that it would have made on its own
even if no new agreement had been negotiated. On their side, the
Americans conceded some degree of differentiation through
customs-classification, thus preventing all their concessions from
being generalized through mfn rules. In the course of the negotiations
the United States authorities became fond of the Canadians, who
knew how to play the game on American lines, and who appeared so
much more reasonable and flexible than the British. Thus the Canadian authorities had won kudos at home and abroad while registering
gains for their own producers and consumers. And, to top it all off,
Mackenzie King could boast—to himself and others—of a great
triumph on the economic appeasement front.

    Far from being a halting-place on the Grand March of trade-
liberalization, nevertheless, the trilateral trade talks of 1938 might

more properly be considered a dead end. All three participants had
learned that it was very hard to negotiate tariffs downward, especially
when their economies were interlocked not only by trade agreements
but by the underlying and over-riding economic realities. To move the
North Atlantic democracies forward there would have to be new
ground rules, a new framework for negotiation, a new willingness to
give concessions and receive imports, and a new readiness to allow

for the generalization of concessions through an honest operation of the mfn principle. In none of these areas did the negotiations, or the agreements, represent any advance over old-fashioned practice. Nor have we found any evidence that the participants realized what would be needed if future negotiations were to be more fruitful and less acidulous.

Let us suppose that war had not broken out, and that new trilateral trade talks had been undertaken in 1941, when the 1938 agreements were to expire. On the form of 1937-38, with "gamesmanship" in the forefront, what might we expect to have occurred? Canada herself would have presumably been much less interested, believing that there was little more to be gained by negotiating with the United States: the 1938 agreement appeared to have exhausted the President's tariff-cutting powers with respect to those goods where Canada was a "principal supplier." Thus the running would have to be made either by the Americans or by the British, neither of whom, as the 1938 talks had shown, was willing or able to concede much more. The 1938 agreements had not changed the political and economic rules of the game. Not much could have been expected from Roosevelt or Hull by way of benevolence; neither American leaders nor officials were capable of transcending the most petty local calculations of political and economic advantage, whether real or apparent. The British, too, had their interests. We might suppose that a protectionist "National Government," with a special concern for the empire and for home agriculture, would still have been in power. And the 1938 agreements would probably have done little or nothing to ease Britain's chief economic problem in international affairs — her enormous and chronic trade deficit with the US, a problem of economic structure and international balance.

Many years ago, Keith Hancock suggested that the tripartite trade agreements were concluded because the North Atlantic powers of the British Commonwealth had realized the folly of their Ottawa ways.[17] In the documents we found little sign of such a principled awakening, but it is true that both the Canadian authorities and the British government had grown more realistic with respect to preferences. Prime Minister Mackenzie King's approach to tariff cuts and rigid preferences was different from that of his predecessor, R.B. Bennett, so that the change of government in Canada had naturally altered that dominion's negotiating posture. However, it should be remembered that Bennett himself had been anxious for a trade agreement with the United States, and had indeed begun such talks in 1934. Canada's switch from Bennett to King, therefore, could better be called a change in emphasis than a deep sea change. In Britain, no one, except perhaps

a few of the most committed "imperialists" like Page Croft and Amery, really believed that the British empire could or should live unto
itself. The Ottawa Agreements had been disappointing to the British,
and subsequent experience with the dominions' importunities had
increased the dismay that Neville Chamberlain and his officials had
felt on leaving the Canadian capital in August 1932. Thus an element
of disenchantment had entered long before 1938, with the effect of
increasing the skepticism with which the National Government and
its officials approached the trade talks. Political considerations, of
course, were crucial by the end of the 1930s and the worries about
Nazi Germany and its friends introduced an element of high international policy that had certainly not been present in Chamberlain's
mind in 1932.

It is not reasonable to suppose that the agreements could ever
have had any pronounced effect on the trilateral trade pattern. The
burden of our refrain throughout the book is that there were insuperable barriers, economic and political, that would have impeded any
negotiators, no matter how skilful and enthusiastic, so that within the
existing negotiating framework, any trade agreements could only be
of marginal effect. None of the three governments could have toler-
ated the domestic political repercussions if it had made really serious
concessions to the other participants, or had given away concessions
to one partner for the sake of the other. As for bargaining about
commodities, many of the relevant goods—cotton, newsprint, certain
non-ferrous metals—were already duty-free, and these already made
up significant proportions of the trilateral trade flows, while the
dutiable goods that were of special interest to negotiators, largely
because of domestic political circumstances, were not very important
in any of the domestic economies. To this generalization, British coal
and cotton textiles were exceptions. But there was never any likelihood that the Americans would do anything serious for the latter, or
that the British would allow the Canadians to disturb the former.
American tobacco might look like an exception, but it too was a
commodity for which the British were never prepared to do anything.
In the final analysis neither such details, nor the reality of the trilateral
trading system, mattered. What mattered, in effect, was to be able to
say something in public— to the press, if one was Roosevelt, or in the
House of Commons, if one was King or Chamberlain—that would
give the domestic electorate the impression that its government was
working hard to make things better for them.

The outbreak of war in September 1939 further diminished the
economic significance of the agreements. With the introduction of
exchange control, the United Kingdom effectively abrogated many

provisions of the Anglo-American agreement: American tobacco, for example, was soon embargoed. The protection of Britain's own pig-farmers and apple-growers came to be seen in different terms, as did trade obligations to the Nordic states. Similarly, the Canadian-American trade arrangements were changed dramatically by wartime improvisations—Mutual Aid, Hyde Park, exchange controls, and the multifarious administrative arrangements that effectively although temporarily interlocked the two North American economies much more thoroughly than any trade agreement could possibly have done. After the end of the war, furthermore, the laborious and limited mutual concessions that any trilateral discussions could produce would look small and uninteresting in comparison with the much more grandiose constructions of the post-war years, as the GATT was devised, as sectoral free trade arrangements developed in North America, and as the European nations moved much more dramatically toward economic integration. It is tempting to believe that the example of trilateral frustration in 1937-38 had some influence on the design of the GATT, and of the abortive International Trade Organization (ITO). Certainly the same senior officials were active in all three countries during both periods, but there is no evidence that any of them saw themselves in the late 1930s as architects of new international structures, or that in the 1940s they deplored the procedures they had been obliged to follow in 1938. Nor were they concerned, in the 1930s, to design new international procedures, much less institutions. Both officials and politicians had a much more limited end in view.

Nevertheless, the prewar agreements and the difficult process of official and unofficial discussion that produced them are not without historical importance. They signal the American obsession about imperial preference and the risk of British exclusiveness in matters of trade and exchange. These obsessions, in turn, were to play an important role in transatlantic economic controversy not only during the war but long afterward. The process also reminds us how natural it was, even with an ardent Anglophile such as Mackenzie King at the helm, for the Canadian economy to move toward North American integration, rather than organizing its trade chiefly within the Commonwealth. We also see how very difficult it was for the three Atlantic democracies to come to agreement on economic matters in peacetime, even when they all wanted so many of the same things.

Still, it is with respect to international relationships that the agreements might most plausibly be called successful, or useful. Acrimonious though the discussions were, and inflexible as the participants so often proved, it is certainly arguable that if the United

Kingdom had refused to have the trade talks, or if she had broken them off during the many tense negotiating moments of 1938, Franklin Roosevelt and his merry men would have been significantly less well disposed toward London after the outbreak of war—with obvious and disturbing implications for the conduct of that war. It may also be conjectured that, given Roosevelt's desire for a rapprochement with Canada, the trade talks made a useful contribution to North American amity, which in turn proved to be very helpful and important for the Commonwealth war effort.[18] Interestingly enough, although the evidence shows that Chamberlain was very much aware of the Anglo-American political dimension, it suggests that he gave little attention to the Canadian-American one. Did he not foresee that Canadian-American relations would matter a great deal in the event of war? Had he given the matter thought, would he have worried that close American-Canadian ties might well mean looser Anglo-Canadian ones? Certainly the desire to keep Canada out of the clutches of the United States had been a motive of the negotiators of the Ottawa Agreements in 1932.[19]

Our final note is one of paradox. The British government persevered in the negotiations because it wanted to keep the Americans sweet lest war should break out. The Americans, too, hoped that the spectacle of amicable transatlantic negotiation, and the successful conclusion of a trade agreement, would demonstrate to the dictators that the democracies could co-operate. Mackenzie King shared this belief, and, like Cordell Hull, really did think that "economic appeasement" through the reduction of trade barriers would be both necessary and sufficient steps to ensure peace.

The trade talks, however, did not prevent war, or even delay it. And we suspect it was the war that, indirectly and after long delays, made possible the progress toward freer and less discriminatory trade—the goal all three governments, in different ways and to differing extents, were seeking. If the trade talks had succeeded in their aim within the realm of high international politics, they would have prevented the longer-run attainment of their goals in the realm of economics. It was the stress of conflict that forced or allowed the Allies to move toward a genuine economic reconstruction, and to find new and different ways by which international trade could be stimulated and redirected along more rational lines. Without the war, the experience of the mid- and late 1930s suggests to us, there would have been no International Monetary Fund, no ITO draft charter, no GATT—because the particular circumstances that encouraged and forced a new kind of co-operation were born from the war, and would not have come to birth without that war.[20] If peace had continued to reign in the North Atlantic Triangle, there would in all likelihood have been less magnanimity, less interest in serious innovation in the international economic environment, less willingness to undertake commitments and bear risks.

Notes

Introduction

1 Allan Fisher, "World Economic Affairs," in Arnold J. Toynbee, *Survey of International Affairs, 1937* [hereafter Toynbee, Survey and year] (2 vols.; London, 1938), I: 62-63.

2 Carl Kreider, *The Anglo-American Trade Agreement: A Study of British and American Commercial Policies, 1934-1939* (Princeton, 1943): 247; W.K. Hancock, *Survey of British Commonwealth Affairs*, vol. II: *Problems of Economic Policy 1918-1939* (2 parts; London, 1940-42), 1: 267; Allan Fisher, "World Economic Affairs," in Toynbee, *Survey, 1938* (3 vols.; London, 1941-53), I: 23-24.

3 See, for example, the excellent books of David Reynolds, *The Creation of the Anglo-American Alliance 1937-41: A Study in Competitive Co-operation* (London, 1981), chapter I, and Gustav Schmidt, *England in der Krise: Grundzuge und Grundlagen der Britischen Appeasement-Politik (1930-1937)* (Opladen Verlag, 1982).

4 Richard N. Kottman, *Reciprocity and the North Atlantic Triangle 1932-1938* (Ithaca, N.Y., 1968), chapters 4-7.

5 Reynolds, *Creation of the Anglo-American Alliance*: 17-18, 20, 32; C.A. Mac-Donald, *The United States, Britain and Appeasement 1936-1939* (London, 1981), e.g.: 51, 85; Robert Holland, *Britain and the Commonwealth Alliance 1918-1939* (London, 1981): 27, 150-51; D.C. Watt, *Succeeding John Bull: America in Britain's Place 1900-1975* (Cambridge, 1984): 86-87; Robert F. Holland, "The End of an Imperial Economy: Anglo-Canadian Disagreement in the 1930s," *Journal of Imperial and Commonwealth History*, 11 (January 1983): 172.

6 J.L. Granatstein, *A Man of Influence: Norman A. Robertson and Canadian Statecraft 1929-1968* ([Ottawa], 1981), chapter III.

7 See, for example, the many references in the *New York Times Index*, 25 (1937) (New York, 1938): 500, 506, 510-11; 26 (1938) (New York, 1939): 418, 421, 423-28; see also *The Official Index to the Times*, January-March 1937: 91, 496; April-June 1937: 469, 489; July-September 1937: 379, 394; October-December 1937: 489-90; January-March 1938: 447; April-June 1938: 481; July-September 1938: 412; October-December 1938: 485-86. See further Kreider, *The Anglo-American Trade Agreement*: 41-42.

8 See S.V.O. Clarke, *Negotiating the Tripartite Stabilization Agreement of 1936* (Princeton, 1977); Ian M. Drummond, *Washington, London, and the Management of the Franc, 1936-39* (Princeton, 1979); C.P. Kindleberger, *The World in Depression 1919-1939* (London, 1973); W.A. Lewis, *Economic Survey 1919-1939* (London, 1949); R. Nurkse, *International Currency Experience* (Geneva, 1944); and Andrew Shonfield, *International Economic Relations of the Western World 1959-1971* (London, 1976).
9 Watt, *Succeeding John Bull:* 87.
10 Ian M. Drummond, *The Floating Pound and the Sterling Area, 1931-1939* (Cambridge, 1981); Drummond, *Washington, London, and the Management of the Franc.*

Chapter 1: An Unpromising Environment

1 Quoted in Keith Feiling, *The Life of Neville Chamberlain* (London, 1946): 325.
2 For background, see two articles by Melvyn P. Leffler, "American Policy Making and European Stability, 1921-1933," *Pacific Historical Review*, 46 (1977): 207-28, and "Political Isolationism, Economic Expansionism or Diplomatic Realism: American Policy Toward Western Europe 1921-1933," *Perspectives in American History*, 8 (1974): 413-61.
3 The "Baltic" lands are here defined to consist of Finland, Estonia, Latvia, Lithuania, Sweden, Norway, Denmark, Poland, and the Netherlands; the last of these nations is included because its commercial ties with Britain resembled those of some of the other states, and because it was equally susceptible to German commercial penetration. The Latin American nations are Chile, Brazil, Uruguay, and Argentina, of which the last was much the most important: in 1936, indeed, that country alone spent fifteen million pounds on British goods, while the very much larger United States spent thirty-seven million.
4 On this point Robert F. Holland, "The End of an Imperial Economy: Anglo-Canadian Disagreement in the 1930s," *Journal of Imperial and Commonwealth History*, 11 (January 1983): 722, is essentially correct.
5 League of Nations, Committee for the Study of the Problem Relating to Raw Materials, *Raw Materials: Report, with Supporting Documents* (8 September 1937) (League Document A.27.1937.11B).
6 Arthur M. Schlesinger, Jr., *The Age of Roosevelt*, vol. II: *The Coming of the New Deal* (Boston, 1959): 188-89.
7 *The Memoirs of Cordell Hull* (2 vols.; New York, 1948), I: 357. On the origins of the Reciprocal Trade Agreements Act, see Lloyd C. Gardner, *Economic Aspects of New Deal Diplomacy* (Madison, Wisconsin, 1964): 39-46.
8 Schlesinger, *Age of Roosevelt*, II: 255-60; Gardner, *Economic Aspects of New Deal Diplomacy:* 39-40. See also, on Sayre's internationalism, his papers in the Library of Congress, Washington, and his *Experiments in International Administration* (New York, 1920), preface.
9 That is, a duty based on the value of the product, not its physical quantity (yards, pounds, or whatever), such duties being termed "specific."
10 Schlesinger, *Age of Roosevelt*, II: 189.
11 Public Record Office, Kew, England [PRO], Foreign Office [FO] 414/274/127-42, W.D. Allen, "Memorandum Respecting the United States and British Interests," 15 March 1937.
12 Hull, *Memoirs*, I: 525.

13 Allan Fisher, "World Economic Affairs," in Toynbee, *Survey, 1937*, I: 56, 63, 108.

14 Schlesinger, *Age of Roosevelt*, II: 190.

15 This figure is derived by summing total import values for wheat, flour, maize, rice, meats, dairy products, fruit, tobacco, and sawn lumber. If it were possible to include all the manufactures that were affected by the new ten per cent general levy of February 1932, a higher figure would result. See United Kingdom, *Annual Abstract of Statistics*, 75 (1930), table no. 236.

16 See United States, *Statistical Abstract of the United States, 1930*, table no. 534.

17 Both the Australian government and the Canadian understood the situation perfectly well, although when R.B. Bennett ruled in Ottawa he did not find it convenient to say so in public. See Ian M. Drummond, *Imperial Economic Policy, 1917-1939: Studies in Expansion and Protection* (London, 1974).

18 FO 414/274/127-42.

19 Consisting of Great Britain's dominions, such as Australia and South Africa, and dependent territories, like India, Malaya, and Nigeria, whose currencies were pegged to the British pound and who kept their foreign exchange reserves wholly or partly in London. See Ian M. Drummond, *The Floating Pound and the Sterling Area 1931-1939* (Cambridge, 1981).

20 PRO, Treasury Records [T] 160/750/F.14239/1, minute of 10 April 1935.

21 See S.V.O. Clarke, *Negotiating the Tripartite Stabilization Agreement of 1936* (Princeton, 1977); Ian M. Drummond, *London, Washington, and the Management of the Franc, 1936-39* (Princeton, 1979), and on war debts Sir Frederick Leith-Ross, *Money Talks* (London, 1968).

22 PRO, Board of Trade Records [BT] 11/755, memorandum of Eden and Cranborne, 20 April 1937.

23 National Archives of Canada [NA], King Papers, J4, vol. 179, file 1644, folios C127491-96, memorandum of Eden, "The Economic Aspect of Foreign Policy," 28 May 1937.

24 FO 371/20658/A446, minutes of Jebb, 21 January 1937.

Chapter 2: Talks about Talks

1 Richard N. Kottman, *Reciprocity and the North Atlantic Triangle 1932-1938* (Ithaca, N.Y., 1968): 121-22.

2 *Foreign Relations of the United States, Diplomatic Papers* [FRUS], 1934 (5 vols.; Washington, 1951-52), I: 797-98, memorandum of Sayre, 14 September 1934; Kottman, *Reciprocity and the North Atlantic Triangle*: 120-21. Roosevelt aide Norman Davis informally suggested an Anglo-American-Canadian trade treaty to the British in March 1933, but the idea was not taken up in Washington or London; see Kottman, *Reciprocity and the North Atlantic Triangle*: 46.

3 Public Record Office, Kew, England [PRO], Treasury Records [T]160/F.14239/1, Chalkley to Leith-Ross, 26 June 1935, and minutes of meeting, 22 May 1935.

4 National Archives, Washington, State Department Records [State] RG 43, box 61, memorandum of Grady, 21 June 1935, in "Preliminary Studies and Negotiations, 1935-6."

5 State, RG 43, box 61, "First Progress Report of the British Empire Committee," n.d., in "Preliminary Studies and Negotiations, 1935-6."

6 State 611.4131/120, memorandum of Grady, 21 June 1935; State 611.4131/125, memorandum of Grady, 16 October 1935.

7 State, RG 43, box 61, memorandum of conversation, 15 November 1935.

8 PRO, Board of Trade Records [BT] 11/589/3, minute of 20 February 1936.
9 PRO, Foreign Office Records [FO] 371/20659/105: 271-309, minutes of Board of Trade, 13 March 1937, and of W.D. Allen, 15 March 1937.
10 T 160/750/F.142392, Waley to Wills (Board of Trade), 18 May 1936.
11 T 160/750/F.14239/1, memorandum of Waley, 16 April 1936.
12 *Foreign Relations of the United States, Diplomatic Papers* [FRUS], 1936 (5 vols.; Washington, 1953-54), I: 666-68, memorandum of Fowler, 17 June 1936.
13 State RG 43, box 62, file UK/8000/1937, "Chronology."
14 FRUS, 1936, I: 669-71, memorandum of Eldridge, 24 June 1936; State 611.4131/186, memorandum of Hawkins, 24 June 1936.
15 State 611.4131/125, 134 1/2, memorandum of Feis, January 1936.
16 State 611.4131/140, 141A.
17 State 611.4131/157, memorandum of Atherton, 1 April 1936.
18 T 160/750/F.14239/2, Troutbeck to Waley, 8 October 1936.
19 BT 11/589/11, minute of unidentified officer, 7 April 1936.
20 T 160/750/F.14239/2, memorandum of Waley, 10 October 1936. Emphasis supplied.
21 State RG 43, box 62, file UK/8000/1937, "Chronology"; State 611.4131/191A, 193; Kottman, *Reciprocity and the North Atlantic Triangle:* 139-40.
22 FO 371/20659/105, memorandum of Board of Trade, 13 March 1937.
23 T 160/F.14239/1, 30 September 1936.
24 State 611.4131/1/197, memorandum of Feis, 31 October 1937.
25 T 160/750/F.14239/3, Overton to Waley, 13 October 1936.
26 State 611.4131/205, memorandum of Hawkins, 16 November 1936.
27 T 160/750/F.14239/3, minutes of Waley and other officials, 24-28 November 1936. See also Ian M. Drummond, *The Floating Pound and the Sterling Area, 1931-1939* (Cambridge, 1981), chapters 9-10.
28 T 160/750/F.14239/3, minutes of interdepartmental meeting, 3 December 1936.
29 FRUS, 1936, I: 702-03, memorandum of Bingham, 18 December 1936.
30 Franklin D. Roosevelt Library, Hyde Park, New York, Roosevelt Papers, PSF Diplomatic, box 46, file GB 1937-8, Bingham to Roosevelt, 5 January 1937.
31 FRUS 1936, I: 704-06, memorandum of Hawkins, 26 December 1936.
32 FRUS, 1937, II: 1-2, memorandum, Hull to UK Embassy, 17 January 1937.
33 State 611.4131/237, memorandum of Sayre, 26 January 1937.
34 PRO, Prime Minister's Office [Premier] 1/291, Runciman to Baldwin, 8 February 1937.
35 PRO, Dominions Office Records [DO] 35/876/T766/11, C.W. Dixon to British high commissioners in the dominions, 5 March 1937.
36 Carl Kreider, *The Anglo-American Trade Agreement: A Study of British and American Commercial Policies, 1934-1939* (Princeton, 1943): 35.
37 DO 35/876/T766/9, minutes of 25 February 1937.
38 On Marler, see *Memoirs of H.L. Keenleyside* (2 vols.; Toronto, 1981-82), I, 252ff.
39 FO 371/20659, telegram of US government, 2 March 1937.
40 In the old British monetary system, there were twenty shillings in a pound and twelve pence in a shilling, so that two shillings and six pence corresponded to twelve and one-half of the "new pence" that are now used in the United Kingdom.
41 A hundredweight of 112 pounds, as normally applied in the United Kingdom until the advent of decimalization in the 1970s.
42 Hereafter we shall follow normal usage by employing the abbreviation "mfn" to replace the cumbersome "most-favoured-nation" label for tariff rates that are extended to those nations whose treaty commitments entitle them to claim the

lowest rate of duty extended to any other independent nation. The United Kingdom and the dominions had always argued that imperial preferential rates were not subject to extension in this way, because they were concessions extended "inside the family."

43 FO 371/20659/267, minute of Ashton-Gwatkin, 11 March 1937.

44 See David Reynolds, *The Creation of the Anglo-American Alliance 1937-41: A Study in Competitive Co-operation* (London, 1981): 16.

45 As explained in chapter 1, McKenna goods were the manufactured items on which Britain had imposed tariffs, generally at a rate of 33 1/3 per cent, during the First World War.

46 Kottman, *Reciprocity and the North Atlantic Triangle:* 217-19.

47 FO 371/20659/A2970, minute of Ashton-Gwatkin, 6 April 1937.

48 FO 371/20659/A2970, minute of Eden, 13 April 1937.

49 State 611.4131/256, 257.

50 State 611.4131/274, Sayre to Chalkley, 2 March 1937.

51 PRO, Cabinet Office Records [CAB] 27/620, meeting of Cabinet Trade and Agriculture Committee, 6 April 1937.

52 CAB 27/619, meeting of Cabinet Trade and Agriculture Committee, 12 April 1937.

53 See DO 114/93/T766/41, enclosure 2.

54 DO 35/876/T766/27, Dominions Office to Chalkley, 13 April 1937; FO 371/20649/207, memorandum of Board of Trade, 13 April 1937.

Chapter 3: King and the British

1 Ian M. Drummond, *Imperial Economic Policy, 1917-1939: Studies in Expansion and Protection* (London, 1974): 378-79; Norman Hillmer, "Anglo-Canadian Relations 1926-1937: A Study of Canada's Role in the Shaping of Commonwealth Policies" (Ph.D. thesis, Cambridge University, 1974): 186-87.

2 National Archives of Canada [NA], King Papers, Diary, 15-30 October 1935; *The Memoirs of Cordell Hull* (2 vols; New York, 1948), I: 525.

3 Richard Hofstadter, *The American Political Tradition and the Men Who Made It* (New York, 1964): 312.

4 See Hull, *Memoirs*, I: 526; II: 1480.

5 See C.P. Stacey, *Canada and the Age of Conflict: A History of Canadian External Policies* (2 vols; Toronto, 1977-81), vol. II: *1921-1948, The Mackenzie King Era:* 173 and, more generally, Norman Hillmer, " 'The Outstanding Imperialist': Mackenzie King and the British," Canada House Lecture Series, no. 4 (London, 1980).

6 *Foreign Relations of the United States, Diplomatic Papers* [FRUS], 1936 (5 vols.; Washington, 1953-54), I: 666-68, memorandum of Fowler, 17 June 1936.

7 FRUS, 1936, I: 783-85, memorandum of Hickerson, 4 June 1936.

8 FRUS, 1936, I: 786-90, memorandum of Hull, 3 November 1936.

9 King Papers, Diary, 12 November 1936.

10 King Papers, Diary, 18 January 1937.

11 NA, Hume Wrong Papers, vol. 3, folder 15, Marler to King, 5 February 1937.

12 FRUS, 1937, II: 13-14, memorandum of Hull, 18 February 1937.

13 King Papers, J1, vol. 237, folios 204304ff, External Affairs to Marler, 18 February 1937.

14 National Archives, Washington, State Department Records [State] 611.4131/234 1/2, note of United Kingdom government, 27 January 1937. See also PRO, FO 371/20658/247, 248, 249, minutes of Foreign Office, 19-21 January 1937.

15 BT 11/755, minute of 21 January 1937.
16 State 611.4131/230, memorandum of Sayre, 1 February 1937.
17 "When you sit around the table with a Britisher," President Roosevelt remarked in 1936, "he usually gets 80 per cent out of the deal and you get what is left." Quoted in David Reynolds, *The Creation of the Anglo-American Alliance 1937-41: A Study in Competitive Co-operation* (London, 1981): 25.
18 PRO, Cabinet Office Records [CAB] 23/87, Cabinet conclusions, 20 January 1937.
19 PRO, Dominions Office Records [DO] 35/876/T766/9, 22 February 1937.
20 PRO, DO 114/77, King to Floud, 4 January 1937.
21 See Drummond, *Imperial Economic Policy*: 414-17.
22 King Papers, Diary, 5 March 1937; Franklin D. Roosevelt Library, Hyde Park, New York, Roosevelt Papers, PSF box 33, "Permanent Conference on Economic and Social Problems," 6 March 1937.
23 King Papers, Diary, 8 November 1935.
24 King Papers, Diary, 6 March 1937; State 500.A19/61, memorandum of Hull, 5 March 1937.
25 Roosevelt Papers, PSF box 33, King to Roosevelt, 8 March 1937.
26 NA, Norman Robertson Papers, vol. 7, file 46, Hull to King, 2 April 1937.
27 Robertson Papers, vol. 7, file 46, memorandum of Robertson, "Imperial Preferences and the United States," 15 April 1937.
28 DO 35/876/T766/11, C.W. Dixon to British high commissioners in the dominions, 5 March 1937.
29 DO 35/876/T766/28, C.W. Dixon to British high commissioners in the dominions, 23 April 1937.
30 Cambridge University Library, Cambridge, England, Stanley Baldwin Papers, vol. 97: 184ff, Tweedsmuir to Baldwin, 8 April 1937.
31 NA, Records of the Department of External Affairs [External], vol. 746, file 167, memorandum of Skelton, 15 April 1937.
32 External, vol. 746, file 167, memorandum of Robertson, 14 May 1937.
33 Norman Hillmer, "The Pursuit of Peace: Mackenzie King and the 1937 Imperial Conference," in John English and J.O. Stubbs, eds., *Mackenzie King: Widening the Debate* (Toronto, 1978): 164-65; Rainer Tamchina, "In Search of Common Causes: The Imperial Conference of 1937," *Journal of Imperial and Commonwealth History*, 1 (October 1972): 99.
34 DO 114/93/T766/41, enclosure 3, p. 17.
35 DO 114/93/T766/41, enclosure 3, p. 17.
36 Carl Kreider, *The Anglo-American Trade Agreement: A Study of British and American Commercial Policies, 1934-1939* (Princeton, 1943): 36.
37 DO 35/876/T766/46, memorandum of Bankes-Amery, 21 May 1937.
38 FO 371/20660/187ff; PRO, CAB 27/619, meeting of Cabinet Trade and Agriculture Committee, 26 May 1937.
39 CAB 32/128, Imperial Conference 1937, minutes, eighth meeting of principal delegates, 27 May 1937.
40 DO 114/93/T766/41, Runciman to dominion prime ministers, 27 May 1937.
41 FO 371/20060/240-8, minutes, meeting of Cabinet Trade and Agricultural Committee, 28 May 1937.
42 King Papers, Diary, 15 May 1937.
43 King Papers, Diary, 26 May 1937.
44 DO 114/T766/50, no. 17, King to Stanley, 5 June 1937.
45 FO 371/20660/A4106, minute of J.M. Troutbeck, 10 June 1937.

46 King Papers, J4, vol. 179, file 1643, folios C127491-96, memorandum of Eden, "The Economic Aspect of Foreign Policy," 28 May 1937.
47 Robertson Papers, vol. 6, file 38, memorandum of Robertson, "Notes on the Anglo-American Trade Agreement," 30 May 1937.
48 State 611.4131/296, US Legation to State, 24 May 1937.
49 State 611.4131/303, Bingham to State, 2 June 1937.
50 Robertson Papers, vol. 6, file 38, memorandum of Robertson, "Notes on the Anglo-American Trade Agreement," 30 May 1937.
51 State 611.34131/306, memorandum of Sayre, 3 June 1937.
52 DO 35/877/T766/68, Lindsay to Eden, 8 June 1937, and attachments.
53 BT 11/780 XM/09172, Lindsay to Vansittart, 25 June 1937.
54 King Papers, Diary, 7 June 1937.
55 FO 371/20660/A4056 and A4106, notes of Anglo-Canadian meetings, 1 and 7 June 1937. For the materially different Canadian minutes of the latter meeting, see Robertson Papers, vol. 7, file 46. See also King Papers, Diary, 7 June 1937 and, on King's aims and motives, Hillmer, "Pursuit of Peace": 151-53, 158-61, 165.
56 External, vol. 1837, file 508, pt. 1, British High Commission to Department of External Affairs and reply, 4 and 7 June 1937.
57 King Papers, Diary, 7 June 1937.
58 King Papers, Diary, 11 June 1937.
59 DO 114/T766/75, Foreign Office to Lindsay, 24 June 1937. See also FO 371/20667/15-24.
60 FO 371/20661/10-11, note of president of the Board of Trade, 18 June 1937.
61 DO 114/T776/75, Cadogan to Lindsay, 24 June 1937. See also FO 371/20667/15-24 and DO 35/877/T766/73, note of conversation with Robertson, 18 June 1937.
62 DO 114/T766/75, Cadogan to Lindsay, 24 June 1937.

Chapter 4: Canadian Complications

1 See Rainer Tamchina, "In Search of Common Causes: The Imperial Conference of 1937," Journal of Imperial and Commonwealth History, 1 (October 1972): 100.
2 C.A. MacDonald, The United States, Britain and Appeasement 1936-1939 (London, 1981): 25, minute of J.M. Troutbeck, 1 April 1937. See also Public Record Office, Kew, England [PRO], Dominions Office [DO] 35/876/T766/27, Dominions Office to Chalkley, 13 April 1937; PRO, Foreign Office [FO] 371/20659/207, memorandum of Board of Trade, 13 April 1937; FO 371/20659/A2847, minute of R. Craigie, 15 March 1937 and passim; more generally, R.F. Holland, Britain and the Commonwealth Alliance 1918-1939 (London, 1981), chapter 2; Ritchie Ovendale, "Appeasement" and the English Speaking World: Britain, the United States and the Policy of "Appeasement," 1937-1939 (Cardiff, 1975), passim.
3 PRO, Cabinet Office Records [CAB] 27/620, no. 47, 18 June 1937.
4 Foreign Relations of the United States, Diplomatic Papers [FRUS], 1937 (5 vols.; Washington, 1954), II: 44-46, US Embassy to Hull, 2 July 1937. See also National Archives, Washington, State Department Records [State] 611.4131.
5 FRUS, 1937, II: 46-68, memorandum of Hull, 7 July 1937.
6 FRUS, 1937, II: 49-52, British Embassy to Department of State, 10 July 1937.
7 FRUS, 1937, II: 52-56, British Embassy to Department of State, 15 July 1937.
8 State, 611.4131/352, 352 1/2.
9 Harvard University Library, Cambridge, Massachusetts, J.P. Moffat Papers, vol. 39, Diary, 20 July 1937. On Moffat, see David Reynolds, The Creation of the Anglo-

American Alliance 1937-41: A Study in Competitive Co-operation (London, 1981): 28.

10 FRUS, 1937, II: 58-62, memorandum of Hawkins, 21 July 1937.

11 DO 35/877/T766/96, Lindsay to Foreign Office, 22 July 1937.

12 National Archives of Canada [NA], King Papers, Diary, 26 July 1937.

13 See J.L. Granatstein, *A Man of Influence: Norman A. Robertson and Canadian Statecraft 1929-1968* (Ottawa, 1981): 403, fn. 31.

14 King Papers, Diary, 26 July 1937. The point is picked up by Robert F. Holland, "The End of an Imperial Economy: Anglo-Canadian Disagreement in the 1930s," *Journal of Imperial and Commonwealth History*, 11 (January 1983), who asserts (172) that the "reluctant dominions were 'pilloried' . . .by the UK into an American agreement, largely paid for by the scrapping of Canadian agricultural preferences in the British market and the benefits which accrued to UK industry and the Foreign Office." It would be difficult, in fact, to detect any relevant Canadian agricultural preferences that were scrapped. Although the preference on apples was reduced, the wheat preference was of no value to Canada, whose officials, indeed, had first suggested its abolition. Australia might more properly be said to have been "pilloried," but she, too, had no interest in the retention of the wheat preference, and wept no tears at its departure. Nor could British industry be said to have benefited: the eventual cuts in American tariffs on manufactures were not large enough to be helpful, and the potential loss of sales in Commonwealth markets was at least large enough to offset any such benefits.

15 King Papers, Diary, 27 July 1937; NA, External Affairs Records [External], vol. 746, file 16, memorandum of King, July 1937.

16 King Papers, Diary, 27 July 1937; External, vol. 746, file 16, memorandum of King, July 1937.

17 DO 114/93/22, Floud to Dominions Office, 30 July 1937.

18 DO 35/877/T766/109, Dominions Office to Floud, 31 July 1937.

19 Norman Hillmer, "The Pursuit of Peace: Mackenzie King and the 1937 Imperial Conference," in John English and J.O. Stubbs, eds., *Mackenzie King: Widening the Debate* (Toronto, 1978): 163-67.

20 DO 35/877/T766/117, Chamberlain to King, 2 August 1937.

21 See PRO, Prime Minister's Office [Premier] 1/291.

22 King Papers, Diary, 5 August 1937.

23 See DO 35/877/T766/112, nos. 23 and 24, Floud to Dominions Office, 1 August 1937.

24 Moffat Papers, Diary, 3 August 1937; Moffat Papers, vol. 12, memorandum of Armour, 6 August 1937.

25 FO 371/20662/80, memorandum of 3 August 1937.

26 Moffat Papers, vol. 12, memorandum of Armour, 6 August 1937.

27 Moffat Papers, Diary, 3 August 1937.

28 On the period see Granatstein, *A Man of Influence*: 60-65.

29 FO 371/20660/A4056 and 4106, British notes of Anglo-Canadian meetings, 1 and 7 June 1937; NA, Norman Robertson Papers, vol. 7, file 46, Canadian minutes, 7 June 1937.

30 King Papers, Diary, 7 June 1937.

31 DO 114/T766/117, no. 26, Dominions Office to Floud, 2 August 1937.

32 DO 114/T766/96, no. 19.

33 DO 114/T766/1/5, King to Floud, 7 August 1937.

34 King Papers, Diary, 6 and 7 August 1937.

35 FRUS, 1937, II: 161-62, "confidential letter to Mr. King," in Hull to Armour, 12 August 1937.

36 FO 371/20662/18, minutes of 27 July 1937.

37 FO 414/274/13, record of statement by Chalkley and Stirling at State Department, 8 July 1937; DO 35/877/T766/106, memorandum of meeting at the State Department, 15 July 1937.

38 FO 371/20662/18, minutes of 27 July 1937.

39 State, Hickerson files, memorandum of State Department, 25 August 1937.

40 State, Hickerson files, memorandum of Hickerson, 1 September 1937; External, vol. 746, file 169, memorandum of Skelton, 30 August 1937.

41 PRO, Board of Trade Records [BT] 11/806, Board of Trade to Chalkley, 31 August 1937.

42 DO 35/880/T166/1/26, memorandum of 31 August 1937 and Floud to King, 5 August 1937; FO 371/20662/35, minutes of 27 July 1937; DO 35/877/T766/12, Floud to Dominions Office, 30 July 1937.

43 FO 371/20662/2789, Floud to Dominions Office, 2 September 1937; DO 35/877/T766/146, Dominions Office to Washington Embassy, 9 September 1937.

44 FO 371/20662/2789, Floud to Dominions Office, 2 September 1937; DO 35/877/T766/146, Dominions Office to Washington Embassy, 9 September 1937.

45 State, Hickerson files, Hickerson to Armour, 4 September 1937; King Papers, Diary, 13 August 1937.

46 DO 35/880/T766/1/23, Floud to Harding, 1 September 1937.

47 Moffat Papers, Diary, 14 September 1937.

48 See Drummond, *The Floating Pound and the Sterling Area, 1931-1939* (Cambridge, 1981): 233-34.

49 DO 35/880/T766/1/30, Mallet to Foreign Office, 23 September 1937.

50 DO 35/880/T766/1/30, British Embassy, Washington to Foreign Office, 24 September 1937.

51 DO 35/880/T766/1/30, British Embassy, Washington to Foreign Office, 24 September 1937.

52 FRUS, 1937, II: 66-68, memorandum of W.W. Butterworth, 22 September 1937; see also pp. 68-72, memorandum of Sayre, 23 September 1937, American chargé d'affaires in London to Hull, 27 September 1937, Department of State to British Embassy, Washington, 28 September 1937.

53 FRUS, 1937, II: 68-70, memorandum of Sayre, 23 September 1937.

54 DO 35/877/T766/153, memorandum of Bankes-Amery, 28 September 1937. The author is presumably counting not only the five dominions, including the Irish Free State (not Newfoundland), but also India and Southern Rhodesia.

55 DO 35/880/T766/1/32, Floud to Dominions Office, 30 September 1937.

56 DO 35/880/T766/1/388, Floud to Harding, 30 September 1937.

57 External, vol. 746, file 167, memorandum of Robertson, 1 October 1937.

58 External, vol. 746, file 167, memorandum of Robertson, 4 October 1937.

59 Robertson Papers, vol. 7, file 40, memorandum of Skelton, 5 October 1937.

60 King Papers, Diary, 8 October 1937.

61 Robertson Papers, vol. 7, file 40, memorandum of Robertson, 8 and 9 October 1937.

62 King Papers, Diary, 9 October 1937.

63 FO 371/20663/103, minutes of 15 October 1937.

64 State, Hickerson files, memorandum of J.D.H. Hull, 13 October 1937.

65 State 611.4231/2044, memorandum of Sayre, 12 October 1937.

66 DO 114/T766/1/34, British Embassy, Washington to Foreign Office, 12 October 1937.

67 Robertson Papers, vol. 7, file 40, Wrong to Robertson, 14 October 1937.

68 State 611.4231/2047, Armour to Hull, 14 October 1937.

69 DO 114/T766/1/141, Floud to Dominions Office, 15 October 1937.

70 Robertson Papers, vol. 7, file 43.

71 CAB 27/620, meeting of Cabinet Committee on Trade and Agriculture, 19 October 1937.

72 DO 35/881/T766/1/61, memorandum of Chalkley, 20 October 1937.

73 DO 35/880/T766/1/48, Dominions Office to Floud, 22 October 1937.

74 FRUS, 1937, II: 73-74, Bingham to Hull, 27 October 1937.

75 King Papers, Diary, 28 October 1937.

76 FRUS, 1937, II: 75, Chalkley to Hawkins, 29 October 1937.

77 DO 114/97, memorandum of Bankes-Amery, minute of Malcolm MacDonald, 24 October 1937.

78 BT 11/806, R.M. Nowell to Chalkley, 13 September 1937.

79 CAB 24/271, Cabinet Paper [CP] 251 (37), report of Committee on Trade and Agriculture, 22 Oct 1937.

80 To 3/- per hundredweight, from the existing 4/6.

81 A cut in the pear duty from 4/6 to 3 shillings, in the tinned grapefruit duty from 15 to just under 10 per cent on a specific basis, a similar cut in the fruit salad duty, and so on.

82 CAB 23/90, Cabinet conclusions, 27 October 1937.

83 DO 114/93, nos. 4 and 5, Dominions Office to the High Commissions in the dominions, and to the government of New Zealand.

84 DO 35/880/T766/1/55, Dominions Office to Floud, 1 November 1937.

85 DO 114/T766/1/59, no. 43, Floud to Dominions Office, 2 November 1937; see also King Papers, Diary, 2 November 1937.

86 DO 114/T766/1/60, no. 44, Floud to Dominions Office, 2 November 1937.

87 DO 114/93/T766/1/60, no. 45, Dominions Office to Floud, 4 November 1937.

88 DO 114/93/T766/1/60, no. 6, Dominions Office to High Commissions in Australia and South Africa and to the New Zealand government, 4 November 1937. The Canadian suggestion was 3/6 per hundredweight on US apples; Whitehall had originally proposed 3 shillings per hundredweight.

89 FRUS, 1937, II: 78-81, British Embassy, Washington, to Department of State and Bingham to Hull, 5 November 1937.

90 FRUS, 1937, II: 81-83, Bingham to Hull, 11 November 1937.

91 D.C. Watt, *Succeeding John Bull: America in Britain's Place 1900-1975* (Cambridge, 1984): 85, Hickerson to Moffat, 8 November 1937.

92 FRUS, 1937, II: 81-83, Bingham to Hull, 11 November 1937; see also 83-85, memorandum of Sayre, 16 November 1937.

93 Franklin D. Roosevelt Library, Hyde Park, New York, Roosevelt Papers, OF 48, Wallace to Roosevelt, 15 November 1937.

94 DO 114/93/T766/165, no. 7, British Embassy, Washington, to Foreign Office, 17 November 1937. See also FRUS, 1937, II: 85, Department of State to the British Embassy, Washington [16 November 1937].

95 Great Britain, House of Commons, *Debates*, 5th series, vol. 329, 18 November 1937.

96 DO 114/93/T766/165, no. 9, Dominions Office to high commissioners in dominions, and to New Zealand, repeating no. 523 to British Embassy, Washington, 17 November 1937; FRUS, 1937, II: 83-85, memorandum of Sayre, 16 November 1937.

97 Keith Feiling, *The Life of Neville Chamberlain* (London, 1946): 308.

98 King Papers, Diary, 17 November 1937.

99 FRUS, 1937, II: 83-85, memorandum of Sayre, 16 November 1937.

Chapter 5: From "Contemplation" to "Negotiation"

1 National Archives, Washington, State Department Records [State] 611.4131/722A, Sayre to Roosevelt, 6 January 1938.
2 State 611.4131B/763 1/2.
3 State 611.4131/822, memorandum of Beale, 11 January 1938.
4 State 611.4131/654, Beale to Hawkins, 31 December 1937.
5 Allan Fisher, "World Economic Affairs," in Toynbee, *Survey, 1938*, I: 18.
6 State 611.4131/480, 488, 567, 568, 74605.
7 State 611.4131/1217.
8 State 611.4131/1410, 1417, 1460, 1497.
9 State 611.4131/1501, 1521, memoranda of 30 March and 2 May 1938.
10 State 611.4131B/1546, 1588.
11 State 611.4131/591, 692, 696, 817.
12 State 611.4131/492, US consul in Birmingham to Hull, 22 November 1937.
13 State 611.4131/1486, minute of 30 April 1938.
14 State 611.4131/1225, memorandum of US Consulate in London, 25 February 1938.
15 Carl Kreider, *The Anglo-American Trade Agreement: A Study of British and American Commercial Policies, 1934-1939* (Princeton, 1943): 38; Allan Fisher, "World Economic Affairs," in Toynbee, *Survey, 1937*, I: 105-06.
16 State 611.4131/581, Chalkley to Hawkins, 14 December 1937.
17 State 611.4131/614/638 1/2, Chalkley to State, 20, 22, and 26 December 1937.
18 Public Record Office, Kew, England [PRO], Foreign Office Records [FO] 371/21489.
19 PRO, Board of Trade Records [BT] 11/960, 962; Fisher, "World Economic Affairs," in Toynbee, *Survey, 1937*, I: 105.
20 BT 11/961.
21 PRO, DO 35/878/T766/210, memorandum of Bankes-Amery, 16 December 1937; DO 114/232, high commissioner in Ottawa to Dominions Office, 30 December 1937.
22 National Archives of Canada [NA], Norman Robertson Papers, vol. 7, file 48, memorandum of Robertson, 16 December 1937.
23 See Ian M. Drummond, *Imperial Economic Policy 1917-1939: Studies in Expansion and Protection* (London, 1974): 365-67.
24 DO 35/881/T766/1/71, Dominions Office to high commissioners in the dominions, 25 November 1937.
25 DO 35/881/T766/66, "List of Dutiable Items on which Concessions are Desired by Canada."
26 DO 35/881/T766/1/114, British high commissioner, Ottawa, to Dominions Office, 1 February 1938.
27 DO 35/881/T766/1/124, British high commissioner, Ottawa to Dominions Office, 14 February 1938.
28 State 611.4131/897A, State Department to US Embassy in United Kingdom, 27 January 1938.
29 Fisher, "World Economic Affairs," in Toynbee, *Survey, 1937*, I: 107.
30 FO 371/1215, memorandum, "Apples and the Trade Agreements Program," 4 February 1938.
31 State 611.4131/1286, memorandum of 8 March 1938.
32 On rye, oatmeal, various pork products, canned shellfish and vegetables, corundum, hardwood, agricultural machinery, belting, some sorts of iron and steel furniture, cash registers, glass working and laundering machinery, office machin-

ery, vacuum cleaners, flooring, boots, shoes, piping and elastic cords, perfumery, sports goods, and silk stockings.

33 Among them bacon, canned milk, wheat flour, canned vegetables, Douglas fir lumber, automobile tires and tubes.

34 For a refined statement see State 611.4131/1373A, B.

35 British minutes on Robertson's two talks with Overton and on his talk with Hickerson are in DO 35/881/T766/1/132, United Kingdom-US Negotiations, Misc. 18; Robertson's own memorandum is in Robertson Papers, vol. 9, file 68, "Memorandum of Conversations," 2 March 1938.

36 NA, Department of External Affairs Records [External], vol. 1846, file 822, part 1, memorandum of Robertson, 14 March 1938.

37 NA, King Papers, Diary, 17-18 November 1937.

38 FO 371/20670/A2082, minute of W.D. Allen, 19 March 1937; minute of Sir R. Vansittart, 31 March 1937.

Chapter 6: Discussions to Some Purpose

1 Public Record Office, Kew, England [PRO], Foreign Office Records [FO] 414/275/97-107, memorandum of Eden and Stanley, 14 February 1938.

2 FO 414/275/97-107.

3 National Archives, Washington, State Department Records [State] 611.4131/1142.

4 The "main Anglo-American Trade Agreement Committee" apparently met only six times.

5 PRO, Board of Trade Records [BT] 11/949, CRT 12771, "main committee minutes," 24 February, 26 April, 13 May, 29 July, 6 and 25 August. Additional British minutes are in BT 11/962, CRT 14796/38, and in various volumes of British Foreign Office [FO] and Dominions Office Records [DO] in the PRO. For American minutes, see State, RG 43 box 62, file "UK Negotiations 1938: Minutes, General Sessions."

6 Far fewer items were to receive the maximum reduction than London had thought on the basis of the American offers of the previous June. One cause of the discrepancy was that London had "measured the reductions of duty by comparing the rates now offered with the rates at present in force, which have in some cases been reduced in the US trade agreements with other countries." In stating possible concessions the Americans had also not explained that they were using the much higher statutory or Smoot-Hawley figures as fixed in 1930, rather than the effective rates at the time of the offer.

7 BT 11/934, UK-USA Negotiations, general minutes 14, 26 April 1938.

8 BT 11/934, UK-USA Negotiations, memorandum, 4 May 1938. There would be reductions of 40 per cent or more on $13 million worth of trade; $10 million would fall in the range 30-39 per cent; $11.6 million from 20 to 29 per cent; $24 million on 20 per cent or less. The Americans were also prepared to bind the duties on goods to the value of $4 million and in addition to bind the 50 per cent reduction in the whiskey duty that they had already conceded to Canada.

9 BT 11/917, memorandum of UK delegation, 6 May 1938; DO 35/879/T766/310, "Note . . . ," 17 June 1938.

10 BT 11/917, UK-US Negotiations, general minutes 15, 6 May 1938.

11 BT 11/934, Overton to Brown, 7 May 1938.

12 BT 11/934, "Draft Note on United States Negotiations," early May 1938.

13 M. Ruth Megaw, "Australia and the Anglo-American Trade Agreement, 1938," *Journal of Imperial and Commonwealth History*, 3 (January 1975): 200.

14 BT 11/934, Overton to Board of Trade, 4 May 1938.

15 FO 371/31496/224-27, Lindsay to Cadogan, 10 May 1938.

16 FO 371/21496/221-23, minutes of 19-26 May 1938.

17 FO 371/21497/21-26.

18 FO 371/21495/186.

19 DO 35/879/T766/310, "Note . . . ," 17 June 1938.

20 FO 371/21501/177, TAC(36) 53, "Note by the President of the Board of Trade," 16 July 1938. By mid-July the United States was offering reductions of some $55 million in British trade (as against $47 million in May), and conventionalization on another $80 million worth. Over 600 rates would be reduced, and there would be substantial gains for whiskey, cottons, woollens, linens, jute, earthenware, and foodstuffs. Britain was offering reductions covering roughly 10 million pounds (about $50 million) and conventionalization covering about 36 million pounds ($180 million), of which raw cotton, already firmly on the free list, accounted for just under half.

21 Richard N. Kottman, *Reciprocity and the North Atlantic Triangle 1932-1938* (Ithaca, N.Y., 1968): 249.

22 PRO, Cabinet Office Records [CAB] 24/278, Cabinet Paper [CP] 184 (38), 22 July 1938; CAB 27/621, no. 55, 19 July 1938.

23 David Reynolds, *The Creation of the Anglo-American Alliance 1937-41: A Study in Competitive Co-operation* (London, 1981): 16.

24 FO 371/21501/172.

25 Allan Fisher, "World Economic Affairs," in Toynbee, *Survey, 1938*, I: 28.

26 C.A. MacDonald, *The United States, Britain and Appeasement 1936-1939* (London, 1981): 80, 86. See generally B.J. Wendt, *Economic Appeasement: Handel und Finanz in der britischen Deutschland-Politik 1933-1939* (Düsseldorf, 1971), for example: 331.

27 Reynolds, *Creation of the Anglo-American Alliance*: 15.

28 CAB 24/278, CP 184(38) and 185(38), 19 and 22 July 1938; CAB 27/619, no. 16, 21 July 1938.

29 David E. Koskoff, *Joseph P. Kennedy: A Life and Times* (Englewood Cliffs, N.J., 1974): 171-72.

30 *Foreign Relations of the United States, Diplomatic Papers* [FRUS], 1938 (5 vols.; Washington, 1955-56), II: 39-42, Hull to Kennedy, 25 July 1938.

31 Kottman, *Reciprocity and the North Atlantic Triangle*: 249-54.

32 See FO 371/21502/11-31.

33 To 3 shillings, or "in the last resort," to 2/6 per hundredweight.

34 CAB 23/94, Cabinet conclusions, 28 July 1938. See also CAB 24/278, 184(38) and 185(38), 19 and 22 July 1938, and CAB 24/279, CP 225(38).

35 FO 371/21505/4, 12 September 1938. See also FO 371/21505/156, minute of 20 September 1938.

36 MacDonald, *The United States, Britain and Appeasement*: 111, memorandum of Halifax, 11 October 1938.

37 Kottman, *Reciprocity and the North Atlantic Triangle*: 259.

38 Reynolds, *Creation of the Anglo-American Alliance*: 34 and chapter 1.

39 National Archives of Canada [NA], Norman Robertson Papers, vol. 746, file 167, Robertson to Skelton, 29 September 1938; FO 371/21506/22, King to Chamberlain, 30 September 1938.

40 FO 371/21503/13, US DES CAN MINUTES 11, 12 August 1938; FO 371/21503/55, Board of Trade to Overton, 20 August 1938.

41 DO 35/882/T766/1, 17 September 1937. Britain would concede a 3 shilling duty on non-Empire apples, but Canada seemed unable to envisage less than 3/3 per cwt.

42 FO 371/21505/52, Overton to Board of Trade, 14 September 1938.
43 CAB 24/279, CP 225 (38); DO 35/881/T766/1/149, US DES CAN MINUTES 10, 2 August 1938. The Americans wanted Canada to grant free entry for anthracite from December to April, but London argued that would impose unacceptable burdens on South Wales. For wheat flour, where Washington wanted consolidation of the 10 per cent duty, the British replied that they needed to retain a weapon against European competition. Ten per cent might not be enough. For planed softwood and plywood, the United States supplied 5 and 8 per cent respectively of Britain's imports; thus if the general British duty were cut, the sacrifice of revenue would be out of all proportion to the possible benefits to United States trade. The Americans wanted a reduction in duty on motor cars rated at 20 to 25 horsepower, but the British government still feared subsidized competition from Germany's Opel, a subsidiary of America's General Motors, which was developing a model in that range. The Americans were also demanding concessions on citrus juices, canned grapefruit, and pineapples—concessions that the Australians were saying could not be granted.
44 FO 371/21505/10, Lindsay to Foreign Office, 9 September 1938.
45 FO 371/21505/23, 13 September 1938.
46 CAB 27/619, no. 17, 13 October 1938.
47 FRUS, 1938, II: 53-55, memorandum of Sayre, 9 September 1938.
48 FO 371/21504/345, minutes of 7 September 1938.
49 FO 371/21503/205, minute of 31 August 1938.
50 FO 371/21505/345, minute of 7 September 1938.
51 FO 371/21505/156-63, memorandum of 6 September 1938. See also FO 371/21505/142, US DES CAN MINUTES 55, 3 September 1938.
52 DO 35/879/T766/449, minute of 30 September 1938.
53 J.L. Granatstein, *A Man of Influence: Norman A. Robertson and Canadian Statecraft 1929-1968* (Ottawa, 1981): 406, Robertson to Skelton, 29 September 1938.

Chapter 7: The Dominions in the Later Stages of the Negotiations

1 With apologies to Frederic L. Crews, whose *Pooh Perplex* (New York, 1963) brightened many days in the 1960s.
2 J.L. Granatstein, *A Man of Influence: Norman A. Robertson and Canadian Statecraft 1929-1968* (Ottawa, 1981): 69-70.
3 Ibid.: chapter 3.
4 Ibid.: 76, Robertson to his mother, 29 September 1938.
5 Ibid.: 70, memorandum of Moffat, 25 September 1941.
6 Ibid.: 74, Robertson to Pearson, [July ? 1938].
7 Ibid.: 77, Robertson to Skelton, 29 September 1938.
8 Ibid.: 74, Robertson to Pearson, [July ? 1938].
9 National Archives of Canada [NA], Norman Robertson Papers, vol. 8, file 62, Robertson to Skelton, 14 June 1938.
10 Richard N. Kottman, *Reciprocity and the North Atlantic Triangle 1932-1938* (Ithaca, N.Y., 1968): 258; Franklin D. Roosevelt Library, Hyde Park, New York, Morgenthau Papers, Diary, 15 September 1938.
11 Public Record Office, Kew, England, [PRO], Dominions Office [DO] 35/881, US DES CAN MINUTES 2, 16 April 1938.
12 Robertson Papers, vol. 9, file 68, Robertson to Skelton, 10 May 1938.
13 PRO, Foreign Office Records [FO] 371/21501/193, memorandum of July 1938.

14 Robertson Papers, vol. 8, file 62, Robertson to Skelton, 25 May 1938.
15 DO 35/881, US DES CAN MINUTES, 3, 7 Jue 1938.
16 NA, Department of External Affairs Records [External], vol. 746, file 167(5), Robertson to Skelton, 7 July 1938.
17 External, vol. 746, file 167(5), Skelton to Robertson, 14 July 1938.
18 DO 35/881, US DES CAN MINUTES 5, 15 July 1938.
19 DO 35/881, US DES CAN MINUTES 6, 19 July 1938.
20 FO 371/21501/193, July 1938.
21 DO 35/881, US DES CAN MINUTES 9, 24 July 1938; DO 35/881/T766/1/185, "Note . . . for the use of the Secretary of State . . . ," August 1938.
22 Robertson Papers, vol. 8, file 63, Robertson to Skelton, 17 August 1938.
23 Robertson Papers, vol. 8, file 62, Skelton to Robertson, 24 August 1938.
24 Robertson Papers, vol. 8, file 63, Skelton to Robertson, 15 September 1938; NA, King Papers, Diary, 14 September 1938.
25 King Papers, Diary, 26 September 1938.
26 M. Ruth Megaw, "Australia and the Anglo-American Trade Agreement, 1938," *Journal of Imperial and Commonwealth History*, 3 (January 1975): 191-99, 201, 207. Megaw supersedes Raymond Esthus, *From Enmity to Alliance: U.S.-Australian Relations 1931-1941* (Melbourne, 1964): 49-61.
27 National Library of Australia, Sir Earle Page Papers, MS 1633/737/3, 11; MS 2633/214, 222.
28 Megaw, "Australia and the Anglo-American Trade Agreement": 199-201.
29 PRO, Treasury Records [T] 161/841/S 40927/03/6, 3rd conclusions, May 1938.
30 PRO, Cabinet Office Records [CAB] 24/277, CP 162(38).
31 United Kingdom, Cmd 5805, "Memorandum of Conclusions," 20 July 1938.
32 Ian M. Drummond, *Imperial Economic Policy 1917-1939: Studies in Expansion and Protection* (London, 1974): 339-53.
33 Megaw, "Australia and the Anglo-American Trade Agreement": 201.
34 Megaw, "Australia and the Anglo-American Trade Agreement": 204.
35 PRO, T160/770/F 15883.
36 DO 35/878/T766/260, Archer to Bankes-Amery, 5 April 1938.
37 External, vol. 746, file 167, Robertson to Skelton, 19 May 1938.
38 DO 114/93/49, Floud to Dominions Office, 30 April 1938; DO 35/881, US DES CAN MINUTES 1, 15 April 1938.
39 FO 371/21489/107-9, 113; FO 371/21489/35-8, 14 January 1938; DO 35/878/T766/260/2, Archer to Bankes-Amery, 5 April 1938; DO 35/879/T766/310, memorandum of Archer, "Note on Recent History . . . ," 17 June 1938. What rate should be charged on non-empire apples? Britain's agriculture minister wanted nothing lower than 3/6 per hundredweight, but the Cabinet had decided that if necessary one could go as low as 3 shillings. The British delegation thought that Canadians might acquiesce in a British apple duty of 3 shillings with safeguards. On 26 April 1938, however, the Americans reverted to their demand of the previous year, ignoring everything that the United Kingdom and Canadian delegations had said since: they were again asking for a duty of 2/6 per hundredweight, without any seasonal limitation. In subsequent discussion they continued to press for a substantial tariff cut, although at the end of May they said they would concede the seasonal arrangement so long as the duty fell to 2/6.
40 PRO, Board of Trade Records [BT] 11/949, no. 5, 6 August 1938.
41 Robertson Papers, vol. 4, file 7, Robertson to Skelton, 30 May 1938.
42 DO 35/879/T766/310, Archer, "Note on Recent History . . . ."
43 FO 371/21500/311, Board of Trade to UK Delegation, 15 July 1938.

44 FO 371/21489/269-73.

45 Given the fact that United States timber cost more, American exporters would presumably opt for the specific rate, whose incidence would be substantially less than 10 per cent—the rate that the cheaper Baltic timber would probably continue to pay. However, the *ad valorem* rate might have to be set at 7.5 per cent, and the alternative specific rate at 22 shillings.

46 FO 371/21490/215-17, Dominions Office to British high commissioner, Ottawa, 24 January 1938.

47 No less than 24 shillings per standard.

48 FO 371/21491/142ff, British high commissioner, Ottawa, to Dominions Office, 11 February 1938.

49 FO 371/21494/197, Overton to Brown, 2 April 1938.

50 BT 11/917, Overton to Brown, 4 April 1938.

51 FO 371/21494/282, 286, Brown to Overton, 5 April 1938.

52 Robertson Papers, vol. 9, file 68, Robertson to Skelton, 8 April 1938.

53 DO 35/881/T766/1/143, minute of 9 April 1938.

54 DO 35/881/T766/1/143, Overton to Brown, 7 April 1938.

55 The United States formally proposed that the duty on sawn, planed, or dressed softwood be reduced to 7.5 per cent. If and when Congress abolished the excise tax on imported lumber, and "so long as the duty charges on British [i.e. Canadian] lumber did not exceed 50 cents per 1,000 board feet," American softwood should get free entry to the United Kingdom. Harry Hawkins then told the British that Congress would not abolish the excise; he suggested a 5 per cent duty on American softwood, and free entry so long as the duty on "British" [again Canadian] lumber did not exceed 50 cents per 1,000 board feet.

56 DO 35/881/T766/1/156, memorandum of Archer, 27 May 1938.

57 DO 35/881/T766/1/156, minute of Bankes-Amery, 31 May 1938.

58 DO 35/881, US DES CAN MINUTES, 30 June 1938.

59 FO 371/21500/325, Foreign Office to UK Delegation, 2 August 1938.

60 DO 35/881, UK Delegation to Board of Trade, 14 July 1938.

61 DO 35/881, UK delegation to Board of Trade, 18 July 1938.

62 DO 35/881, US DES CAN MINUTES, 15 July 1938.

63 FO 371/21499/323.

64 T 160/754/F14239/16, letters and minutes, 23 September 1938, Board of Trade to UK Delegation, 24 September 1938.

65 FO 371/21499/336, 1 November 1938.

66 FO 371/21499/232, 9 July 1938.

Chapter 8: The End at Last

1 National Archives, Washington, State Department Records [State] 611.4131/1795, meeting of Sayre and Roosevelt, 19 September 1938; State 611.4131/1782, Lindsay to Hull, 27 September 1938.

2 State 611.4131/1807A, Hull to Lindsay, 5 October 1938.

3 Public Record Office, Kew, England, [PRO], Foreign Office Records [FO] 371/21506/168-9, Hull to Lindsay, 6 October 1938; *Foreign Relations of the United States, Diplomatic Papers* [FRUS], 1938 (5 vols.; Washington, 1955-56), II: 58-59, memorandum of Sayre, 6 October 1938.

4 FRUS, 1938, II: 58-59, memorandum of Sayre, 6 October 1938; FO 371/21506/63, Lindsay to Board of Trade, 9 October 1938.

5 *FRUS*, 1938, II: 61, memorandum of Sayre, 8 October 1938.
6 State 611.4131/1805, Kennedy to Hull, 7 October 1938.
7 FO 414/275, no. 20, Lindsay to Foreign Office, 8 October 1938.
8 FO 371/21506/13-16, minutes of 6 October 1938.
9 PRO, Cabinet Office Records [CAB] 24/621, no. 56; FO 371/21506/121, TAC(35)56, "Note by the President of the Board of Trade," 10 October 1938.
10 The Americans wanted Britain to conventionalize free entry for maize, to eliminate the 3-year limitation on the ham quota, give lard duty-free entry, bind the 10 per cent duty on wheat flour, and reduce the duty on softwood plywood to 5 per cent. Hull wanted, furthermore, new concessions on light electric motors, typewriters, and silk stockings, and he was asking Britain, "subject to the approval of the Cabinet and Parliament," to reduce the tobacco preference when imperial obligations expired in 1942 — a year after the proposed Anglo-American trade agreement would end. And he wanted Britain to extend the lumber concessions already offered to include the more valuable sorts of planed softwood. CAB 24/621, no. 56; FO 371/21506/121, TAC (35)56, "Note by the President of the Board of Trade," 10 October 1938.
11 CAB 27/619, no. 17, 13 October 1938; FO 371/21507/83, Cabinet Paper [CP] 225(38), 14 October 1938; FO 371/21506/109-18, Balfour, "Anglo-United States Trade Negotiations," 13 October 1938; FO 371/21507/157-89, TAC (36), 17th meeting, 13 October 1938.
12 CAB 23/96, Cabinet conclusions, 19 October 1938.
13 C.A. MacDonald, *The United States, Britain and Appeasement 1936-1939* (London, 1981): 111, memorandum of Halifax, 11 October 1938.
14 CAB 23/96, Cabinet conclusions, 19 October 1938; for more discussion of Chamberlain's attitudes at this time see MacDonald, *The United States, Britain and Appeasement*: 110.
15 State 611.4131/1828, Kennedy to Hull, 18 October 1938.
16 State 611.4143/1850, Lindsay to Hull, 25 October 1938.
17 FO 371/21506/89-90, Foreign Office to UK Delegation, 15 October 1938.
18 FO 371/21507/203, UK Delegation to Board of Trade, 1 November 1938.
19 CAB 23/532, Cabinet conclusions, 7 November 1938.
20 State 611.4131/1855A, B, Hull to Kennedy, 13 November 1938. Having been frozen out by Hull, Kennedy must have found that his competitive juices were now flowing. He called Hull to say that the ambassador could get further concessions, if only the secretary would "let him take the ball." David E. Koskoff, *Joseph P. Kennedy: A Life and Times* (Englewood Cliffs, N.J., 1974): 173-74.
21 PRO, Treasury Office Records [T] 160/750/F.14239/1, Phillips to Hopkins, 28 September 1935 and memorandum of Waley, 1 October 1935.
22 FO 371/21491/38-39, 81ff.
23 FO 371/21491/38-39, 81ff.
24 FO 371/21492/29, 51, US Article XV.
25 FO 371/21494/65, US-UK minutes, 24 February 1938.
26 T 160/F.14239/04, various minutes of 22 March 1938; FO 371/21494/23, Treasury to Bewley, 31 March 1938.
27 FO 371/21494/302, Bewley to Treasury, 6 April 1938; FO 371/21496/151, Bewley to Treasury, 20 May 1938.
28 FO 371/21495/71, 109, Board of Trade to Lindsay, 25 and 27 April 1938; Franklin D. Roosevelt Library, Hyde Park, New York, Morgenthau Papers, Diary, vol. 124: 277, memorandum of Taylor, 11 May 1938.
29 FO 371/21496/153, Treasury to Bewley, 8 June 1938.

30 Morgenthau Papers, Diary, vol. 147: 92-93, remarks of White and Taylor, 21 October 1938.

31 FO 371/21498/27, 24 May 1938.

32 T 160/F.14239/04; FO 371/21499/413-4, UK Delegation to Board of Trade, 7 July 1938; FO 371/21500/304, Waley to Board of Trade, 13 July 1938.

33 T 160/F.14239/04.

34 Morgenthau Papers, Diary, vol. 147: 99.

35 National Archives, Washington, US Treasury, RG 56, box 2, chronological D11, memoranda of Taylor (written by White), 29 April and 11 May 1938.

36 On the general question of sterling's movement and US nervousness, see Ian M. Drummond, *The Floating Pound and the Sterling Area, 1931-1939* (Cambridge, 1981): chapter 10.

37 Morgenthau Papers, Diary, vol. 139: 14, 110-111, transcript of conversation, 8 September 1938; FO 371/21505/10, Lindsay to Foreign Office, 9 September 1938.

38 Morgenthau Papers, Diary, vol. 147: 74ff, 91, 121, 146ff. On the Tripartite Agreement of 1936, see Drummond, *Floating Pound and the Sterling Area*, ch. 9, and S.V.O. Clarke, *Negotiating the Tripartite Stabilization Agreement of 1936* (Princeton, 1977).

39 Morgenthau Papers, Diary, vol. 150: 2ff, memoranda of Morgenthau and Taylor, 14 November 1938.

40 Morgenthau Papers, Diary, vol. 150: 12-13, 14 November 1938; State 611.4131/2058, 14 November 1938.

41 T 160/754/F.14239/19, Lindsay to Foreign Office, 14 November 1938.

42 Quoted in C. P. Stacey, *Canada and the Age of Conflict: A History of Canadian External Policies* (2 vols.; Toronto, 1977-81), vol. II: *1921-1948, The Mackenzie King Era*: 226. See also A.A. Offner, *American Appeasement: United States Foreign Policy and Germany, 1933-1938* (Cambridge, Mass., 1969), 170-71.

43 For the texts, see United Kingdom, *State Papers 1938*: 183ff, 327ff. It should be noted that the agreements are not treaties. If they had been, they would have required Congressional ratification in the United States. The Trade Agreements Act of 1934 allowed the president to make such agreements without having to submit them to Congress.

Chapter 9: Conclusion: The Trials of Trilateralism

1 Calculated from data in United Kingdom, *Statistical Abstract, 1946*, table 220. Canadian data are from M.C. Urquhart and K.A.H. Buckley, eds., *Historical Statistics of Canada* (1st ed., Toronto, 1965), series F351, 352, 353.

2 Urquhart and Buckley, *Historical Statistics of Canada*, series H623, 624.

3 Arthur Annis, commenting on the authors' "A Shaft of Baltic Pine: Negotiating the Anglo-American-Canadian Trade Agreements of 1938," a paper presented to the Canadian Historical Association Annual Meeting, Ottawa, 10 June 1982. Published in P.L. Cottrell and D.E. Moggridge, *Money and Power: Essays in Honour of L.S. Pressnell* (London, 1988), 199-225. See also Robert B. Bryce, *Maturing in Hard Times: Canada's Department of Finance through the Great Depression* (Kingston and Montreal, 1986), 100.

4 Ian M. Drummond, *British Economic Policy and the Empire 1919-1939* (London, 1972): 52-54.

5 Ingo Walter and Kaj Areskoug, *International Economics* (New York, 1981): 207.

6 Public Record Office, Kew, England, [PRO], Cabinet Office Records [CAB] 23/99,

Cabinet conclusions, 3 May 1939, where it is sadly recorded that the proposals made on 3 March 1938 had yet to elicit any response from Berlin.

7 See CAB 23/93, Cabinet conclusions, 8 February 1939, where this decision is noted.

8 CAB 23/97, Cabinet conclusions, 1 February 1939.

9 CAB 23/100, Cabinet conclusions, 5 July 1939, discussing Cabinet paper CP 149(39) in the presence of Sir Richard Hopkins. This appears to have been the first occasion on which the Cabinet was formally briefed on the financial situation should war break out. When the Cabinet did decide, on 22 August, to let the pound float freely downward, it resolved to warn the Americans, though not to consult them, and perhaps to warn the French, who had pegged the franc to sterling some months before. CAB 23/100, Cabinet conclusions, 22 August 1939.

10 CAB 26/627, FP(36)80, memorandum of a conversation between Sir Arthur Willert and Roosevelt, 25 and 26 March 1939. On Lord Halifax's pessimism with respect to a change in the neutrality legislation, see CAB 23/100, Cabinet conclusions, 12 July 1939.

11 See CAB 23/96, Cabinet conclusions, 30 November 1938, when it was agreed that Lord Halifax should sound out the Americans with respect to a three-million-pound Chinese loan, and CAB 23/97, Cabinet conclusions, 18 January 1939, when the American response was finally received.

12 So were the tin and rubber prices, but in form the situation was different in that the tin and rubber control schemes were managed by international committees, not by governments.

13 PRO, Foreign Office Records [FO] 371/22797/72, memorandum of Ashton-Gwatkin. For the reservations that later surfaced with respect to the balance-of-payments implications, see FO 371/22797/88, minute of Gwatkin, 23 April 1939.

14 FO 371/22797/128, Foreign Office to Lindsay, 15 May 1939, and FO 371/22797/150, Lindsay to Foreign Office, 17 May 1939.

15 FO 371/22797/180, minutes of interdepartmental meeting of officials, 19 May 1939.

16 CAB 23/99, Cabinet conclusions, 4 June 1939; CAB 23/100, Cabinet conclusions, 21 June 1939. The elaboration of the agreement, and the tracing of the necessary congressional steps on the American side, can be followed in FO 371/22797/72-241, and FO 371/22798/13-170. Ambassador Kennedy demanded that the British should buy 650,000 bales, although only 500,000 bales seemed to be justified. The final figure was 600,000 bales. Similarly, the price-basis was adjusted in the Americans' favour at the last moment.

17 W.K. Hancock, Survey of British Commonwealth Affairs, vol. II: Problems of Economic Policy 1918-1939 (2 parts; London, 1940-42), 1: 267;

18 Interview with Charles Ritchie, 22 September 1985.

19 Norman Hillmer, "Personalities and Problems in Anglo-Canadian Economic Relations Between the Two World Wars," Bulletin of Canadian Studies [British Association of Canadian Studies], 3 (June 1979): 17-18.

20 The most recent scholarly account is L.S. Pressnell, External Economic Policy Since the War, vol. I: The Postwar Financial Settlement (London, 1986), chapters 1-4, where the main prior contributors to the literature on this topic are also cited.

Bibliography

I. Official Manuscript Sources

(i) Public Record Office, Kew, England
Board of Trade Records
Cabinet Office Records
Dominions Office Records
Foreign Office Records
Prime Minister's Office Records
Treasury Records

(ii) National Archives of Canada, Ottawa
Department of External Affairs Records
Department of Finance Records
Department of Trade and Commerce Records

(iii) Department of External Affairs Historical Section, Ottawa, Canada
Department of External Affairs Records

(iv) United States National Archives, Washington, D.C.
Department of State Records
Treasury Records
Records of the Office of the Special Representative for Trade
Records of the Office of the Special Adviser to the President in
    Foreign Trade
Department of Commerce Records
Bureau of Foreign and Domestic Trade Records

II. Private Papers

(i) National Archives of Canada, Ottawa
Bennett Papers
King Papers

Robertson Papers
Wrong Papers

(ii) National Library of Australia, Canberra
Page Papers

(iii) Library of Congress, Washington, D.C.
Hull Papers
Sayre Papers

(iv) F.D. Roosevelt Library, Hyde Park, New York
Roosevelt Papers
Morgenthau Papers

(v) Harvard University Library, Cambridge, Massachusetts
Moffat Papers

(vi) University of Birmingham Main Library
Neville Chamberlain Papers

(vii) Cambridge University Library
Baldwin Papers

(viii) Queen's University Archives, Kingston, Canada
Buchan (Tweedsmuir) Papers

III. Interviews

Sir Harry F. Batterbee
Sir Charles W. Dixon
Lord Garner
Sir Stephen Holmes
Malcolm MacDonald
Charles Ritchie

Index